NAPOLEON AND HITLER

NAPOLEON
AND
HITLER

A COMPARATIVE BIOGRAPHY

Desmond Seward

HARRAP

London

First published in Great Britain 1988
by HARRAP LTD
19-23 Ludgate Hill, London EC4M 7PD

ISBN 0 245-54636-7

Designed by Langley Iddins

Printed and bound in Great Britain by
Mackays of Chatham plc

for Nigel and Georgina Parker

Acknowledgements

I must first of all thank Mr Daniel Frank of New York, who gave me the idea for this book.

I am very grateful to Susan, Viscountess Mountgarret for help at every stage – many useful suggestions, reading the typescript and checking the proofs – and to Mr Derek Johns for his editorial criticisms and unfailing encouragement.

I also owe much to the staffs of the British Library and the London Library for their patient assistance.

Contents

I certainly deprecate any comparison between Herr Hitler and Napoleon: I do not wish to insult the dead.

Winston Churchill, speech at Harrow in December 1940[1]

Misinterpretation has been the common fate of most prophets and thinkers in every sphere . . . Clausewitz invited misinterpretation more than most.

Sir Basil Liddell Hart, Strategy

Introduction: The Supermen

Others besides Winston Churchill may think it blasphemy to compare Napoleon and Hitler. Certainly there are many differences – not least the relative duration of their careers. The Emperor was forty-four when he fell from power, the age of the Führer when he achieved it. Yet undeniably there are resemblances too; their rise from obscurity, their military domination over Europe, their tyranny and contempt for human life, their megalomania and inability to compromise, their hubris. No one can ever be really sure that a nuclear war or an economic collapse will not occur, creating just the sort of chaos from which their like might emerge again. An examination of the two men's careers and a pinpointing of the qualities they share may provide a means of identifying future 'saviours', as well as casting fresh light on both, and especially upon Hitler.

In 1941 Professor Pieter Geyl of the University of Utrecht was by some miracle released from Buchenwald, returning to internment. in occupied Holland. He spent the rest of the war working on his great study of Napoleon's historians, *Napoleon: For and Against*. In this he says that one cannot avoid comparing the Emperor and the Führer, since the resemblances are 'too striking'; that he had 'hated the dictator in Napoleon long before the evil presence of Hitler began darkening our lives', but has 'nowhere worked it out'.

He also admits that 'one almost feels as if one should ask pardon of the Emperor for mentioning his name in one breath with that of the other'. While scarcely trying to emulate Geyl, this book is a modest attempt to work out the comparison.

No one will dispute that Hitler was more evil than the Emperor, did evil on a far greater scale. A liberal like Lord Acton could call Napoleon 'the most splendid genius that has appeared on earth', and he still inspires some very unlikely people. No one denies that he created modern France, while nothing remains of the Führer's Germany save the autobahns. Hugh Trevor-Roper likens the latter's mind to 'some barbarian monolith, the expression of giant strength and savage genius, surrounded by a festering heap of refuse'.

Even so, the resemblances are inescapable. Each was a foreigner in an adopted country, self-made – the Emperor an uprooted squireen, the Führer a rootless *petit-bourgeois.* They appeared from nowhere to become 'saviours' of their new countries; Napoleon was not a Frenchman but a Corsican who kept an Italian accent till he was nearly thirty, while Hitler never lost his Austrian accent. Each was a loner despising the rest of humanity. The Emperor believed that any man – or woman – could be bought, while Hitler declared 'I have come not to make men better but to make them worse.' (Mme de Staël described the 'hall-mark of Bonaparte's rule' as 'profound contempt for the riches of human nature'.) Napoleon and Hitler loathed intellectuals, suppressing freedom of thought by means of censorship and secret police. Emperor and Führer restored briefly their countries' prosperity and self-confidence, and then conquered most of Europe through ruthless diplomacy and war. Both destroyed themselves by invading Russia. Hitler echoed Napoleon's fear (voiced on St Helena) that 'the Cossacks will rule Europe', and was very conscious of his predecessor's failure – after his armies had survived the winter of 1941 he boasted:'We mastered a destiny which broke another man 130 years ago.'

Admittedly Hitler's hero, in so far as he ever had one, was Frederick the Great, as creator of the *Preussensgeist* – that terrifyingly dynamic compound of militarism and State service, of discipline and precision. In the Führer's eyes Napoleon never achieved anything like such distinction. Yet while he sometimes looked to the old King for inspiration he must have been keenly aware how many of his problems had been those of the man whom he described to Himmler as 'that unique military genius, the Corsican Napoleon'.

The Emperor and the Führer were gamblers who kept the game playing until the very end, whatever the cost to their peoples. 'Conquest has made me what I am, conquest alone can maintain me,' Napoleon told Bourrienne. 'Small change' was what he called the French dead at Eylau. Both conscripted relative children into their armies, Napoleon the 'Marie Louises' (fifteen-year-olds) in 1814, Hitler the Hitler Youth in 1945. The Emperor bragged 'A man like me cares little about losing the lives of a million men', the Führer 'I can send the flower of German youth into the hell of war without the slightest pity.' Napoleon's threat 'I shall bury the world beneath my ruin' was repeated by Hitler – 'We may be destroyed but, if we are, we'll drag the world down with us, a world in flames.' The former anticipated the Führer in preparing a *Götterdämmerung*- like fight to the death in his capital. In 1814 he ordered that Paris must never be evacuated even if this meant its destruction.

In some ways Hitler achieved more than the Emperor. Trevor-Roper calls him 'the Rousseau, the Mirabeau, the Robespierre and the Napoleon of his revolution; he was its Marx, its Lenin, its Trotsky and its Stalin'. Of these Hitler had most in common with Napoleon. But one must agree with Geyl that the Emperor can only benefit from comparison with the Führer – the worst of his crimes cannot possibly match Adolf Hitler's murder of the Jewish people.

11

There is a subtle link between the pair, which emerges only when they are compared. It is contained in the writings of that baneful genius Carl von Clausewitz, one of the brilliant group of soldiers who rebuilt the Prussian army after its humiliating defeat by Napoleon in 1806. Something of an outsider on account of bourgeois origins and spurious nobility (his father had merely assumed the 'von'), he was never entirely at ease in the exclusively noble Prussian officer corps, although he joined it at the age of twelve, while his interest in new ideas incurred suspicions of 'Jacobinism'. His primary concern was to produce a military science capable of meeting and overcoming the 'nation in arms' concept developed by the French; he foresaw further great wars, and was determined that Prussia should emerge triumphant from them. He remained essentially a Prussian expansionist, his views on Poland anticipating in some ways those of Hitler. It has been claimed that his influence in Germany was among the causes of both world wars. As a 'military philosopher' he tried to see both sides of every question, and since he had a mind shaped (at second hand) by Kant, his meaning is often over-subtle or ambiguous – he himself wrote that his work was 'open to endless misconceptions'. The Führer was to be the ultimate misinterpreter of Clausewitz.

A comparison of the Emperor and Hitler reveals the enormous influence on the latter of Clausewitz's view of Napoleon. Most of the Führer's biographers refer to his being a disciple of the Prussian general, yet not one has sufficiently examined this aspect, let alone Hitler's indirect debt to the Emperor through the latter's writings. Clausewitz had had first-hand experience of Napoleonic methods – from the other side – having been on Kutuzov's staff in 1812, at Blücher's headquarters in 1813 and chief of staff to General Walmoden's Russo-German corps (part of Bernadotte's Army of the North) in 1814. He venerated Napoleon as a genius, for breaking 'the rules of civilised warfare'. Even if he never totally understood the Emperor's strategic method, he none the less grasped the basic ideas behind it, and has been described as 'distilling Napoleon into theory'.

There is no doubt that the Führer studied Clausewitz – even if that passionate Clausewitzian, the late Raymond Aron, could not bear to believe it.[2] *Vom Kriege* ('On War'), Clausewitz's master-piece, was almost certainly among the 'books on war' which he is reported to have read before 1914. In *Mein Kampf* he quotes it with savage approval, and in a speech at Munich in 1934 accused his audience of never having read Clausewitz, or if they had, of not knowing how to apply him to modern circumstances. On at least one occasion he reminded his generals that he knew Clausewitz, while Keitel stated at Nuremburg that during the war Hitler had spent whole nights studying him.[3] Admittedly, as Aron emphasizes, there have been many enthusiastic readers of Clausewitz, but few careful ones. It is unlikely that the Führer ever understood properly the theories of this most complex of military philosophers, which may be why historians have underestimated his influence on Hitler. Yet the Führer acknowledged Clausewitz alone as his intellectual master. It is only reasonable to suppose that he was fascinated by the many desperate situations so closely paralleling his own which are described and analysed in *Vom Kriege* – the 1812 campaign, and Napoleon's last-ditch defensive battles in 1814 being the most obvious. As a man who habitually read into a situation what he wished to believe, he may very well have extracted from the book merely what he wanted. Even so, a careful study of *Vom Kriege* casts considerable light on Hitler's mind and on why he reached a number of historic decisions.

It is the enigma presented by the Führer that makes him unique, not only the vast scale of his wickedness. (By contrast Mussolini was an open book.) Yet we know far more about him than about earlier tyrants. The enigma consists in his possessing so many undeniable gifts and likeable qualities, besides those which can be immediately recognized as evil. It is this extraordinary mixture which gives the man and his career their ultimate horror. Only by appreciating Hitler's good points can one appreciate the full extent of his savagery and depravity.

Napoleon is almost as baffling for much the same reason, and he was given time to fabricate his own legend on St Helena, shaping his own image in history. (For all that, none of the many thousand books about him agree.) Luckily, the Führer was not given the opportunity similarly to sift the facts in his own favour. However, if the Emperor possessed a surprisingly similar combination of good and evil qualities, he is less of an enigma.

There is an aspect of the two men which tends to be overlooked, their European dimension. The years from the Napoleonic wars to Hitler's mark the height of the European hegemony over the rest of the world, a hegemony that has now vanished, perhaps for ever. Admittedly, the Emperor began the irreversible destruction of the old hierarchical, Christian Europe and the Führer completed it. Even so, the legend which Napoleon afterwards disseminated from his exile on St Helena included a vision of a united Europe of the future. It can be argued that to some extent he prepared the way for unification; his creation of a single West German state (the Con- federation of the Rhine) and of a single North Italian state (the Kingdom of Italy) undoubtedly contributed. And though Hitler ruined Europe, destroying its dominance, he did at least demolish some of the obstacles which stood in the way of a united continent. Napoleon called the continent 'a rotten old whore whom I shall treat as I please', while in 1943 Goebbels recorded the Führer's 'unshakeable conviction that the Reich will be master of all Europe' – two years later, just before his death, Hitler said of the continent, 'I had to rape it in order to possess it.'

No doubt, as Geyl emphasizes, 'under Napoleon, French civilisation (albeit stifled and narrowed by him) still accompanied the conquest, while the character of the conquest that it has been the lot of our generation to undergo is not compatible with any civilisation at all'. The French brought their social and legal revolution with them, so that everyone became equal before the law in much of western Europe. Even so, they imposed these benefits as conquerors. Hippolyte Taine, perhaps the most formidable intellect among all the critics of the man he called the 'Diocletian of Ajaccio', shudders at what might have happened had he triumphed over the Russians in 1812:

> At best a European empire secretly undermined by a European resistance, an external France imposed by force on an enslaved continent, with French commissioners and military governors at St. Petersburg and Riga as at Danzig, Hamburg, Amsterdam, Lisbon, Barcelona and Trieste; every available Frenchman employed from Cadiz to Moscow in maintaining and administering the conquest; every available young man conscripted each year and, should he escape, reconscripted by decree, the entire male population employed in oppression; no other prospect for an educated or an uneducated man, no other career military or civil, but extended duty as soldier, excise officer or policeman in the role of spy or bully, employed to hold down the subjected and extort taxes; to confiscate and burn merchandise, to catch smugglers and crush the obstinate.

Taine wrote in the 1880s, never dreaming that a very similar German hegemony would be established sixty years later, which would offer as its highest careers those of spy and bully.[4]

Essentially each man was an opportunist on a colossal scale. 'His ideas about the history of the Revolution were astonishingly superficial and defective,' the former deputy Jean Charles Bailleul wrote of Napoleon. 'He used just so much of it as he needed to construct a régime which was neither old nor new. This misunderstanding, whether deliberate or unintentional, of men and principles had a

most disastrous effect on his career.'[5] Hermann Rauschning – also
a contemporary observer – said of Hitler in 1939: 'He damped
down the Socialist tendencies in the movement and brought the
Nationalist ones into the foreground. He was out to gain powerful
patrons and friends who could help the movement into power.'
Rauschning discerned that his movement had 'no fixed aims, either
economic or political, either in home or foreign affairs'. Both in
Napoleonic France and in Hitlerian Germany, there was only one
leader. Everything, whether human beings or principles, was
subject to his devouring, insatiable egotism.

This book is an investigation of megalomania. In 1811 Napoleon
asked an aghast Fouché: 'How can I help it when all this power is
sweeping me on to world dictatorship?' After conquering Russia he
intended to assemble an army at Tiflis, and then send it through
Afghanistan into India. In 1942 Hitler told Albert Speer that after
Russia's defeat 'a mere 20 or 30 divisions' would be all that was
necessary to conquer India. As young men the Emperor and the
Führer had little in common – a Corsican soldier and a failed
Austrian 'artist'. What united them at their zenith was the
demonic process of corruption by power.

(N.B. The superior numbers throughout the text refer to the Notes
on pp. 304-7.)

Corsica . . . I have a feeling that some day that little island will astonish Europe.

Jean-Jacques Rousseau, Du Contrat Social (1762)

What I dread is that Germany doesn't know that she was licked. Had they given us another week, we'd have taught them.

General John J. Pershing, November 1918

1

The Poor Devils

No one in their right mind could have believed that either would become rulers. Stendhal met an old officer who had served with Napoleon Bonaparte before 1789. He remembered 'a young windbag arguing interminably whatever the subject, determined to reform anything and everything', adding that he had known scores of similar 'ranters'. In the autumn of 1909 a tramp in a Vienna doss-house saw a nightmarish apparition called Adolf Hitler, with a thin, starving, bearded face and burning eyes, an apparition naked save for a pair of trousers.

Yet the sons of the noble Carlo de Buonaparte (a lawyer by profession) and the *Zolloberamstrat* Aloïs Hitler both came from assured if contrasting backgrounds, despite the Führer's description of himself as 'a poor devil'. One father was a nobleman, the other a *petit-bourgeois*, but each advanced his standing. They did so by making shrewd use of opportunities offered by the State.

Napoleon's noble blood has been exaggerated. The Buonaparte family derived a scanty income from a few small farms, their peasants calling them by their Christian names. Only the accident of Corsica's conquest by the French in 1769 and the creation of Corsican nobility transformed them into patricians, for all Carlo's purchasing certificates of nobility from the Tuscan government; they were never more than gentry of the pettiest sort, well-to-do peasants with a coat-of-arms. Carlo's desertion of the Corsican cause and assiduous wooing of the new French régime in the person of the island's governor, the Comte de Marboeuf – a keen admirer of his wife – secured posts and privileges, in particular expensive State education for his children.

Aloïs Hitler also made the best of his chances. Born in 1837, he came from a long line of alarmingly intermarried peasants in Upper Austria, on the borders of Bohemia and Bavaria, whose name was probably Czech in origin – Hidler or Hidlarcek. He was illegitimate, the bastard of a cook named Maria Anna Schickelgrüber, his father's identity being unknown. Five years after his birth his mother married a local ne'er-do-well, Johann Georg Hiedler, who over thirty years later acknowledged Aloïs as his son, possibly for the sake of Aloïs's career; the parish priest was persuaded to alter the baptismal register so that the name became Hitler instead of Schickelgrüber. The couple were so poor that at one point they slept in a cattle-trough. When he was thirteen the boy ran away to Vienna, apprenticing himself to a cobbler before entering the customs service. Despite his lack of education, he was a success, rising to the rank of senior inspector.

However different the two fathers, each had a profound influence. Carlo taught his son that, as a nobleman, he was superior to other men – a belief which received a rude shock in the presence of the great nobles of *ancien régime* France. Aloïs bequeathed his fear of becoming déclassé, of sinking back into the mud and being a man of no consequence.

'Napoleone' was born in Ajaccio on 15 August 1769. He grew up there and in the country round about, exploring its dense heathland on a pony or visiting the family farms with his brothers and sisters. When in the city he led a band of friends in vicious fights against the local urchins. He left Corsica at the age of nine to go to a French military boarding school at Brienne, and therefore saw little of his parents. Carlo died from cancer of the stomach in 1785. 'It would be useless for me even to try to express the pain which I felt,' he wrote on St Helena. 'In everything he was the prop of our youth.' This was not true. As a small boy he had been sent to fetch Carlo from taverns where he was gambling, and even at a distance was aware that his father was a spendthrift. He was unquestionably fond of his strong-minded mother Letizia Ramolino. Yet there was a period during the late 1790s when, dazzled by his success, he questioned his paternity because of his forebears' lack of military talent. The only possible alternative to Carlo was the governor, the Comte de Marboeuf, a gallant old soldier whose admiration of Letizia had been remarked on. But she was as strict a Catholic as she was beautiful and, barely literate, had absorbed the traditions of a people who punished adultery with death.

At Brienne the young Bonaparte excelled in mathematics while acquiring a taste for ancient history – notably Plutarch and Polybius, which he read in translation. According to Louis de Bourrienne, his contemporary at school, he was self-absorbed and solitary, unpopular because of his acid tongue. He himself recalled that he found 'unspeakable charm in reading and pondering far away from my companions' noisy games', admitting 'I was not liked in school.' On the other hand, he claims to have been the leader in snow fights during the winter of 1783-4, commenting that the authorities stopped them because so many boys were injured by stones concealed inside the snowballs. When he was teased about his Italian accent and odd name he retorted, 'Had there been only four French to one Corsican, Corsica would never have been conquered, but there were ten to one.' His hero was

General Paoli, who led the islanders 'against tyrants, luxury and courtiers'. Throughout his early years he was a Corsican nationalist, secretly hating the people whose king he was being trained to serve.

Napoleon went to the École Militaire at Paris in October 1784, to spend a year before being commissioned into the artillery regiment of La Fère the following September. He remembered how at the École 'We were magnificently fed and waited on, treated at all times like officers with vast incomes, greater than those of the richest Corsican families, larger than any pay we would ever receive.' Here he acquired a grasp of the theory and practice of gunnery in accordance with the new cannon of Gribeauval. Yet despite his good record at the École Militaire, there are indications that he did not work quite so hard there as he afterwards suggested, and was prone to pick quarrels.

It was his first experience of Paris, in those days still at the height of its *ancien régime* elegance and gaiety. Superficially the monarchy appeared secure, the social order rock-solid. The French and the Americans had just defeated and humiliated Britain. The country seemed prosperous, and the government's imminent bankruptcy was skilfully concealed. The capital itself was particularly cheerful, with over 600 cafés and restaurants – both comparatively recent inventions. As Alexis de Tocqueville observes, 'France in those days was a nation of pleasure seekers, all for the joy of life.' However, the young gunner officer was scarcely 'all for the joy of life'. In May 1786 he seriously contemplated suicide. He still hated the French, lamenting that his fellow-Corsicans were suffering beneath 'the oppressors' hand' and how 'I am compelled by duty to like people whom it is natural for me to hate'. Later he returned to Paris on several occasions before the Revolution, losing his virginity to a young prostitute whom he picked up in the Palais Royal in November 1787. He had already been in love, with Caroline du

Colombier, but the affair went no further than 'eating some cherries together'. There was more to depress him than mere home-sickness or the sufferings of Corsica. Although he was well paid for a subaltern, much of his pay had to go to his widowed mother, since she and his family were now in some poverty. His prospects of pro-motion were remote.

He tells us how his brother Joseph remembered him visiting Corsica in 1786 with a trunk 'much larger than the one holding his clothes', packed with books which included translations of Plutarch, Plato, Cornelius Nepos, Livy and Tacitus, together with the works of Montaigne, Montesquieu and Raynal. He was also pasionately fond of the poems of Ossian, a bogus Celtic bard whose true name was James Macpherson, of which a French prose trans-lation had appeared in 1771. Yet, as he recalled, he was obsessed by Rousseau ('my hero') and the cult of feeling. 'Always alone in the midst of people, I return home to give myself in my dreams to unspeakable melancholy.'

Napoleon was a supporter of the French Revolution from the moment the Estates-General was replaced by a Constituent Assembly in May 1789. He believed that it meant the rebirth of France and, more important, of his Corsican homeland. Louis XVI's inept attempt to escape in June 1791, the Flight to Varennes, turned him into a firm republican. However, to begin with he spent most of his time in Corsica, plunging into political intrigue, working for a Revolutionary Corsica which would be firmly allied to France. His occasional visits to the mainland made him uneasy. He was dis-gusted by the anarchy which he found in 1791, and revolted by 'the lowest scum' whom he saw storming the Tuileries in August of the following year.

Even so, he welcomed the Revolution as 'a general rising of the people against the privileged classes'. In his view 'The new France gave to the world the remarkable phenomenon of 25 million souls, all equal, governed by the same laws, the same rules, the same government. All the changes were in harmony with the good of the people, with its rights, with the progress of civilisation.'

In Corsica General Paoli, the island hero who had returned to lead its patriots once again, came to regard 'Citizen Buonaparte' as a danger. He was too pro-French, too much of a revolutionary. In June 1793 Napoleon and his family fled from Corsica. 'This is no country for us', he told his mother.

The former nobleman became a Jacobin of the deepest dye. He was accepted by other Jacobins because of the poverty and obscurity of the Bonaparte family. He was appointed commander of the artillery during the siege of Toulon from September to December 1793. Toulon, nauseated by the local excesses of the Terror, had rebelled against the Convention in Paris and invited the English to occupy it. Here Napoleon found himself. 'On this occasion', he wrote many years later, 'I displayed for the first time those brilliant military gifts which have since earned such renown for the French army.' His skilful siting of the batteries and devastating employment of their guns, firing red-hot cannon-balls 'to burn the despots' ships' (his words), made it impossible for the enemy fleet to use the harbour, and the fall of royalist Toulon was due entirely to him. Throughout the siege he slept at the batteries, on the ground next to his guns. He personally captured an English general, was bayoneted in the leg, had two horses shot beneath him. He reported to the Minister of War, 'I promised you brilliant successes and, as you see, I have kept my word.' The Convention was so impressed that it promoted him to Brigadier-General, giving him command of the Army of Italy's artillery. He then crushed another royalist plot at Toulon.

While Major Bonaparte's cannon had been shelling Toulon a thirteen-year-old Prussian officer saw action on the Rhine against the French army. Carl Philipp Gottlieb von Clausewitz was serving as a *Fahnenjunker* (ensign) in the Prinz Ferdinand Regiment, and he must have watched the enemy's new-style Revolutionary troops, burning with fanaticism, singing the *Marseillaise* as they charged. One day he was going to write a book which would be read either as a brilliant treatise on war or, in the words of Liddell Hart, as 'a Prussian *Marseillaise* which inflamed the blood and intoxicated the mind'.

For a long period Napoleon was a committed Jacobin, declaring 'Marat and Robespierre, those are my saints.' It was true that he had a family to support – his adored mother, his brothers Joseph, Lucien, Louis and Jerome, his sisters Elisa, Caroline and Pauline – and his Corsican clan loyalty was such that as he prospered they would prosper with him. Yet his ideological commitment was perfectly genuine; indeed, he was so extreme in his opinions that he earned the reputation of being a 'Terrorist' – one of those responsible for the Terror. He never denied that he had held such views, admitting on St Helena, 'I was very young and my opinions were not settled', claiming that Robespierre 'possessed more foresight and policy than is generally appreciated'. He made firm friends with the 'Incorruptible's' brother Augustin – in so far as it was in his nature to make friends – and the younger Robespierre is known to have admired the little general.

'Everyone had accepted the thought of death,' he told Count Bertrand in 1821, just before he died. 'It was present every day in front of our eyes. They had grown used to the idea.' On another occasion he observed that had the Bonaparte family been a little richer or more distinguished his career would never have taken off. He deliberately coarsened his manners and appearance to curry favour with the *sans-culottes,* acquiring a filthiness of vocabulary which he was never able to lose in his days of glory. Barras recalls how he discerned in Bonaparte a striking resemblance to Marat, the bloodiest Jacobin of them all. Barras gives a description of Napoleon dancing attendance on the wife of an especially influential friend of the younger Robespierre, carrying her gloves and fan to ingratiate himself. He also has a hilarious account of the citizen general's behaviour at a dinner given by some local Revolutionary Committees to the Convention's commissioners, members of the former dining in one room, the commissioners in another – 'already playing the double role natural to him, he somehow managed to alternate between the commissioners' dinner, which he was happy and proud to attend, and that for the *sans-culottes* in the other room into which he went as though to apologise for not being with them'.

Bonaparte's first serious study of politicians was during his Jacobin period. The nine (later twelve) members of the Committee of Public Safety formed a joint dictatorship inspired by Rousseau's theory of the General Will – that the very best and wisest men decide what is to be done in the public interest, since representative democracy is impossible. They had taken over the government of France in April 1793 and ruled by martial law, sending opponents to the guillotine or massacring them, in order to save the Revolution from the armies of *ancien régime* Europe. The 'Terror' was Danton's invention; in coldly objective terms it meant the use of the strongest methods available to ensure the effectiveness of the Nation-in-Arms. The Law of Suspects extended the death penalty not only to obvious enemies like returned émigrés but to those who failed it, such as generals who let themselves be defeated. Danton declared that the Republic would never be safe so long as a single opponent was left alive; even 'indifferents' must be hunted down. Considered insufficiently extreme, Danton himself was sent to the scaffold by his colleagues. Henceforward Maximilien de Robespierre dominated the Committee. One of Robespierre's friends, Armand de Saint-Just, had warned that in certain circumstances the General Will could grow 'depraved', in which case it would establish itself in any conceivable form – 'in twenty years the throne might even be re-established'. (In *The Origins of Totalitarian Democracy* J. S. Talmon comments: 'It took less than twenty years for Napoleon to make the claim that he embodied the general will of the French nation and to find theoretical support for it.') The Terror unleashed a truly awful slaughter, until even Jacobins grew frightened. The coup of 9 Thermidor [27 July] established a milder régime, the Robespierrists going to the guillotine.

As has been seen, Napoleon always retained a soft spot for Robespierre, pointing out that 'Marat, Billaud de Varennes, Fouché and others were infinitely more ferocious'. He had particular respect for another formidable member of the joint dictatorship, Lazare Carnot, the Committee's 'architect of victory', whose ruthlessness and gifts of organization made the undisciplined French levies so extraordinarily effective. A Burgundian who in 1789 had been a sapper captain and a Chevalier of St Louis, he hated noblemen even more than Robespierre; Bonaparte says the latter had to stop Carnot sending too many of them to the guillotine.

The coup of Thermidor and fall of Robespierre was a shattering blow for Napoleon. Arrested the following month as a Robespierrist, for some weeks he was in very real danger of being guillotined like his former leader. The Thermidorians were Jacobins themselves, men who had been Terrorists, who had voted for the execution of Louis XVI. They finally seized power because they went in fear of their own lives. It is revealing that they regarded Citizen Bonaparte as being potentially a rabid extremist. His situation was so alarming that a Lieutenant Junot (a former sergeant whose bravery had impressed him during the siege of Toulon) offered to arrange his escape from prison. Fortunately, his commanding general persuaded the commission of inquiry that the Directory could not afford to lose so talented a soldier, and saved his life.

When released Napoleon made the mistake of refusing a posting to the Vendée (to fight royalist guerrillas) and was put on the half-pay list. He had been short of money before, but this was his first experience of real poverty. For a time he received no pay at all. Living in a seedy hotel near the Place des Victoires, he ate at cheap eating houses, wrapping the sums he paid with in paper to conceal how little he was spending. His uniform was ragged and he could not afford gloves. His brother Joseph sent him small sums which saved him from starving. Only a miraculous loan stopped him drowning himself in the Seine.

After 10 Thermidor 1794 and the fall of Robespierre there seemed small chance of Bonaparte ever soldiering again with the French army. He made fruitless inquiries about joining the Turkish service. Bourrienne saw much of him at this time and says he 'was always pensive, frequently anxious and depressed . . . None of his plans came to anything. Not one of his petitions received an answer. The ill treatment soured him. He was tormented by his need for activity, finding it unbearable to be just one of the crowd.' A lady friend of Stendhal (one of his earliest and most perceptive biographers) remembered meeting the unemployed citizen general early in 1795:

> Truly he was the thinnest and oddest being I ever met in my whole life. He wore huge "Spaniel's Ears" down to his shoulders, in the fashion of the day. Italian eyes with a piercing and occasionally gloomy look are not set off by such a mass of hair. Far from receiving the impression of a man of fiery genius, one is more apt to feel that this is someone it would be alarming to meet too close to a wood late at night.

The Paris in which Napoleon very nearly starved was a comparatively happy one, much happier than under Robespierre. He wrote to his brother Joseph in July 1795:

> Here luxury, pleasure and the arts are reviving astonishingly. Yesterday *Phèdre* was played at the Opera for the benefit of a retired actress; although the prices trebled there was an immense crowd by

two o'clock. Carriages and dandies are reappearing, and remember their eclipse only as a long dream . . .

Everything that can delight and make life pleasant is available. One has no time to think and how could one be gloomy in the midst of so gay a round and such a display of wit. The ladies are everywhere: in the theatre, out driving, in the libraries. You see lovely creatures in the scholar's study.

For all his Jacobinism and rejection of privilege, Napoleon never forgot what Carlo had instilled into him – that he was a nobleman. He only condemned privilege because it was expedient to do so, or when it was in hands other than his own. Later, despite his insistence on an 'open road for talent', he could not resist assuring Metternich that he was of aristocratic birth and ancient family (much to the latter's amusement). This conviction was an important element in his self-respect and belief that he was destined to be a leader. By contrast Adolf Hitler had no pretensions to nobility. When he came to dominate the European continent he would place Hungary first among 'the sickest communities of New Europe', apparently because it was still ruled by its aristocracy. One night in 1941 he would recall resentfully that in the world of his youth 'every man existed only by virtue of his origin'. Unlike Bonaparte – who secretly venerated blue blood – he condemned the nobles of *ancien régime* France as 'degenerates'.

Hitler's favourite reading was pro-German from a very early age, although he was an Austrian. This was a popular illustrated history of the Franco-Prussian War of 1870-1, in consequence of which 'I was forced to accept the fact, though with a secret envy, that not all Germans had the good luck to belong to Bismarck's Reich'. He would only learn why when he went to the Realschule (secondary school) at Linz, where he was to be fascinated by the lessons of a Dr Poetsch. Young Hitler was going to acquire (as he put it later), 'a feeling of intense love for my German-Austrian home and a profound hatred of the Austrian state, together with a conviction that the House of Habsburg did not, and could not, have any love for us Germans'.

He had been born on 20 April 1889 in Braunau am Inn, a little town on the Austro-Bavarian border where Aloïs was stationed. Two years later the Hitlers moved to the much bigger town of Passau, but early in 1895 Aloïs retired and bought a farm at Hafeld near the small market town of Lambach, thirty miles south-east of Linz, where he kept bees and tended his orchard. The farm began to lose money, so after a brief sojourn in Lambach, the Hitler family moved into a cottage with a garden in the substantial village of Leonding near Linz, where Aloïs continued to keep bees. Adolf had 'pleasant memories of woods and fields'.

His timid, mousy mother, Klara Poezl – one of the few people of whom he was genuinely fond – resembled Letizia only in her piety. Of the same peasant stock as Aloïs – she was his second cousin – Frau Hitler was twenty-three years younger than her gruff, tyrannical husband, of whom she went in awe. She had been his foster-daughter during his first marriage before going to Vienna as a servant. She returned to be his housekeeper while his second wife was dying, marrying him after her death. Aloïs was over fifty when Adolf was born. There was another son who just survived infancy, Edmund, born in 1894, together with a daughter, Paula, born two years later. She also had two stepchildren, from her husband's second marriage; Aloïs the younger, born in 1882, and Angela, born the following year. A quiet, gentle and affectionate woman who doted on her children, Klara was extremely hard-working and her house was spotlessly clean.

Their savage-tempered father beat the boys every day, the

principal victim being Aloïs, who ran away when he was fourteen, to become a waiter in Paris. Adolf seems to have had marginally better treatment. According to him, he infuriated his father by refusing even to think of a career in the customs service, and by wanting to be an artist. 'Naturally the resulting situation was not pleasant', Hitler recalled in *Mein Kampf.* 'The old gentleman was bitterly annoyed; and indeed so was I, although I really loved him.' He adds: 'It nauseated me to think how one day I might be fettered to an office stool, that I would not be able to dispose of my own time but forced to spend my entire life filling out forms.'

The Realschule at Linz was a worthy product of the highly efficient Austrian educational system, and should not be underestimated. Clearly it possessed some excellent masters, as is shown by Adolf's enthusiastic response to Dr Poetsch's teaching. The curriculum omitted Latin and Greek and was designed to equip pupils for commercial or technical careers; it included German, French, History, Geography, Mathematics, Chemistry, Physics, Natural History and Drawing. Despite his intelligence (which was recognized by all those who taught him), young Hitler did poorly at all subjects save drawing, for which he received excellent marks; surprisingly, even his history was only 'adequate'. The reason for this lacklustre performance seems to have been pure laziness.

When the Führer looked back in *Mein Kampf* on his days at the Realschule he none the less says that 'the ridiculously easy school tasks which we were given made it possible for me to spend more time in the open air'. It was an hour's walk from his home to the school, and in bad weather he would go there by train; later he lodged in Linz, with five other boys. A fellow-pupil, Joseph Keplinger, records 'We all liked him, both in the classroom and in the playground', adding 'He had guts.' The masters disagreed. One, Dr Hümer, thought him 'notoriously cantankerous, wilful, arrogant and irascible', recording that 'the gaunt, palefaced youth

. . . demanded of his fellow-students their unqualified subservience, fancying himself in the role of leader.' Another master recalled Adolf Hitler talking to trees as they waved in the wind, and making up replies. Probably he was not particularly strong, if good at gymnastics, and he may have suffered from chest trouble. The earliest-known sketch of him, when he was sixteen, shows a consumptive face, even though he did not suffer from tuberculosis. In *Mein Kampf* he states that he left the Realschule because a doctor told his mother that he should stay away from school for at least a year.

Adolf claims to have felt 'deeply bereaved when old Aloïs Hitler died suddenly from a stroke in January 1903, but one is inclined to doubt it – he certainly did not mourn him in the way Napoleon did Carlo. Aloïs had been a success, and received an obituary in Linz's leading newspaper, which paid tribute to the way he had risen in the world. He left his widow well provided for, so that she was able to maintain her standard of living. Now she was able to spoil her beloved Adolf to her heart's content: when he left school in 1905 she let him moon around, indulging his taste for foppery. He dressed smartly by the standards of his class, and carried an ivory-topped cane. Just as Napoleon had set his heart on becoming a soldier, so he was determined to become a famous artist and go to Vienna and study at the Academy of Fine Arts. He went to the opera and paid one or two trips to the capital. He had acquired a friend with similar tastes, Gustl Kubizek, who shared his passion for music.

In December 1907 Klara Hitler died. She had been suffering from cancer for the past year and a mastectomy failed to halt the disease. The doctor who had attended her, Dr Edward Bloch, recalled 'In all my long career I never saw anyone so prostrate with grief as Adolf Hitler.' He had been a kind physician, and although he was a Jew Hitler never forgot that, allowing him to emigrate years later.

When he was nearly eighteen and a half, in September 1907,

Adolf Hitler had taken a room in Vienna near the Westbahnhof, the railway station for Linz – much to the sorrow of his failing mother, by then in constant pain. The landlady was an aged Polish crone, the tiny apartment cramped and verminous. Nevertheless, his friend Kubizek came to stay there with him for a time. Almost as soon as he had installed himself in Vienna Adolf suffered the first major setback of his life. He failed the entrance examination to the Academy of Fine Arts, news which 'struck me like a bolt from the blue'. He thought of becoming an architect but did not have the qualifications to study. Nevertheless, he stayed in Vienna, sight-seeing, going to the opera in cheap seats, not even considering a career other than art or architecture, let alone a job. His father had left him a little money, and probably his mother did too; after her death he was paid an orphan's pension. He had in all 83 kronen a month, which was as much as a junior schoolmaster's salary. His mother's indulgence had provided him with an excellent wardrobe. He neither smoked nor drank – unusual for an eighteen-year-old – while, as a German study puts it, he incurred 'no flirtatious expenses'.

When he was twelve he had been to a performance of *Lohengrin*, the first opera he ever heard. 'I was fascinated at once. My youthful enthusiasm for the Bayreuth master knew no limits. Again and again I was drawn to hear his operas.' He dated his ambition to be a politician from the moment he saw *Rienzi* – whose plot is the tragedy of medieval Rome's great tribune. He considered *Tristan* to be Wagner's masterpiece. In January 1942 he recalled nostalgically 'At the beginning of this century there were people called Wagnerians. Other people had no special name. What joy each of Wagner's works has given me!' He went to the Vienna State Opera whenever he could. It is impossible to exaggerate the composer's influence on Hitler, who compared him with Frederick the Great and Martin Luther. Through Wagner he attuned himself to the

Germanic intellectual climate of the early twentieth century, a climate largely dominated by Schopenhauer and Nietzsche. Wagner had enthusiastically accepted the former's interpretation of music as the immediate language of the will, while it was no accident that the latter dedicated *The Birth of Tragedy* to the composer. It was from Nietzsche, however indirectly, that the Führer took his rejection of what he later termed 'the effeminate Judaeo-Christian pity ethic', although the philosopher had despised nationalism and anti-Semitism, and eventually Wagner himself. Wagner's combination of selfishness, cynicism and romanticism appealed deeply to the young Adolf.

Hitler's first-known flirtation was pure fantasy. During his mother's last illness she moved to Urfahr, a suburb of Linz. Here, walking with his friend Kubizek one day, he saw a tall, statuesque, blonde maiden, 'a real Valkyrie'. Adolf immediately told Kubizek, 'I'm in love with her!' She was two years older than him, and her name was Stefanie Jansten; she had studied at Munich and Vienna, and she had a whole host of admirers. He began to dog her foot-steps, and once during a flower festival she threw a rose at him, but he never spoke to her. He sent her a letter saying that he was about to study at the Academy of Fine Arts and that she must wait for him to come back and marry her. She was puzzled, since she did not know the writer. He composed poems in her honour, and dreamt about her for months. He told Kubizek that he contemplated drowning himself in the Danube, but since he wanted a joint performance, a suicide pact, and she did not know him the scheme had certain difficulties.

The Vienna in which he found himself was the capital of an empire containing many nationalities, much of which had been acquired by dynastic marriage. It was the successor of the old Holy Roman Empire *(Heilige Römisches Reich Deutscher Nation)* and yet in some ways it was the first modern international state, its territories constituting a symmetrical economic unit – even if its component races detested each other. Full of feudal pomp, dominated by an ancient and august dynasty and by a proud aristocracy, it was at the same time the city of Freud, of Gustav Klimt and Oskar Kokoschka, of Richard Strauss, Mahler and Alban Berg, of Robert Musil and Hugo von Hofmansthal, and of Karl Kraus. Yet the young Hitler could see little to admire, although he admits that there was a certain glamour.

> In the centre and in the Inner City one felt the pulse-beat of an empire which had a population of 52 million, with all the perilous charm of a state made up of multiple nationalities. The dazzling splendour of the court acted like a magnet on the wealth and intelligence of the whole empire . . . Vienna presented an appearance which made one think of her as an enthroned queen whose authoritative sway united the conglomeration of heterogeneous nationalities that lived under the Habsburg sceptre.

But, he goes on, 'the radiant beauty of the capital city made one forget the sad symptoms of senile decay which the state manifested as a whole.'

He was horrified by the *Reichsrat* (Parliament). 'A turbulent mass of people, all gesticulating and bawling against one another, with a pathetic old man shaking his bell and making frantic efforts to call the House to a sense of its dignity.' He could not help laughing. Next time he visited it, the chamber was empty save for a few yawning deputies. He admits 'In the light of my then attitude towards the House of Hapsburg I would have considered it a crime against liberty and reason to think of any kind of dictatorship as a form of government', that at that time he could not imagine any régime other than a parliamentary system. Yet he concluded 'If the Parliament was useless, the Habsburgs were worse.' There is no doubt that much of his hatred of democracy derived from what he saw in Vienna.

In *Mein Kampf* Hitler writes of poverty in Vienna.

> Dazzling riches and loathsome destitution were mingled in violent contrast . . . Thousands of unemployed loitered in front of the palaces on the Ring Strasse; and below the *Via Triumphalis* of old Austria the homeless huddled together in the murk and filth of the canals . . . I shudder even today [1923] when I think of the woeful dens in which people dwelt, the night shelters and the slums, and all the tenebrous spectacles of ordure, loathsome filth and wickedness.

He knew what he was talking about, but it was his own fault that he had experienced such things. He refused to consider any career other than one studying art or architecture. A second attempt to enter the Academy in September 1908 failed, his sketches being rejected as below standard; the finality and the humiliation must have been shattering. Yet instead of trying to find a job – he could easily have become a clerk or a shop assistant – he severed his links with his few friends, moved to another room and began to study politics. The politicians who attracted him were all extreme German nationalists. They included Karl Lueger, mayor of Vienna and leader of the Christian Social Party; an unfrocked Cistercian monk called Jorg Lanz von Liebenfals, 'Prior of the Order of the New Temple'; and Georg Ritter von Schönerer, leader of the Pan-German Movement. All three were anti-Semitic. To a young man sinking inexorably down the social scale – for all his delusions of grandeur – a sense of superiority over *anyone*, let alone Jews, provided a desperately needed sense of status. His own hopeless circumstances induced extremism. Schönerer's repudiation of the Habsburgs and of Catholicism also appealed to him, even if he was not yet quite ready to abandon a religion so dear to his mother.

It cannot be too much stressed that, like the young Napoleon, Hitler's ideas were those of his time. There has been controversy about the scope and depth of Adolf's reading, whether he read as voraciously as he claimed or merely absorbed knowledge through magazines and popular digests. Certainly it was undisciplined and, if he expressed admiration for Goethe and Schiller, his literary taste was often execrable, as for example his passion for the cowboy-and-Indian novelettes of Karl May.

While young Adolf disagreed with Karl Lueger's programme of saving the Habsburg empire by regenerating Vienna, and regretted that his Christian Socialist Party was 'only outwardly anti-Semitic', he was none the less impressed by his tactical skill. He contrasted it with Georg von Schönerer's political ineptitude. Lueger 'saw only too clearly that in our epoch the political fighting power of the upper classes is quite insignificant . . . he chose as the social basis of his new party that middle class which was threatened with extinction'. He was also struck by Lueger's cunning handling of the Catholic Church, and how he recruited many of the younger clergy. 'Dr Lueger's special talent' in Hitler's view was 'his rare gift of insight into human nature and he was very careful not to take men as something better than they were in reality'.

By the autumn of 1909 Hitler's resources were insufficient to support him. He had spent the money left by his parents, and could no longer afford to rent a room. He slept in coffee-houses, on park benches or in doorways, pawning what was left of his elegant wardrobe to buy food, queuing up at soup kitchens. Winter came early that year, and it was a bitter one. Starving, without an overcoat and frozen, his feet became so blistered by ceaseless trudging through the snow that he could barely hobble. In December, at the very end of his strength, unwashed and lousy, with matted hair and a beard, he was admitted to the *Asyl für Obdachlose* (Institute for the Homeless), near the Danube. Here his rags were taken away for delousing and he received a ticket entitling him to a bed and bread and soup for five days – perhaps longer, if he looked for a job.

We know something about Hitler at this time from Reinhold Hanisch, a German-speaking tramp from Bohemia who was in the next bed and wrote down an account in the 1930s – 'I was Hitler's Buddy.' He describes Adolf as a nightmarish figure even after his rescue from the streets, with a thin, famished face, burning eyes, a beard and long hair, who dressed in a cast-off black overcoat (a present from a Jewish second-hand clothes merchant) and a greasy old bowler-hat. Discovering he was 'an artist', Hanisch said that there was a market for painted postcards and small pictures, that if Adolf would paint some he would sell them. The little enterprise was a success and they moved to better accommodation, the *Männer-heim* (Home for Men), near the Jewish quarter of Leopoldstadt. A cubicle could be rented for three kronen a week, there was a canteen and reading-rooms, and facilities for washing clothes. In the summer of 1910 Hitler quarrelled with his partner, though he continued to live at the Männerheim until 1913, supporting himself by his paintings. But for Hanisch he would probably have gone under.

Before Hanisch suggested painting they had lived by begging, carrying luggage at the Westbahnhof – one wonders if Adolf saw any old friends arriving from Linz – or by shovelling snow. When he returned to Vienna in triumph at the Anschluss in 1938 he told his cronies that one night, after a fierce blizzard, he was clearing the snow away from outside the Kaiserhof Hotel and watched Archduke (later Emperor) Karl and Archduchess Zita going in over a red carpet. The spectacle and the strains of cheerful music which emerged made him bitter at the sheer injustice of life; he swore that one day he too would enter the Kaiserhof along the same carpet. The trouble with this reminiscence is that Karl and Zita were not married until 1911, by which time he could support himself and did not have to shovel snow. There is no need to question his dislike of the Habsburgs. In *Mein Kampf* he states that the German-Austrian people had come to feel strongly that the historical mission of the House of Habsburg as rulers of the First Reich had ended after the Franco-Prussian War when the Second, Hohenzollern, Reich came into existence.

He was determined to avoid military service with the Habsburg army. After five years in Vienna he decided to flee. But where was he to take refuge? Despite his rural upbringing, he was essentially a creature of cities, of artistic capitals. There were only two other artistic capitals in the German-speaking world, Dresden and Munich. Saxony was comparatively far away, while he had been born on the Bavarian border. Munich was the obvious place to go. In May 1913, on a sunlit Sunday, he therefore arrived at the Hauptbahnhof in Munich, on the train from Vienna. He had come to a city almost as romantic and musical. Its Wittelsbach royal family were perhaps not so worthy of reverence as the unifying Hohenzollerns, but at least they were Germans who ruled over Germans. As a devout Wagnerian, he approved of the late Ludwig II's idolatry of his hero, admiring deeply the King's fantastic palaces and castles. He may even have respected Ludwig III and Crown Prince Rupprecht, who both spoke that broad Bavarian dialect he found so soothing. There were three fine opera houses where he could hear his favourite music. As Hanisch observes quaintly, 'In music Richard Wagner brought him to bright flames.'

However, Hitler could not afford to go the opera very often. He found lodgings in the house of a tailor, Herr Popp, for which he paid in part by shopping, fetching coals and beating carpets. His main income seems to have come from working as a tourist guide. He continued to paint his postcards, though they did not sell as well. Often he was behind with his rent. His basic diet was bread and sausage. However, he managed to go fairly often to a coffee-house or a *bierkeller* where he could talk politics. And he read voraciously – 'all political stuff and how to get on in Parliament', according to Frau Popp. We know from a photograph of August 1914 that he smartened himself up, shaved off his beard, dressed neatly. He established surprisingly friendly relations with the Popps. Later he wrote how happy he had been, because of 'the charm of the marvellous Wittelsbach capital, which has attracted probably everybody who is blessed with an awareness of beauty instead of commercial instincts'.

Much has been made of his evading military service – when finally forced to appear before a board at Linz he was rejected as unfit – but it was not from cowardice: he did not wish to serve in a Habsburg regiment. He considered war inevitable; people feared 'the very existence of the German nation was at stake'. 'On 3 August 1914 I presented an urgent petition to His Majesty King Ludwig III requesting to be allowed to serve in a Bavarian regiment.' He joined the List Regiment (reserve infantry), and at the end of October was in action at the first battle of Ypres. He was so happy in the army that an officer commented that the List Regiment was Hitler's 'homeland'. He himself wrote: 'I look back on those days with wistful pride.' He became a dispatch runner, noted for ability to take messages through the heaviest bombardment. In December 1914 he won the Iron Cross Second Class. In October 1916 he was wounded in the leg and sent home for several months, during which he visited Munich and Berlin and was horrified by the defeatist mood (which he blamed on Jews and enemy propaganda); he began to contemplate a career in politics after the War. He was only too pleased to get back to the Front, and received a certificate of bravery from his regiment in May 1918, being awarded the Iron Cross First Class the following August – a decoration seldom given to non-commissioned officers. Oddly, he never rose above the rank of corporal, being considered deficient in 'leadership qualities', but he was perfectly content with his lot.

In October 1918 Corporal Adolf Hitler was caught in a British gas attack. 'My eyes were like glowing coals and all was darkness around me.' He was sent to a hospital in Pomerania. A chaplain visited the patients on 10 November, and, in tears, told them that the War had been lost. The shock sent Hitler blind again. 'Darkness surrounded me as I staggered and stumbled back to my ward and buried my aching head between the blankets and the pillow. I had not cried since the day I stood beside my mother's grave . . . my hatred grew – hatred for the originators of this dastardly crime.' His world had indeed come to an end. The War had all been in vain.

From 1918 to 1920 Adolf Hitler's prospects were bleaker than ever. The Hohenzollern Reich had collapsed, and the social order looked as though it would follow it. Berlin was taken over by the communist Spartacists under leaders like Rosa Luxemburg, while Bavaria became a socialist republic under Kurt Eisner. Understandably, middle-class Germans were terrified. The country swarmed with refugees from Soviet Russia, with grim tales of Bolshevik atrocities against the bourgeoisie. (Before 1914 German had been Russia's commercial language, so they had no difficulty in communicating their experiences.) The Freikorps came to the rescue of the middle class, unofficial paramilitary bands of veterans from the trenches. In Berlin they put down the Spartacists bloodily, 'executing' Rosa Luxemburg; in Munich they killed many Reds long after Eisner's government had been toppled and he himself assassinated. In mid-1919 the Peace Treaty of Versailles came as almost as bitter a blow as the Armistice of November 1918; Germany had to pay crippling reparations, allow the French to occupy the Rhineland, surrender her colonies, and reduce her army to 100,000 men. Most of the army refused to believe it had been defeated – the bearing of the Prussian Guard as it marched back into Berlin beneath the Brandenburger Tor was scarcely that of beaten men. There grew up the legend of the *Dolchstoss*, the Stab-in-the-Back; that the enemy had triumphed only because the troops had been betrayed at home by greedy financiers, agitators hoping for a revolution and Jews – regardless of the fact that large numbers of them had fought gallantly for Germany.

The drastic reduction in troop numbers could well mean Corporal Hitler's discharge. A ruined Germany was not going to buy many painted postcards. It was not impossible that he might sink back into the beggary he had known in Vienna during that dreadful winter of 1909.

Nothing could have been more different than the early careers of Napoleon Bonaparte and Adolf Hitler. One, a regular officer and a former petty noble, had destroyed his career prospects through dabbling in extremist politics. The other, a war-time ranker and sometime tramp, had fought loyally in defence not only of his country but of the old-established order – and, ironically, had seen far more of life and death in the front line. All they had in common was failure and the prospect of penniless oblivion.

I saw the world spin away beneath me, as if I had been borne up into the air.

Napoleon Bonaparte

I was forced now to scoff at the thought of my own personal future, which hitherto had been the cause of so much worry to me.

Adolf Hitler, Mein Kampf

2

The Way Up

Nothing could have been more different from Napoleon's rise to power than that of Adolf Hitler. Napoleon succeeded, a mere four years after being given command of an army, in becoming master of France at thirty. He did so because of his genius as a soldier and by a coup d'état. After Hitler returned to civilian life it took him thirteen years to capture Germany, through his political skill and by constitutional means. Yet while the two ascents differed, the backrounds to them bore some striking resemblances.

The Directory ruled France from 1795 until 1799. Power rested in the hands of five Directors, who were elected by the Council of Five Hundred and Council of Ancients. The 'Thermidorians' who had toppled Robespierre and now held power passed a law that two-thirds of the Council's members must have been members of the Convention which had preceded the Directory, making the régime unpopular from the beginning. There was a pervading fear of coups – whether by the Right (who might bring back the monarchy) or by the Left (who wanted the restore the Terror). It was an ineffectual government. There was runaway inflation, while the military situation began to deteriorate.

The Weimar Republic was an equally unhappy régime. Its constitution too was bicameral, but the President had semi-monarchical powers. The burden of the reparations to the victorious allies, the threat of communist revolution and terrible inflation, made it no less fearful. Its governments seemed powerless. The Right despised it.

The world of the Directory was gay and elegant but scarcely admirable. It was perhaps the most decadent period in all French history, dominated by selfish financiers and bankers. Paris swarmed with speculators and *grandes horizontales*. Weimar had much in common with the Directory. It too was gay and elegant, a time of artistic ferment. Similarly, money was everything. Georg Grosz's caricatures of profiteers flaunting newly acquired wealth were all too accurate, while war heroes begged at street corners.

Albert Speer describes in his memoirs the mood of all too many German middle-class intellectuals during the 1920s:

> Spengler's *Decline of the West* had convinced me that we were living
> in a period of decay strongly similar to the late Roman Empire:
> inflation, decline of morals, impotence of the German Reich. His
> essay 'Prussianism and Socialism' excited me especially because of
> the contempt for luxury and comfort it expressed.

Speer feared 'Spengler's dark predictions', did not believe his prophecy of the coming of a new Roman Emperor and thought communist revolution inevitable.

♔
N

By the autumn of 1795 royalists in Paris felt strong enough to seize power. The troops in the capital were mutinous, their commander, General Menou, parlying with the insurgents – most of them National Guardsmen. Menou was replaced by a Director, Barras, who knew that he himself could not cope. After releasing several hundred 'guillotine-lickers', Jacobin extremists, he sought out the little Robespierrist gunner who had been so effective at Toulon. There was some difficulty in finding him, since he was not at his usual shabby restaurant (later Barras claimed he had been negotiating with the royalists) but at the last moment he was appointed to be second-in-command. It was 9.00 p.m. on 13 Vendémiaire [5 October], and the crucial attack was expected early next morning. He at once sent a Major Murat and his squadron galloping off to an artillery park near Neuilly to bring up cannon. When the enemy attacked in the small hours they were cut to ribbons, in the Rue St Honoré, the Place du Carrousel and the Pont Royal; those who took refuge in the church of Saint-Roch were evicted at bayonet-point. Fighting continued until 9.00 a.m. on 14 Vendémiaire when the remaining royalists finally bolted, much to Napoleon's contempt – 'forgetting the military honour of Frenchmen'.

Bonaparte's reward was promotion to full general and command of the Army of the Interior. His real career was about to begin. However, he was too gauche socially to make the most of his opportunities, having no contacts in the ruling circle other than Barras.

This lack was made good by Citizeness Tascher-Beauharnais. A former Vicomtesse, she was a 32-year-old Créole whose husband, a second-rate nobleman, had been guillotined during the Terror because of his inadequate performance as a general of the Republic. Her best friend was Barras's favourite mistress, Thérèse Thallien – there were not implausible rumours that the pair had danced naked before him – and the Director was certainly one of her lovers. She seems to have slept with many of the régime's 'great and good'. Fouché, who ran the security services, was so impressed by her wide acquaintance ('she knows all Paris') that he paid her a retainer for useful gossip. When she was on the brink of financial ruin her instinct told her that the little general was a coming man, and she swiftly awakened his voracious sexuality. (An achievement she would live to regret; he is known to have had at least sixteen mistresses.) However, her most useful service to him in career terms was to introduce him to the Directory's establishment and to convince Barras that her new lover was devoted to him.

As commander of the Army of the Interior he had responsibility for law and order in Paris, where he swiftly purged its police of royalist personnel and shut the Jacobin Panthéon Club. On 9 March 1796 he married Josephine Tascher-Beauharnais; he was under the delusion that she was very rich, he needed her contacts and her house and he was also genuinely in love with her. A week before he had been given command of the Army of Italy, an appointment which his brother Lucien described as 'Barras's dowry' for Josephine. His orders were to mount a campaign over the Alps as part of an overall offensive against Austria; his role was to distract the enemy while Jourdan and Moreau, whose armies numbered 160,000 men, marched on Vienna – Bonaparte had only 36,000 troops and was not expected to advance very far. The plan was drawn up by Carnot, once the Terror's 'architect of victory'.

General Bonaparte arrived at his headquarters in Nice at the end of March 1796. His chilly reception by his generals is legendary; so too is the way he brought them to heel. They had thought he was no better than an intriguer who owed everything to Barras's favour, that the projected campaign was unworkable. Augereau, who had begun life as a footman and served in the Russian Army; Masséna, who had been a smuggler; La Harpe, a tough Swiss mercenary; Sérurier, who had become an ensign in 1754, when he was twelve; Berthier, who had been promoted colonel in 1778 during the American war – none of these were men to be easily cowed by a 'wild haired little runt' of twenty-six. Yet, as Augereau admitted, something about Bonaparte frightened them. (Each was to become one of his marshals.) What angered Napoleon was not his generals' attitude but the poor equipment and morale of his men, who were ragged and starving. His first step was to distribute a week's supply of bread, meat and spirits, while he complained to Paris about their miserable condition. Yet they were good material, many being mountaineers from Dauphiné (like today's Chasseurs Alpins), or southern hillmen. On St Helena he claimed to have issued the following order of the day:

> Soldiers! You are badly fed, almost naked. I am going to lead you into the most fertile plains in the world where you will find big cities and wealthy provinces. You will win honour, fame and riches.

He had never led an army in the field before. He faced 70,000 Austrians and Sardinians, well-equipped regulars full of confidence, who controlled the Alpine passes. Going into the mountains, he attacked the Austrians at Montenotte on 12 April, inflicting 3,000 casualties, hitting them again at Dego two days later. In between these victories he smashed the Sardinians at Millesimo, capturing an entire corps. These battles were fought in the rain, nearly two thousand feet up. He routed the last Sardinian army at Mondovi on 21 April, whereupon their king asked for an armistice. It was the first example of *blitzkrieg* – the lightning war which destroys an enemy in a flash.

Next came the turn of the Austrians, whom Bonaparte broke at the bridge of Lodi over the river Adda on 10 May, he himself leading the final charge over the bridge. He began to suspect that a brilliant destiny lay before him. ('I saw the world spin away beneath me, as if I had been borne up into the air,' he told General Gourgaud years later.) On 15 May he rode into Milan, capital of the Austrian duchy of that name. In July Field Marshal von Würmser attacked on two fronts in an attempt to relieve Mantua. Napoleon defeated Quasdanovich at Lonato on 3 August and Würmser himself two days afterwards at Castiglione, capturing 20,000 men with 50 cannon. Despite reinforcements, Würmser had to take refuge in Mantua.

Ironically, the main French offensive against Austria had ground to a halt – Jourdan defeated by Archduke Karl, Moreau retreating. A new Austrian general, Alvinzi, attacked Bonaparte in November, but after a battle lasting three days was routed at the bridge of Arcole. He returned in January 1797, to be beaten again at Rivoli. Mantua surrendered in February.

Napoleon now advanced into the Tyrol, aiming for Vienna. He reached Semmering, only 100 kilometres from the Imperial capital. On 18 April the Emperor sued for peace, whereupon Bonaparte went back to Italy and took Venice. At the Treaty of Campo Formio France secured the greatest diplomatic triumph of her entire history. The Austrians surrendered Belgium, besides recognizing the French puppet régime in northern Italy known as the Cisalpine Republic and the incorporation into France of the left bank of the Rhine. They were compensated with Venice.

Napoleon returned to France at the end of 1797 to receive an ecstatic welcome. He had won 18 pitched battles, captured 170 enemy colours and given his country a position surpassing that under Louis XIV at his most glorious. In addition he had sent home large consignments of bullion, together with countless art treasures. The street in which he lived was renamed 'Rue de la Victoire'.

While he was at Milan he had issued a proclamation, on 20 May 1796:

> Respect for property and personal security; respect for the religion of countries: these are the sentiments of the government of the French republic, and of the army of Italy. The French, victorious, consider the nations of Lombardy as their brothers.

His achievement appeared a little differently to those who were not French. William Pitt may have been biased, but a speech which he gave some years later (on 3 February 1800) to the House of

Commons gave an undeniably objective account of 'the horrors committed in Italy during the campaign of 1796-97'. He reminded Members of Parliament that:

In testimony of this fraternity, and to fulfil the solemn pledge of respecting property, this very proclamation [of Milan] imposed on the Milanese a provisional contribution to the amount of twenty millions of livres, or near one million sterling; and successive exactions were levied on that single state to the amount, in the whole, of near six millions sterling. The regard to religion and to the customs of the country were manifested with the same scrupulous fidelity. The churches were given up to indiscriminate plunder. Every religious and charitable fund, every public treasure was confiscated. The country was made the scene of every species of disorder and rapine. The priests, the established form of worship, all the objects of religious reverence, were openly insulted by the French troops . . .

The Prime Minister continued:

But of all the disgusting and tragical scenes which took place in Italy, in the course of the period I am describing, those which passed at Venice are perhaps the most striking.

He accused the French of deliberately goading the Venetians into rising against them and into issuing a proclamation hostile to France, Napoleon had then invaded Venice, installing a government on the 'democratic' French model, which he guaranteed with a treaty. Pitt states, accurately, that as soon as the treaty had been signed the French sacked and plundered the Arsenal and the Doges' Palace, besides demanding huge sums in cash from the inhabitants. He adds:

not more than four months afterwards, this very republic of Venice, united by alliance to France, the creature of Buonaparte himself, from whom it had received the present of French liberty, was by the

51

same Buonaparte transferred under the treaty of Campo Formio, to 'that iron yoke of the proud House of Austria', to deliver it from which he had represented in the first proclamation to be the great object of all his operations.

Understandably, the Directory were extremely uneasy about General Bonaparte. Not only was he hero-worshipped but he had shown alarming independence, ignoring its instructions – as when he demanded the surrender of Lombardy by the Austrians or declared war on Venice. Not only had he kept semi-regal state in his headquarters in the castle outside Milan, dining in public and never emerging without an escort of 300 lancers, but he had paid journalists to project his image to the French at home as well as among his men in the field. The *Courrier de l'Armée d'Italie* (on sale in Paris, and distributed free to soldiers) praised the exploits and personality of 'The First General of the Great Nation.' Other newspapers which he subsidized wrote in the same strain. Yet the Directors had only survived because of him; when royalists tried to bring down the Directory in 1797 Bonaparte's men led by Augereau purged the Councils at bayonet-point on 18 Fructidor (4 September). Many of the Republic's generals were suspected, with reason, of royalist or Jacobin sympathies. Moreover, when Napoleon returned to Paris he assumed a studiedly modest air, dressing in civilian clothes.

Bonaparte was ordered to plan the invasion of England. He approached the project in no light-hearted manner. But after personally reconnoitring the Channel coast he concluded by 23 February:

To carry out a descent on England without mastery of the sea would be the boldest and most difficult operation ever undertaken . . . The right moment to prepare for this exhibition has been lost, perhaps for ever.

Instead he proposed an expedition to Egypt. This was more than a mere flight of romantic fancy, and was inspired by calculations which were far from purely military. The overall strategy was to cut Britain's main trade route to India – even to provide a base from which to recommence the struggle for the sub-continent lost by France years before. More subtly, the expedition would enhance his prestige at home. The French were attracted by the glamour of the East, they had not forgotten that the first French colonies had been the Crusader states, and that St Louis had tried to conquer Egypt, while there was a fashionable taste for Egyptology. Above all, it was far away, removed from the sordid atmosphere of the Directors' domestic politics. Whatever Napoleon may have said afterwards, he had no intention of 'assuming the turban' and becoming a new Caliph. His ultimate motives for the Egyptian adventure were political, and he had every intention of returning to France.

At first the expedition was a triumphant success. Malta was captured en route, its unfortunate Knights being evicted from the island which had been their home for 250 years. The land of the Pharaohs was conquered with ease, the feudal army of its Mameluke rulers being routed in a colourful victory beneath the Pyramids. An Institut Egyptien was founded on the model of the Institut de France. French savants made such brilliant archaeological discoveries as the Rosetta Stone – the key to Egyptian hieroglyphs. There were rumours that, like Alexander the Great, Bonaparte was contemplating the conquest of Persia and India. The harsh reality was that Turkish troops and the British Navy soon confined him to Egypt. Nelson blew the French fleet out of the water at the battle of the Nile in August 1798, and his ships ruled the Mediterranean. Napoleon marched into Syria, and was checked at Acre. He was trapped. Should he try to return to France there was every chance of his being intercepted and imprisoned in Britain until the defeat of France.

At the end of 1918 Corporal Hitler, his eyesight restored, left hospital in Pomerania and rejoined his regiment at Munich. It is likely he went by way of Berlin, where he may even have seen the Freikorps crushing the Spartacists. (When their machine-guns fired down the streets terrified Berliners queued up in long lines behind lamp-posts to escape the bullets.) He was certainly in Munich during the fighting which finally destroyed the Bavarian Socialist Republic, though he stayed in the List Regiment's barracks throughout. As a reliable man with 'sound' political views, he was ordered to attend a course of lectures meant to 'inculcate certain fundamental principles on which the soldier could base his political ideas' – i.e. loyalty to Reichswehr and Fatherland – after which he was made an 'instruction orderly' with the task of lecturing the troops. In *Mein Kampf* he tells how as a schoolboy he had suspected he might be an orator, while during his days in the flop-house he had sometimes ranted at the inmates; Hanisch says that the sight of a rabble-rouser on the silent screen (in Kellerman's *The Tunnel*) drove him all but demented. Now 'I was able to confirm what I had hitherto merely felt, namely that I had a talent for public speaking.'

In September 1919 he was ordered to investigate one of the little political parties which had recently emerged, the National Socialist German Workers' Party (NSDAP). The President was a machinist from the local railway works, Anton Drexler. Its message was the need to synthesize nationalism and socialism. Shortly after, Hitler joined the party as its fifty-fifth member, an indication of its size. The new recruit spoke again and again, his first important speech being at the party's first public meeting in October, attended by 111 people. He spoke for thirty minutes in the small beer-cellar. The impression he made convinced him beyond doubt that 'I could speak.'

Early in 1920 he was entrusted with the Party's propaganda. By skilful use of posters and leaflets he attracted an audience of two thousand people to 'the first great mass-meeting under the auspices of the new movement'. Here he presented the Party's programme. Among its national policies were the inclusion of all Germans in a *Grossdeutschland*; the abrogation of the Treaty of Verseilles; denying German nationality to Jews; and the prohibition of immigration. Socialism was represented by demands for the confiscation of war profits, profit-sharing, increased old-age pensions; agricultural land reform, replacing the regular army by a citizens' militia, and the confiscation of unearned income. He was rewarded by wild applause. On 1 April 1920 he left the Reichswehr, in the autumn the movement became the Nationalist Socialist German Workers' Party (*Nationalsozialistische Deutsche Arbeiterpartei*, or NSDAP), in December a newspaper was bought, the *Völkischer Beobachter*, and on 29 July 1921 after driving Drexler out Hitler became leader of the Party – that evening a member saluted him with the words '*unser Führer*'.

There was more to this swift success than his genius as a demagogue and innate political skill. The régime and political climate in Bavaria were by nature sympathetic to forceful right-wingers. Both the Reichswehr and the Freikorps smiled benevolently on him, the latter providing many recruits. Among the 'officers and gentlemen' who joined him were Ernst Röhm, Hermann Goering and Franz-Xavier, Ritter von Epp. All had distinguished war records; Captain Röhm (who entered the Party even before Hitler) had been badly wounded in front-line fighting in the trenches before serving on the General Staff. The air-ace Major Goering (a Prussian, the only one of the three who was not a Bavarian) was admired throughout Germany as last squadron-leader of Richthofen's *Jagdstaffel*, whose bravery and 43 'kills' had been recognized by the Pour le Mérite, the supreme Hohenzollern award for gallantry. Major General von Epp, last commander of the Bavarian Royal Guard and now commander of the Bavarian Reichswehr, had been knighted for his bravery. Paradoxically, the 'undeserved defeat' of 1918 had enhanced the glamour of the military, already high enough in German esteem. By an odd irony the Reichswehr (most of whose officers were devoted monarchists) was the Weimar Republic's guarantee of stability, its safeguard against coups by Right or Left. And if the Freikorps did not exactly endear themselves to Reds, they were much appreciated by the Right. Militarism was in fashion, bands playing everywhere. Inevitably the new Party acquired a paramilitary organization, uniforms, ranks and the swastika standard being soon adopted. It also took to street fighting; the communists, already adepts at this, provided a perfect target for aggression, an activity which attracted still more veterans. Furthermore, while it had some distinguished members and a command structure, the Party was essentially egalitarian, offering the same comradeship which had existed in the trenches. On the whole the Bavarian middle classes were inclined to welcome an organization like the NSDAP as a defence against Russian-style revolution.

Until 1924 Germany was in chaos. Weak Social Democrat governments in Berlin and the state capitals were constantly threatened by a right-wing putsch or Bolshevik revolution. Most army officers, senior civil servants and academics were monarchists, while communists still hoped for a Soviet system. Early in 1923 the French occupied the Rhineland. In the same year inflation assumed astronomic proportions; the German mark collapsed, ruining a large part of the middle class overnight. Major Buchrucker, a war hero, attempted a right-wing coup in Berlin but was crushed by General von Seeckt, commander-in-chief of the Reichswehr. For a time Seeckt contemplated installing himself as Chancellor. Led by Ernst Thälmann, the communists rose in Hamburg, while left-wing extremists gained control of Saxony and Thuringia. Every-

where there were noisy demands for the dictatorship of the pro-
letariat, Red 'militia' being put down bloodily by the Reichswehr in
several areas.

The political (if not financial) situation in Bavaria differed from
that in the rest of Germany. Here the reaction in this Catholic and
largely agricultural state against Eisner's short-lived socialist
republic had brought to power a régime of the extreme Right, its
key figures being the prime minister Gustav von Kahr, the local
commander of the Reichswehr, General Otto von Lossow, and the
chief of police Hans von Seisser. They detested Social Democrats.
There were rumours that Bavaria would secede from the Reich to
which it had only been united for fifty years, rumours of a new
Austro-Bavarian state under the able Crown Prince Rupprecht.
Army officers began to take a new oath of loyalty, to Bavaria. Moreover, all right-wing paramilitary groups were encouraged, including National Socialists.

The Party's membership, organization and influence increased
rapidly during 1922-3. Two paramilitary groups were absorbed,
Röhm's Kriegsbanner and Friedrich Weber's Oberland Bund.
Major Goering, who lived in Munich with his Swedish wife Karen,
was given command of the stormtroopers; these were being trained
to use fists instead of guns, like Italian Fascists. Hitler acquired a
peculiarly effective rabble-rouser in the vicious person of Julius
Streicher, a ranting schoolmaster from Nuremberg noted for
sadistic treatment of his pupils. Every party member was encouraged by Mussolini's march on Rome.

By March 1923 General von Lossow was offering to support a
Fascist-style march on Berlin. However, in May he changed his
mind, threatening Hitler with arrest if he attempted one, forcing
him to give his word that he was not planning a putsch. Adolf did
so. He spent the early summer planning one, and waiting for a
further deterioration in Germany's overall situation.

In August 1923 Hitler addressed a full-scale parade of his storm-troopers for the first time. To the music of two military bands they marched on to the great Königsplatz in Munich, where a joint rally by various paramilitary groups was taking place. He denounced the 'November criminals' who had betrayed Germany in 1918, and his voice hoarse with excitement, ended by screaming *'Deutschland erwache!'* – 'Germany, awake!' According to Karl Ludecke, who was present, this strangely delivered speech had an undeniably impressive impact.

In September he held another parade at Bayreuth. He took the opportunity to visit Richard Wagner's 86-year-old widow and son at the Villa Wahnfried. Both welcomed him ecstatically, Cosima kissing him and Siegfried explaining that they admired him deeply. (In January 1942 he was to recall 'In addition to all Wagner's gifts, Cosima was femininity personified and her charm had its effect on all who visited Wahnfried.') He was also greeted by the composer's son-in-law, Houston Stewart Chamberlain, the son of an admiral in the Royal Navy, who believed that Germany's sacred mission was to convert the world to Wagnerian Teutonism. He told Hitler that he was 'God-given'. The latter undoubtedly read Chamberlain's book *Foundations of the Nineteenth Century,* and the writer's attitude must have contributed to his mixed feelings about the English. Afterwards Chamberlain wrote to him, telling him that he had played John the Baptist to Adolf's Messiah. Hitler treasured the memory of this delightful first visit to his hero's shrine, to which he was to return again and again. 'I was on Christian-name terms with them all,' he recounted years later. 'I love them all and I also love Wahnfried . . . the ten days of the Bayreuth season were always one of the blessed seasons of my life.' Wagnerian encouragement confirmed him in his sense of destiny.

The Nazi putsch of 1923 has generally been dismissed as crack-brained. Nevertheless, it was not entirely impracticable. The plan was to secure control of the Bavarian government and then, with Munich for a base, march on Berlin and seize power – like Mussolini's march the previous year. The Weimar Republic's authority seemed so brittle, disorder so widespread, that the scheme appeared to have a fair chance of success. General Ludendorff, second only to Hindenburg as a military leader during the war, agreed to accompany the march.

On the evening of 8 November Kahr, Lossow and Seisser attended a meeting of three thousand civil servants in the huge Bürgerbräukeller in Munich. Hitler slipped into the hall with a small bodyguard. Kahr was addressing the assembly when at 8.30 p.m. sixty steel-helmeted storm-troopers burst in, setting up machine-guns at the exits. Pandemonium broke out. Hitler, wearing a trenchcoat, jumped on to a table and fired two shots from a revolver. There was silence. He bellowed, 'The National Revolution has begun! There are six hundred men occupying this hall. No one is to leave. The Reichswehr barracks and the police barracks have been occupied. The Reichswehr and the police have joined the swastika flag. The Bavarian government is deposed! The Reich government is deposed!' None of this was true, but his hearers believed him. Kahr, Lossow and Seisser were taken into an office. Hitler waved his revolver, yelling at them, 'I have three bullets for you gentlemen and one for me!' They were unimpressed, but then Ludendorff entered and they agreed to do anything he wanted, accepting ministerial posts in the Reich's new government – which Hitler was to head, and in which Ludendorff would be commander of the Reichswehr. All that remained to be done was to march on Berlin.

However, Kahr and his two colleagues succeeded in leaving the Bürgerbräukeller, changed their minds and set about crushing the putsch. Next morning Hitler and Ludendorff – the former under the impression that he was about to become dictator of Germany – led three thousand armed men (their rifles were without firing-pins) into the centre of Munich. Then the police opened fire. General Ludendorff simply walked straight on and through the police, who dared not stop so imposing a figure. However, Scheubner-Richter, marching arm in arm with Hitler, fell to the ground mortally wounded and wrenching his leader's arm from its socket. In all 16 stormtroopers died and three policemen were killed; there were many wounded, Goering receiving a terrible injury in his groin. Hitler, half fainting with pain and nearly deranged, was driven to a friend's house in the nearby village of Uffing, where he hid in the attic. (He hoped to escape to Austria, regarding his political career as finished.) Here he was arrested on 11 November and taken to the prison at Landsberg.

Hitler was in despair after his arrest, terrified for weeks at what might happen to him – perhaps a life sentence. In prison at Landsberg he went on a long hunger-strike, refusing to speak. However, he succeeded in turning his trial – which began on 24 February 1924 – into the trial of Kahr, Lossow and Seisser rather than of himself. He rejected the charge of treason, and denounced the 'November criminals'. At moments the packed courtroom applauded him, and even the judges were won over. Lossow called him a liar, but it made no difference. Hitler was helped by Ludendorff standing beside him in the dock. (The Marshal was acquitted.) He played his cards brilliantly, presenting himself as a war veteran and, 'patriotic front soldier' who wanted to be 'the destroyer of Marxism'. Throughout the hearing flowers and chocolates arrived by the gross from new admirers. By the end of the trial the entire courtroom was under the spell of his oratory, even if some must have smiled at his description of himself as a 'man who is born to be a dictator'. He received the minimum sentence, five years, together with a strong recommendation for speedy parole – for which he would become eligible in six months' time – on account of his 'patriotic motives and honourable intentions'.

Landsberg-am-Lech, as Adolf Hitler experienced it, was more like a rest-home than a prison. Admittedly his cell was spartan but it was roomy compared with the cells of modern British and American gaols, and filled with flowers and delicacies; he was constantly receiving whole hams, strings of sausages and rich cakes, which he shared with his fellow-inmates. Among these was Rudolf Hess, the son of a German merchant in Cairo, who had served in the German Air Force during the War. He was able to eat with them in the common-room, and to exercise with them in the gymnasium. Even the unsupplemented prison diet was excellent, and wine or beer could be bought. The attitude of the warders was notably friendly, most of them becoming Nazis. He was allowed to receive letters and newspapers as well as a stream of visitors. He never forgot how 'Houston Stewart Chamberlain wrote to me so nicely when I was in prison'.

He read voraciously, and it often said that in some ways Landsberg fulfilled the function of a university for him. He wrote a book, *Mein Kampf* ('My Struggle'), which he dictated to Hess, who typed it. The work is partly autobiographical, partly a political treatise. It has been variously described a 'a ragbag of ideas' or 'a blue-print for world conquest', neither description being altogether accurate. Certainly it is nauseatingly anti-Semitic, and states unequivocally that one day racially pure Germans will inevitably rule the world. Yet some of the personal detail is vivid and absorbing. The point about *Mein Kampf* is that it was perfectly attuned to the prejudices of those Germans who believed they had been betrayed in November 1918, or of those ruined by the inflation, the author having a demonic facility for finding scapegoats.

Hitler was released from this far from unpleasant sojourn at Landsberg on 19 December 1924. Unquestionably his political situation had deteriorated. The Party had survived, but was tending to split into rival groups, while it was banned throughout

Germany – he himself was not allowed to speak in public until 1927. Worst of all (from the Nazi point of view) Weimar had learnt how to cope with the economic situation and ended the inflation. Prosperity began to return for the first time since 1914, while the diplomacy of the Chancellor, Gustav Stresemann, gained new prestige for Germany. The present writer's father, who was living in Berlin, wrote in August 1926:

> the financial and general position of Germany is improving with astonishing rapidity. At the same rate Germany will have regained her old position within fifteen or twenty years. There is still a shortage of liquid capital, but that is a natural sequel to the German inflation. The feeling towards England is, on the whole, good, but the hatred against France is very bitter.[6]

The paramilitary organizations melted away. The Weimar Republic seemed to have to have found its feet.

The Nazis became a fringe party with a membership of less than 30,000 and considerable financial problems. The writer of the letter quoted above saw a group of stormtroopers demonstrating in Mannheim in 1927, and noticed that their uniforms were cheap and shoddy, their transport ramshackle. There were dangerously individualist interpretations of the Hitlerian gospel, notably by Gregor and Otto Strasser in Berlin, who tried to make the Party concentrate as much on socialism as on nationalism. Adolf outmanoeuvred them by detaching their most able adherent, the hitherto fanatically socialist Dr Josef Goebbels, who wrested control of the Berlin Party organization from them. Although the Nazis survived, they did not have enough money to organize a full-scale rally during 1927. In the elections the following year they secured only 2.5 per cent of the vote, less than a million. Many senior members despaired, like Röhm, who joined the Bolivian army. None the less there were a few useful recruits, such as a slavishly obedient young chicken-farmer called Heinrich Himmler. By 1929 Adolf Hitler, the would-be dictator of Germany, was a figure of some derision.

Again, nothing could have been more dissimilar than the early progress of Napoleon and Hitler. The former was a triumphant conqueror and national hero at twenty-six, the latter still a political adventurer with little more than an abortive coup behind him when he entered his forties.

The risk is terrible yet unavoidable; one can only escape from
anarchy through despotism, and risk finding the same man first a
saviour then a destroyer, in the certain knowledge that from now
on one is going to be the pawn of an unknown will . . . this is the
bitter fruit of social dissolution.

Hippolyte Taine, Les Origines de la France contemporaine

What is the ape to the man? A jest or a thing of shame. So shall man
be to the Superman – a jest or a thing of shame.

Friedrich Nietzsche, Also Sprach Zarathustra

3

Brumaire and Gleichschaltung – 1799 and 1933

At first sight the methods by which Napoleon and Hitler obtained power may seem very different. One did so by a straightforward coup d'état, the other by constitutional means. However, a closer examination reveals considerable resemblances. The aim was exactly the same – to secure total control of the State. Napoleon was supported by an army with (in theory), revolutionary principles, which was in practice inspired by personal loyalty and careerism; Hitler by an army of storm-troopers similarly motivated by personal loyalty and careerism. Both leaders duped numerous formidable politicians who had thought that they could make use of them. The period which it took them to impose their respective forms of tyranny was approximately the same.

The future Emperor never ceased to be sensitive about accusations of illegality. 'There has been much heated discussion and there will be much more of it for years to come as to whether we did or did not break the law and whether we acted like criminals,' he recalled on St Helena. 'The fact is that the country would have been lost without us and we saved it.' 'It was a civil and not a military coup,' he told Bertrand a few months before his death in 1821. 'In reality it was Sieyès and the civilians who were acting. I was little more than their agent.' In his opinion any criticisms were idealistic claptrap. He also claimed, most untruthfully, that no operation could have gone more smoothly.

It has to be admitted that in some respects the Führer's real Brumaire had been the Munich putsch of 1923. Ten years later he had had quite enough of coups d'état. In 1942, after dinner one evening, he explained that to his guests. 'I considered it of the highest importance that I should legitimately take over the Chancellorship with the blessing of the Old Gentleman ['Der alte Herr' – President Hindenberg], he told them. 'For it was only as constitutionally elected Chancellor . . . that I could overcome the opposition of all the other political parties, and finding myself in constant conflict with the Wehrmacht.' He feared that if he took power illegally the Wehrmacht – the armed forces – might launch a coup of their own. By acting constitutionally he was in a position to restrain the activities of the Wehrmacht to its legal and strictly limited function, until he had introduced conscription. He knew that he would then be able to swamp it with Nazi recruits, enabling him to 'overcome all opposition among the armed forces, and in particular in the corps of officers'.

♔
N

By the summer of 1799 the Directory was beginning to collapse. It was showing unmistakable signs of terminal decay, and was unpopular with all save those who had vested interests. Napoleon's Italian conquests of 1796-7 had been lost, Holland and Belgium were threatened, and General Jourdan had been heavily defeated by Archduke Karl, being driven back across the Rhine; France lived in justified fear of invasion by the armies of Austria and Russia. The treasury was empty, and there was galloping inflation, French *assignats* or banknotes being practically worthless. (The gold franc was worth more than 80,000 paper francs, compared with 75 in 1794). There were countless bankruptcies and chronic unemployment – including over 80 per cent of artisans in Paris. Taxation soared; a forced loan of 100 million francs was imposed in August 1799. Manufacture, trade, finance, agriculture – every aspect of French economic life was in decline. Not only was brigandage rife but the Vendée had risen once more for the Bourbons and the Catholic Church, under some extremely formidable guerrilla commanders. The Council of Ancients (or upper house) was dominated by 'moderates', many of whom were royalists; on the other hand, the Council of Five Hundred (or lower house) was controlled by Jacobins. Most of the Directors were personally contemptible, in particular Barras. He had grown more corrupt and dissolute than ever, selling government posts to pay for his gambling and his mistresses; he was plotting to sell the entire country back to the Bourbons for 12 million francs. His principal opponent was the ablest of the Directors, Sieyès, who believed that a new Constitution with a stronger executive was needed to save the Republic.

In fact, the régime had reached the point of dissolution for which General Bonaparte had been waiting in Egypt. Two years before, he had told Talleyrand that the Directory could not survive. On 23 August 1799 he embarked on the six-week voyage back to France, although the Mediterranean was controlled by Nelson's fleet in overwhelming strength, making this a gamble of the utmost audacity. His little ship and her three companion vessels slipped past the blockade, passing at midnight through the British. News of his latest victory, over the Turks at Aboukir in July, had preceded him when he landed at Fréjus on 9 October. He had feared he would be quarantined; instead the crowds shouted, 'We prefer plague to Austrians!' When he reached Paris he was distracted by a terrible quarrel with Josephine over her infidelities, but it ended in reconciliation. Understandably nervous, the Directors gave a public banquet in his honour – at which he gave the ominous toast, 'Union of all the parties.' He was offered any command he chose, but preferred to keep a low profile. He wore civilian clothes and behaved as he had in 1797, attending scientific lectures; however, it was noticed that he made himself especially amiable to anyone who had served with the Army of Italy. He explored the possibility of becoming a Director, but was told he had not yet reached the statutory age of forty.

The Director Sieyès decided to make use of the little general. Now in his fifties, a former priest and once vicar-general of Chartres, he had voted for the execution of Louis XVI but was more a survivor than a revolutionary (*'J'ai vécu'*). A small, thin, dry man with a grave smile and a courteous manner, he thought of himself as a political scientist, a framer of Constitutions. One of the ablest politicians in France, if excessively self-confident, he had contemplated using General Bernadotte, a former Minister for War, despite his Jacobin sympathies, but decided he was an ambitious lightweight – 'While he looks like an eagle in reality he is a goose.' Again, in his own words, 'I must have a sword but who will wield it? Hoche and Joubert are dead. That leaves Bonaparte, who may be less trustworthy and less honest but is more brilliant.' His allies, Talleyrand and Fouché, agreed that Bonaparte was the right man for their purpose.

Napoleon was already building a power base of his own. Lucien Bonaparte had contrived to be elected President of the Five Hundred; he and their brother Joseph sought feverishly for allies and useful contacts. So did Josephine among her smart friends.

Lucien arranged for Sieyès to meet Napoleon at his house in the Rue Verte. The Abbé at once took a dislike to 'that insolent little man', an aversion which was mutual. Nevertheless, they managed to reach an agreement. Joseph tried to enlist Bernadotte – they were brothers-in-law – since he had more influence than any general in Paris after Bonaparte. But Bernadotte had ambitions of his own; he had already advised the Directors to arrest Napoleon for abandoning his command in Egypt without permission – which was a capital offence.

Sieyès had brought another Director, the colourless Roger Ducos, into the plot, aimed at the remaining three. The plan was to force them to resign and then to persuade the Councils to nominate a committee of three who would prepare a new Constitution. A chance to assemble troops had been provided by three regiments petitioning Bonaparte to review them, while countless officers had called on him to pay their respects after his return; it is reasonable to suppose that they guessed something was in the wind. The parade was to take place on the Champs-Élysées on 18 Brumaire (9 September).

At first the coup went well enough. At Josephine's house in the Rue Chantereine (or 'Rue de la Victoire') Napoleon rose very early on the morning of 18 Brumaire, put on an olive green civilian coat and placed a brace of pistols in his pockets. A stream of officers began to arrive. He took each one separately into the little study and asked if he would 'join in a journey' to save the Republic. Most agreed, including General Lefèbvre (military governor of Paris) who promised to 'chuck those legal buggers into the river'. The exception was Bernadotte, who refused to take part in 'this rebellion'; Joseph Bonaparte took him off to lunch in the country outside Paris under the impression that nothing would happen.

Meanwhile Sieyès left the Luxembourg (the Directory's official residence) on horseback, his clumsy horsemanship entertaining vastly another Director not in the secret. He had already persuaded the Council of Ancients to meet early by announcing that a Jacobin plot had been discovered. They agreed to transfer both Councils to Saint-Cloud and to entrust General Bonaparte with the armed forces. Napoleon changed into full dress, and accompanied by twenty officers, rode to the Tuileries at 7.30 a.m. to take an oath of loyalty. Within an hour a decree had been voted by the Ancients giving him command of all troops in and around Paris, including the National Guard.

He then set up his headquarters at the Tuileries. Barras sent his secretary, one Bottot, to find out what was happening. Napoleon lectured Bottot as though he were Barras himself. 'What have you done', he demanded dramatically, 'with that fair France I left so prosperous in your hands? In place of peace I find war. I left you victories, I find defeats! I left you the riches of Italy, and I find nothing but grinding taxation and misery. What have you done with the hundred thousand brave Frenchmen I once knew, my comrades in glory? They are dead.' The three hostile directors – Barras, Gohier and Moulins – were arrested. Barras signed a gracefully phrased resignation forced on him by Talleyrand in return for a promise of half a million francs (which Talleyrand seems to have pocketed), while the other two also gave way.

So far Sieyès could argue that what happened was technically legal, simply a parliamentary manoeuvre. The next problem was to persuade the Councils to appoint three consuls to reform the Constitution. He advised Bonaparte to arrest their hard-line Jacobin members but the general refused. It was the first sign that Sieyès was losing control of his coup.

After the Ancients had assembled on the following afternoon Bonaparte suddenly burst in and gave a long-winded speech during which he denied rumours that he was 'a Cromwell, a Caesar'. He assured them: 'Had I wanted power I have had plenty of opportunities before. I swear that France holds no more loyal patriot. There is danger all around. We must not risk losing the benefits we have bought so dearly – liberty and equality.' He accused Jacobins of wanting to bring back the Terror. He had revealed that he had in mind more than a mere revision of the Constitution. However, there was neither applause nor booing, and his secretary hustled him out of the chamber. When he entered the hall in which the Five Hundred were sitting pandemonium ensued. There were shouts of 'The Constitution or death!' 'Down with the Dictator!' 'Down with the tyrant!' 'Outlaw him!' Someone hit him, another member attacked him with a dagger. He had one of his nervous fits and, half fainting, was dragged out by some soldiers who had followed him in. The Five Hundred at once began to move that he be outlawed – the tactic which had brought down Robespierre. Lucien saved the day by rushing out, leaving the Council without a president, and telling the troops that assassins inside were menacing the Five Hundred with stilettos and that they must clear the chamber. Generals Leclerc and Murat then led in three hundred grenadiers to the roll of drums, with fixed bayonets, and the deputies bolted through the windows. That evening thirty of them were dragged in from the local restaurants and cafés, and forced to vote the acceptance of the Directors' resignations, the appointment of three provisional consuls and the drawing up of a new Constitution.

A hostile observer, William Pitt, gives a résumé of Napoleon's civil as opposed to his military career, which casts a mercilessly accurate light on his political morality. 'When the Constitution of the third year [of Revolution, 1795] was established under Barras, that Constitution was imposed by the arms of Buonaparte.' Similarly, the Prime Minister told the House of Commons, the coup of Fructidor in 1797 had succeeded only because of 'Buonaparte's support for the Directory'. He continued:

> Immediately before this event, in the midst of the desolation and bloodshed of Italy, he had received the sacred present of new banners from the Directory; he delivered them to his army with this exhortation: 'Let us swear, fellow soldiers, by the *manes* of the patriots who have died by our side, eternal hatred to the enemies of the Constitution of the third year.' That very Constitution which he soon after

enabled the Directory to violate, and which, at the head of his grenadiers, he has now finally destroyed.

For some time Sieyès remained under the delusion that it was he who really controlled the new régime in Paris. He himself was one of the three provisional Consuls, his friend Roger Ducos was another, while his old allies Fouché, Talleyrand, Cambacérès and Goudin were the ministers responsible for police, foreign affairs, justice and finance. Admittedly he received a jolt at the very first discussions, when Bonaparte showed an unexpected grasp of financial and foreign affairs; afterwards he told Talleyrand and some other ministers, 'Messieurs, I perceive you have acquired a master.' Yet Sieyès still thought he could handle the General. He dominated the two commissions charged with framing the new Constitution, and was confident of having his way. Despite the coup and despite the General, the new government was political, not military; it was dominated by men who had been in political life for a decade, who had supported the coup against Robespierre. Indeed, Bonaparte attended the meetings at the Luxembourg wearing civilian clothes. Sieyès proposed that ultimate power should be in the hands of a Senate recruited from the wealthy who would appoint the executive and the legislature; the former were to consist of two Consuls – one for home affairs, one for foreign – and a Grand Elector at Versailles with a salary of 6 million francs, whose function would be advisory and ceremonial. To his consternation Napoleon refused to be Grand Elector. 'Who is going to accept an office whose sole duties are to grow fat like a pig on millions a year?' he asked, adding that a government of this sort would be the shadow of a state – 'France would be knee-deep in blood!' Sieyès, 'man of systems', was outraged. Ten days of wrangling ensued, in theory about the Constitution, in practice over political power, during which Bonaparte tried to isolate his opponent. Sieyès retaliated by accusing him of planning to make himself king of France, a dangerous charge which the General defused by pointing out that he had declined to be Grand Elector for life. There were eleven such meetings at the Luxembourg in which Sieyès argued passionately in defence of his belief in rule by assemblies instead of by ministers, let alone individuals.

The new Constitution of the French Republic was published on 24 December 1799. There were three Consuls, appointed for ten years, Bonaparte being First Consul with the power of appointing ministers. The three were to be elected by a Senate who also chose the members of two of the legislative assemblies; the third legislative assembly, the Council of State, was to be appointed by the First Consul. He graciously allowed Sieyès to select the men for the Senate. Nevertheless, the public were astounded to learn that Sieyès was not among the Consuls. Shortly after, he retired to a château deep in the country to enjoy the fortune he had acquired during the last decade. Bonaparte's shadowy colleagues were the elderly Charles-François Lebrun, a treasury mandarin from the days before 1789, and Jean-Jacques Cambacérès, a gifted jurist – useful assistants whose powers were purely advisory.

The choice of ministers reflected the First Consul's total control. His brother Lucien (the former President of the Five Hundred who had saved the day on 19 Brumaire) was Minister of the Interior, keeping an eye on Fouché, who was Minister of Police. The latter's political ally Talleyrand – they detested each other – was Minister of Foreign Affairs. Napoleon did not entirely trust Lucien's obedience or his judgment, so he hobbled him by imposing two director-generals on his department. Other ministers were similarly restricted by assistant ministers or director-generals. He deliberately divided their powers in order to rule them. France had been deprived not only of parliamentary government but of ministerial government as well. There was no mention in the new Constitution of liberty, equality or fraternity.

On 17 February 1800 a plebiscite confirmed France's approval of the new régime – from an electorate of 9 million Frenchmen over 3 million voted in favour, as opposed to a mere 1,562 against. (Lucien Bonaparte had helped to organize this gratifying result; only a million and a half actually voted.) On the day the votes were announced the First Consul moved his official residence from the Luxembourg to the Tuileries, from the residence of the Directors to the palace of the kings of France. He commented, 'It isn't everything to be in the Tuileries – the great thing is to stay here.' It was precisely a hundred days since 18 Brumaire.

The way in which Bonaparte had outmanoeuvred Sieyès is highly significant, since the latter was the first really formidable politician whom he faced as an equal. Hitherto his previous relationship with politicians was that between client and patrons. And Sieyès had been a power in the land since 1789, deeply respected. (Stendhal lists him with Mirabeau, Danton and Napoleon as a founder of modern France.) He, not Bonaparte, had been the originator and planner of 18 Brumaire. Yet he had been outwitted by a series of moves in which his 'ally' used bullying and bribery to isolate him. Bonaparte had demonstrated that he was as gifted a politician as he was a soldier.

The reason before all others why Napoleon's rule was accepted by a majority of Frenchmen was a yearning for peace. They wanted a strong man. Sieyès and the Directory's ousted establishment plotted against him in their country retreats, while the royalists were still very strong indeed, still very hopeful. The Jacobins, meanwhile, looked to Bernadotte and Lazare Carnot. The First Consul knew from Fouché that Paris seethed with plots, that he had plausible rivals – that he was far from secure. If he could reconquer Lombardy, where he had been so triumphant, it would be an unpopular campaign but he would assert his dominance in a 'last war'.

In May 1800 he crossed the St Bernard Pass to invade Lombardy.

Carefully orchestrated propaganda made the most of this mountain journey; bulletins described the First Consul leaping crevasses, jumping from precipices and sliding down the snow – there were frequent comparisons with Hannibal. On 14 June, by a crass miscalculation, he found himself facing General Melas and 40,000 Austrians with only 20,000 men and almost no cavalry. His 70-year-old antagonist drove the French off the battlefield, so certain of victory that he went to bed. In the nick of time General Desaix arrived with the French reserves. He told Bonaparte, 'I think we've lost this battle', receiving the reply 'I think we've won it.' By the end of the day the Austrians were routed. Desaix had been killed leading an infantry charge, so the First Consul took all the credit for the victory which gave him northern Italy. It gave him more, the dictatorship of France.

On hearing the news Pitt's ally, William Windham MP, commented 'Shocking business.' For Marengo had fastened Bonaparte's rule over the French still more firmly. The way lay open for him to make himself Consul for life, and then Emperor.

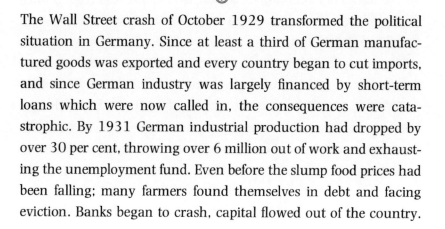

The Wall Street crash of October 1929 transformed the political situation in Germany. Since at least a third of German manufactured goods was exported and every country began to cut imports, and since German industry was largely financed by short-term loans which were now called in, the consequences were catastrophic. By 1931 German industrial production had dropped by over 30 per cent, throwing over 6 million out of work and exhausting the unemployment fund. Even before the slump food prices had been falling; many farmers found themselves in debt and facing eviction. Banks began to crash, capital flowed out of the country.

Yet Germany had to continue paying reparations to the victors of 1918. Everyone sought scapegoats; Prussian junkers who bullied the State into keeping their unviable farms afloat, the banking community and Jews – whether of the capitalist or anti-capitalist sort.

Hitler knew exactly how to exploit the situation. A hundred speakers were trained at a special Party school and then roamed the country delivering inflammatory harangues; storm-troopers contacted old war comrades throughout Germany, trying to enlist them; the party's newspapers were slanted to maximum effect (pillorying the Jews); and the Führer went on whistle-stop tours making speeches of diabolical cunning. He recruited the young unemployed as storm-troopers, giving them food, shelter and a purpose.

The communists played into his hands. On orders from Moscow they refused to consider a Popular Front with the Social Democrats; while their own storm-troopers in leather uniforms rivalled the Nazis' SA (or Sturmabteilung) in pugnacious street fighting, filling the middle classes with dread.

The success of Hitler's tactics was demonstrated in the elections of September 1930, in which the Nazis secured 6.4 million votes and 107 seats in the Reichstag, to become the second largest party after the Social Democrats (compared with less than a million votes and only 12 seats in 1928).

The new Chancellor was Heinrich Brüning of the Catholic Zentrum party, who formed a right-of-centre coalition. Without a majority in the Reichstag, he governed by Presidential decree, Hindenburg using the emergency powers given to him by the Weimar constitution. Austerity measures, such as cutting unemployment benefits and civil servants' salaries, merely succeeded in throwing more people out of work. Yet Brüning had a scheme which might have altered the course of history: he planned that after

Hindenberg had been re-elected President in 1932 the Reichstag should proclaim the restoration of the monarchy with the old Field Marshal as Regent for life, to be succeeded by a Hohenzollern emperor. The Reichstag's support was to be secured by revising the terms of Versailles and ending reparations – and, where the Left was concerned, by emphasizing the threat of Nazi takeover. It would split the Right in two, since all Nationalists and many Nazis would approve; Hitler would be put in an awkward position since he had often pretended he meant to bring back the monarchy. The army would be totally in favour. Brüning's scheme received grudging approval from a few far-sighted Social Democrats who realized it might be the one chance of derailing the Nazi juggernaut. Unfortunately, he was not given time.

In 1931 the Nationalists decided that Brüning was a left-winger. In October all their groups paraded together with the Nazis at Bad Harzburg in a mass rally (the 'Harzburg Front') which demanded the Chancellor's resignation. The Nationalist Party, the Stahlhelm (ex-servicemen), the business magnates and all men of the conservative Right were by now convinced that Herr Hitler and his movement could be harnessed for their own purposes. Although they welcomed his attacks on Bolshevism and democracy, they still did not take him seriously – what they wanted was his movement's votes in the Reichstag, not his wild ideas of 'revolution'.

Meanwhile the Führer suffered an emotional collapse over a woman, for the only time in his life. From the very beginning of his political career there had been speculation about his sexuality, which remains a mystery even today. We know that during his rise to power, and still more after he achieved it, women found him irresistible despite his lack of good looks, but that – far from being a pouncer like Napoleon – he resisted every feminine wile. However, he developed an incestuous passion for his niece Geli Raubal (daughter of his half-sister Angela Hitler), a lively and attractive girl who hoped to become a musician. He seems to have fallen obsessively in love with her in 1929 when she was twenty, installing her in his Munich flat on the Prinz-Regentenstrasse and paying for singing lessons by the most fashionable Wagnerian teachers. Happy enough at first, she began to look increasingly miserable; there were noisy quarrels in public. He was shattered when in September 1931, while he was campaigning, news reached him that Geli had shot herself in their Munich flat. For two months he was a broken man, threatening to abandon politics. There is no need to doubt his sincerity. No one has ever explained convincingly why she committed suicide, though it was after an especially bitter row with her uncle. Many reasons have been suggested, most of them sexual, ranging from suspicions that Hitler was unable to satisfy her in bed to discovering her having an affair with his chauffeur Emil Maurice. The wife of Adolf's friend Hanfstängl was certain he was impotent, while Hanfstängl claimed to have seen pornographic drawings of Geli by the Führer. Apart from the incestuous aspect and the possibility that he was slightly undersexed, the relationship may have been much more normal, or nearer normalcy, than is generally supposed. (Hitler may have given a clue why she killed herself during his fury at Field Marshal Paulus's failure to commit ritual suicide after the fall of Stalingrad in 1943; he spoke of 'a really beautiful woman' who felt insulted by 'her husband' over some triviality and threatened to leave, 'I can go? I'm not wanted?' – and who on being told 'Get out then' wrote a farewell note and shot herself.) He never forgot her, keeping her room just as it was and hanging her photograph in his bedroom.

It is not impossible that the Führer was syphilitic. The symptoms of the undiagnosed malady from which he suffered at the end of the war were not dissimilar from those of tertiary syphilis. Putzi Hanfstängl says that he was rumoured to have been infected with the disease during his early days in Vienna. But Hanfstängl was a gossip who invented what he did not know for the sake of effect. He speculates that Hitler's 'abounding nervous energy which found no normal release sought compensation first in the subjection of his entourage, then of his country, then of Europe'. Yet the Emperor took many mistresses without weakening his drive as a conqueror. On the other hand, it is not inconceivable that Adolf Hitler's sexuality was sublimated in his lust for power.

The key to the political situation was the 'ersatz Kaiser', Field Marshal Paul von Hindenburg, President since 1925, he gave Germans a reassuring impression of dignity and solidity. Born in 1847, he was the archetypal Prussian officer; he had ridden into Paris in 1871, had presided over the annihilation of the Russians at Tannenberg in 1914, had been the symbol of the War Effort and had emerged untarnished from the débâcle of 1918. Unfortunately, not only was his mind failing but he was vain and obstinate; by 1932 he was all but senile, under the influence of his shallow and venal son Oskar. When he stood for President again that year he was incapable of reading a newspaper, let alone of writing a speech. Hitler took out German nationality to stand against him. In the first ballot the Field Marshal only just missed an overall majority, with 18 million votes compared to Hitler's 11 million, the communist Thälmann's 5 million and the Nationalists' 3 million. In the second Hindenburg won over 19 million, securing his majority, though Hitler increased his vote to over 13 million.

The President dismissed Brüning, insisting on a cabinet whom he found congenial. The result was the 'Cabinet of Barons', so called because seven of its ten members were noblemen. The new Chancellor was a Westphalian aristocrat, Franz von Papen, who at best was a cunning intriguer. Like Brüning, he had to govern by Presidential decree since he did not have a majority in the Reichstag. On the pretext that it could not cope with violent communist riots, he dissolved the Prussian parliament and appointed himself State Commissioner for Prussia – over a third of Germany.

At the general election of July 1932 the NSDAP secured 230 seats in the Reichstag, more than any party had ever won during the Weimar Republic, with 37 per cent of the vote. The parties of the Right outnumbered those of the Left but would not have a majority in the Reichstag unless the Nazis joined in a coalition. Papen tried desperately to persuade Hitler to join his cabinet as Vice-Chancellor, in vain. That autumn Papen again dissolved the Reichstag, to continue ruling by decree. In the ensuing election in November the NSDAP lost 34 seats; it looked as though their bubble had burst. Hitler contemplated suicide, writing to Cosima Wagner shortly after Christmas 'I have given up all hope', while Goebbels confided to his diary on 24 December, 'All possibilities and hopes have disappeared.' But in December Papen was ousted as Chancellor by General von Schleicher, who tried and failed to detach Gregor Strasser and sixty 'Socialist' Nazis from their allegiance. Hitler reacted swiftly, forcing Strasser to resign from the NSDAP.

Papen's attempts to form a government were shadowed by the threat of civil war. During a brief second term as Chancellor, Schleicher after failing to form a viable government had tried to persuade the President to declare an emergency. The army would no doubt have obeyed Hindenburg, but the Nazis and the Left would have been at each other's throats almost at once. The President reminded Schleicher that he himself had only recently informed him that such a move would lead to civil war, and that the army and police were simply not strong enough to handle the situation. Schleicher resigned to make way for Papen on 28 January 1933; the mood throughout Germany was growing more nervous by the hour, street fighting becoming even more widespread and vicious. Papen and all the leaders of the Right, together with the industrialists, had been in close touch with Hitler and Goering since the beginning of the month. The situation was still very confused when Papen persuaded the old Field Marshal that the 'Bohemian Corporal' was more effective than appearances might suggest. (When he had first met him in 1931, Hindenburg had commented that the man was better suited to be Minister of Posts than a national leader.) Papen's solution was that he should form a government of 'National Concentration', with Adolf Hitler as Chancellor while he himself as Vice-Chancellor would be the real power.

Herr Hitler modestly agreed that his party should have only two other members in the cabinet: Wilhelm Frick, a former Bavarian policeman, was to be Minister of the Interior (though with no police powers), while Major Hermann Goering, President of the Reichstag, was to be a Minister without Portfolio and Prussian Minister of the Interior for Papen (in the latter's capacity as State Commissioner). Several of Papen's old allies from the 'Cabinet of Barons' returned: Count Lutz Schwerin von Krosigk, Baron von Neurath and Dr Franz Guertner held the portfolios of Finance, Foreign Affairs and Justice. Alfred Hugenberg, leader of the Nationalists, was Minister of Economics, Food and Agriculture, Seldte – head of the Stahlhelm – was Minister of Labour, and General Werner von Blomberg was Minister for Defence. It was a coalition which represented almost the entire German Right rather than a Nazi government. At noon on 30 January Hitler, his eyes filled with tears, emerged from the Kaiserhof, the former Imperial palace. At an audience President Hindenburg had just appointed him Chancellor. That evening he was heard to whisper to himself, 'No power on earth shall ever get me out of here alive.'

Schwerin von Krosigk recalled in his diary how the new Chancellor, despite awkward manners, gained the respect of the cabinet in 1933. Everyone admired his infallible memory and 'the clarity with which he could reduce the most intricate question to a simple – sometimes too simple – formula . . . and his cleverness in approaching a well known and long discussed problem from a new angle'. He asked them to give him advice as experienced politicians. Papen says that at first Hitler was 'invariably polite, even modest'. At a dinner given for him by the head of the Reichswehr he explained to the assembled generals and admirals that while he intended to take control of all policy at home and abroad, he was going to allow the army and navy freedom to rearm and train. This quiet behaviour contrasted with that of the brutally overbearing Goering. Konstantin von Neurath told the British Ambassador that Goering, not Hitler, was the Nazi Party's real fascist.

For the Chancellor was not yet in full control. Indeed, some observers thought he was unlikely to survive. He lacked experience of government, while his followers were disunited; if many thought in terms of nationalism and anti-Semitism, others were genuine socialists. Moreover, the Social Democrats had 133 seats in the Reichstag and controlled the militant trade unions; the communists had 89, besides a formidable force of Red storm-troopers. Not only did Hitler lack a majority in both the Reichstag and the cabinet but the President was known to dislike him – and the army was loyal to Hindenburg.

The President had appointed Hitler Chancellor on the understanding that he would seek a majority in the Reichstag. Hitler used this as an excuse for demanding fresh elections, now that he could manipulate the machinery of government to influence voters. He pretended to the cabinet that they were necessary because the leader of the Catholic parties, Monsignor Kaas, had made 'insuperable objections' to entering a coalition. Hindenburg then agreed to dissolve the Reichstag.

In Prussia Goering, all-powerful as Minister for the Interior, made his own preparations for the elections. Within days of his appointment he had removed 22 out of 32 police chiefs; in February hundreds of inspectors and thousands of sergeants were dismissed, storm-troopers or Stahlhelm members taking their place. He ruled Prussia by decree, ignoring Papen. At the end of February he added 50,000 'special constables', also recruited from storm-troopers and the Stahlhelm, to the Prussian police force. All were ordered to be merciless to 'enemies of the State' – Marxists.

At this time Major Goering was Chancellor Hitler's right-hand man. He was essentially an adventurer, an amoral killer, if gifted with undeniable charm. (It was strong enough to suborn an American serviceman into giving him a poison capsule at Nuremberg.) Although dominated by Hitler, as Goebbels said, he had 'as much to do with the Party [ideology] as a cow with radiology'. Nevertheless, 'Fat Hermann' was genuinely popular with the German masses. He saved several people, including Jews, but from amiability rather than any sense of justice or mercy; he would have sent them to their deaths just as cheerfully, had it been in his interest. Soon he was going to succumb to pathological self-indulgence. However, in 1933 and 1934 he was savagely effective.[7]

The elections would take place on 5 March. Dr Goebbels confided to his diary on 3 February: 'We are able to employ all the means of the State. Radio and Press are at our disposal. We shall achieve a masterpiece of propaganda. Even money is not lacking this time.' Goering extracted millions of marks from industrialists, promising them 'the elections will certainly be the last for the next ten years, probably even for the next hundred'. (Meanwhile Hitler was assuring the electorate they could pass judgment on him after four.) The campaign was exceptionally savage, opposition newspapers being suppressed, candidates beaten up – not just communists but Catholics and Social Democrats as well. Fifty-one people were killed, and hundreds wounded.

On the night of 27 February the Reichstag's debating chamber was burnt out. The arsonist was most probably a young Dutchman called Marinus van der Lubbe (who was later beheaded). Three prominent communists were also accused; nevertheless, in after years Goering bragged that it was he who had arranged the fire. Whoever did it, the Nazis knew just how to exploit the incident. The Chancellor persuaded the President to sign an emergency decree suspending civil liberties; ten thousand communists were then arrested, including Ernst Thälmann.

Despite these advantages, the NSDAP failed to secure a majority. Although it increased its vote by over 5 million, with 288 seats it had to rely on 52 Nationalists. But Goebbels boasted, 'What do figures signify any longer? We are the masters of the Reich and of Prussia . . .'

Bavaria attempted to secede, its Prime Minister planning to appoint the popular Bavarian Crown Prince Rupprecht state commissioner. However, General von Epp and Heinrich Himmler – now police chief for all Bavaria – staged a swift coup with the local stormtroopers, Epp himself becoming state commissioner for Bavaria. State commissioners were appointed in four other states, while all state parliaments were dissolved by decree at the end of March. By then the Reichstag in Berlin had dissolved itself.

On 21 March Chancellor Hitler and President von Hindenburg met at Potsdam for the formal summoning of the Reichstag. Hitler addressed the deputies in the garrison church where Frederick the Great was buried; behind an empty throne for the Kaiser sat Crown Prince Wilhelm in pre-1914 uniform. The Chancellor's speech was so cunningly phrased, the spectacle so regal, that every Nationalist deputy anticipated the imminent restoration of the Hohenzollern monarchy. Two days later the Reichstag met in the Kroll Opera House, where the NSDAP and the Nationalists – supported by the Catholics to whom the Chancellor promised new privilieges for their Church – voted an Enabling Bill which gave the government power to enact laws without the authority of the Reichstag. A law was also passed giving legal status to State Commissioners appointed by the Chancellor. It had taken Hitler just over fifty days to implement his *Gleichschaltung*, or political co-ordination, and to become absolute master of Germany.

The French who applauded Bonaparte's assumption of power were those who had done well out of the Revolution, having acquired lands confiscated from the émigrés or the Church. (Perhaps surprisingly, at least 10 per cent were former nobles.) All feared they might lose their property – some their lives – under a restored monarchy or a fresh Jacobin Terror. They were joined by those who supported him because they were tired of revolution, of chronic instability at home and abroad, of inflation and threats of invasion. Many of this second group, probably most, believed that he would turn out to be a Monk – the general who restored Charles II – rather than a Cromwell. There was a third group, the army, who relished the prospect of war, of loot and promotion, and who welcomed being ruled by a soldier. No one envisaged the creation of a new type of monarchy.

In 1933 Germans supported the NSDAP for very similar reasons. The established political parties had shown themselves to be hopelessly ineffectual, while Hitler was undeniably convincing in his promises of no more inflation and no more unemployment. Those who wanted a Hohenzollern restoration – and there were many of them – believed that he would bring back the monarchy. As for the military, on the whole they were inclined to prefer so aggressive a patriot to any professional politician. Above all Ernst Thälmann's communist street-fighters had been only too eloquent in threatening Bolshevik Terror. Even in the Nazi party, few anticipated the dreadful reality of the Führer State.

The strongest poison ever known
Came from Caesar's laurel crown.

William Blake

Men felt certain in his company that they would get what they
wanted. Which is why they followed him, just as men will follow
anyone who inspires that sort of certainty. Don't actors grow fond
of managers from whom they expect a good part?

Wolfgang von Goethe on Napoleon

4

A New France, a New Germany

After they had come to power, Napoleon and Hitler were faced by
very similar problems. Their countries were in economic chaos,
there was substantial opposition to their régimes, there were difficulties with the Church. The First Consul saw his primary
task as healing the wounds inflicted by the French Revolution,
while Hitler was determined to 'save' Germany from the Jews and
Bolshevism. Both their foreign policies were aggressive in the
extreme. Bonaparte wished to assert France's dominance over
western and central Europe besides retaining her 'natural'
frontiers; Hitler intended to create a Greater Germany and then to
conquer eastern Europe. In addition, each was intent on building a
new type of state with a new social order.

A comparison of this period of their careers will at once reveal
resemblances. Both men enjoyed the advantage of more or less
unlimited power, swiftly removing all constraints, yet they had to
go carefully since at first neither was entirely secure. A serious
military defeat (which very nearly happened at Marengo) would
almost certainly have toppled Napoleon, while Hitler was justifiably
nervous of the generals, who might easily have moved against him.
Nevertheless, they gradually transformed a tenuous control over
their countries into an iron grip, even if the saviour rather than the
despot was more in evidence during the early stages. They showed

extraordinary skill in selecting the right experts to assist them. Nowhere is this more apparent than in their restoration of the French and German economies.

N

The Consulate is generally regarded as a golden age of French prosperity. This was largely due to Napoleon's gifts as administrator and his flair for choosing the right men. Just as he had centralized the administration with the college of prefects, he set up tax offices in every *département*, each staffed by eight collectors, the principal tax being on income. He picked experienced officials to rebuild the country's financial machinery. A sinking fund to buy back stock from the national debt was established, the Bank of France was founded, and paper currency was replaced by gold and silver; the franc would remain stable until 1914. In 1802 the budget was to be balanced for the first time in seventy years. Gold reserves were built up steadily (quite apart from Bonaparte's secret hoard beneath the Tuileries). A Commercial Bank, a Discount Bank and other institutions to assist trade were set up. Industry was encouraged, interest-free loans being granted to a number of manufacturers. Roads and communications were improved, ports built. When famine threatened grain was rushed in from abroad; in winter soup-kitchens and public shelters were erected in Paris. Within three years there was full employment and prosperity was returning. Some of this was due to the end of an economic depression, some to the work of gifted ministers. However, the First Consul was given the credit, much of which he indeed deserved. He had above all restored France's self-confidence.

In 1799 Bonaparte was still only thirty. The Duc de Broglie (Mme de Staël's son-in-law) saw him that year 'striding vigorously through the Tuileries, his right arm in that of his secretary and a little Turkish sword under the other, slim and easy, olive skinned and fierce eyed'. Another secretary, Baron de Méneval – who hero-worshipped him – describes the First Consul as 5 feet 2 inches tall, well built, with piercing grey eyes, good teeth, a straight nose and fine chestnut hair which he now wore short. Méneval adds that 'the nobility and dignity of his head and neck were unsurpassed by the finest antique busts', that he had a charming smile and a loud, cheerful laugh, but that if angry 'his countenance grew stern, even terrible'. The far from worshipping Mme de Staël has a very different picture. Bonaparte had 'a little body and a big head, with something arrogant and awkward about him, at the same time both contemptuous and sheepish, combining the gaucherie of a parvenu with a despot's insolence'. As for his smile, while admitting that it had been praised, she herself found it 'more mechanical than coming from the heart – his eyes never matched the expression of his mouth'. From a window at the Tuileries the German playwright Kotzebue watched him at a review:

> He arrived escorted by generals and aides-de-camp, all splendidly accoutred, while he himself wore the plainest of uniforms without gold lace . . . on several occasions I saw him being stopped, even by women who were allowed to go up and talk to him and hand in petitions . . . if he stayed silent his gravity might seem coldness, giving an alarmingly stern impression. Yet the instant he speaks a kindly smile gives a gracious impression to his mouth.

Frenchmen who saw Bonaparte only from the crowd would no doubt have agreed with Kotzebue that he 'inspired trust'.

We have a more intimate picture of the real man from Mme de Rémusat, Mme Bonaparte's lady-in-waiting. Her testimony is often questioned, since not only is she critical but she also wrote after Napoleon's fall.[8] Yet her picture tallies strikingly with that of

Mme de Staël, while she had far more opportunities for observing him, at close quarters over many years. It is not an attractive portrait. 'I have never known him admire, I have never known him appreciate a noble action,' she tells us. 'Every appearance of good nature met with the utmost suspicion; he placed no value whatever on sincerity and had no hesitation at saying that he judged a man's mettle by the way he lied. Having said this, he then commented with considerable smugness that when he was a child one of his uncles had prophesied he would rule the world since he was such a liar.' 'Monsieur de Metternich', he added, 'is growing into something more like a statesman – he lies very well.' She also informs us that Napoleon dreaded ties of affection and tried to isolate people, that he believed in destroying a man's reputation as the best way of ensuring his loyalty. She quotes him as telling Talleyrand, 'I am mean minded, basically mean. I can promise you that I have no scruples in doing what the world calls dishonourable.' Louis de Bourrienne (his secretary until 1802) also seems to confirm a basic cynicism and suspicion. Recalling Bonaparte during the first years of the Consulate, he writes: 'How often have I heard him say "Friendship is only a word. I care for nobody".' In Bourrienne's words, he was '*très peu aimant*'.

Yet he knew very well how to please. 'I would kiss a man's arse if I needed him', he once remarked. When an erring minister offered him his head he asked 'Just what do you expect me to do with it?' Many years later Metternich, of all people, would recall that 'conversation with him has always had for me a charm difficult to define.'

Mme de Rémusat's analysis of his intellect – which is seldom given in full – has certain resemblances to reminiscences of Hitler:

> It would be very difficult, I think, to find a more powerful or a more
> many sided mind. It owed absolutely nothing to education as in fact
> he was quite ignorant. He read little and what he did he read hur-
> riedly, but he quickly absorbed what he had taken in and with his

imagination built so much on it that he easily passed for a well educated man. His conversation usually consisted of long monologues
though he did not object to people interrupting if he was in a good
mood. His court listened to his slightest word with the sort of respect
normally given to military orders. Listening attentively was a sure
way of pleasing him. And he was very fond of talking about himself.

His attitude to women would hardly appeal to a modern feminist.
Perhaps it was this which antagonized Mme de Rémusat as it had
Mme de Staël. She claims with all too much justification that he
despised them, 'regarding their weakness as an unanswerable
proof of their inferiority and the power they have in society as an
intolerable usurpation'. She blames such an attitude on his
spending too much time with adventuresses during the Directory
and on the Italian campaign. 'He took no notice of a woman unless
she was beautiful or at any rate young. He would quite probably
have been ready to accept the view that in a well-run country we
should be slaughtered when we have borne our children – just as
some insects are destined by nature to a speedy death as soon as
they give birth.' She concedes that he felt genuine affection for
Josephine, and may have been in love two or three times, recording
his irritation at Josephine's jealousy and how he told her she must
put up with it – 'You ought to think it perfectly natural that I allow
myself amusements of this kind.' Admittedly such 'amusements'
were purely physical, scarcely very romantic. On one occasion he
greeted a terrified actress, clutching at the rags of her dignity, with
'Come in. Undress. Lie down.'

Napoleon himself bears out Mme de Rémusat. In his opinion
'We treat women too well and by doing so have spoilt everything.
We have been very wrong indeed to raise them to our own level.
The Orientals are much more intelligent and sensible in making
women slaves.' As he saw it, their sole function was to bear man
children and satisfy his sexual needs. Since no woman could do the

latter when she was ill or having a period, it was natural for men to take several wives. 'What do most ladies have to complain of? Don't we acknowledge they have souls . . . They demand equality! Pure madness! Woman is our property . . . just as the fruit tree belongs to the gardener.' Only inadequate education could make a wife think she was on the same level as her husband. Convinced of 'the weakness of the female intellect', he considered his brother Joseph extraordinary in enjoying the other sex's company as well as their bodies – 'He's forever shut away with some woman reading Torquato Tasso and Aretino.'

However gracefully phrased, his opinion of adultery revealed utter cynicism. In the end it is 'a joke behind a mask . . . not by any means a rare phenomenon but a very ordinary occurrence on the sofa'. He had surprisingly modern views on women as soldiers. 'They are brave, incredibly enthusiastic and capable of the most frightful atrocities . . . In a real war between men and women the only thing which would handicap women would be pregnancy, since the women of the people are just as strong as most young men.' (In this he was far more progressive than the Führer.)

The Consul's assured style of leadership appealed to the majority of Frenchmen. In particular he was able to convince them that they were the best soldiers in Europe; while the troops were flattered by their role as the sword of the nation-in-arms, even civilians were proud of their army's exploits – though they took most pleasure in the belief that victories would lead to security and peace. The soldier's erroneous conviction that there was a Field Marshal's baton in his knapsack was echoed by the bureaucrat's assurance of a career open to talent. A whole host of new Consular officials, pre-fects, tax-collectors, schoolmasters or *auditeurs* to the Council of State – the nucleus for a mandarin civil service – considered they had a stake in society. The *notables,* the rich and powerful, felt that their wealth was safe. The institution of a Consular order of chivalry, the

Legion of Honour, was only the first step in the creation of a new ruling class. 'Monsieur' replaced 'Citoyen' as equality began to go out of fashion. Many of the *émigrés* who were now allowed to return were attracted by the sheer vigour and purpose of the régime. The exceptions were royalists, Jacobins, anyone averse to tyranny, and those who did not care to entrust their future to one man. Yet even critics recognized the Corsican's genius.

Count Chaptal tells us that, when he began to rule, Bonaparte had no idea of administration or of law, had never studied properly, that his knowledge of mathematics was slight. Nevertheless, Chaptal says that during the Consulate (when he presided over several councils a day) Napoleon's comments showed such acumen that they astonished the experts – though even the adoring Méneval concedes that if he never forgot a face the First Consul could not remember names or get his sums right. He could work for eighteen hours without impairing his concentration. All observers, including the most hostile, accept that he was a genius.

According to Count Roederer, a Counsellor of State and a very shrewd observer, Napoleon's knack of getting to the bottom of a problem at once was outstanding. He always asked two questions. 'Is that accurate? Is it useful?' *(Cela est-il juste? Cela est-il utile?)* He had 'a capacity for remembering facts which seemed more than human'.

The First Consul was determined to make use of the Catholic Church. It was in complete disarray, Catholicism appearing to be in greater danger than during the Reformation. In France its bishops, priests, monks and nuns had been killed or driven into exile; a handful of clergy survived in disguise, ministering in cellars or the depths of the forest. The churches of 'Constitutionalist' priests, who had taken a schismatic oath of allegiance to the Republic, were deserted. The previous Pope, Pius VI, had died a prisoner on French soil. As a Deist, Bonaparte believed in a Supreme

93

Being, but whatever he claimed at certain times, he was in no sense a Christian. (Although he once remarked, 'I know men and I tell you Jesus Christ was not a man.') Mme de Rémusat tells us, 'I do not know whether he was a Deist or an atheist but in private conversation he constantly ridiculed everything concerned with religion.' However, she adds, 'Bonaparte made use of the clergy even if he disliked priests.'

He recognized that the vast majority of the French were Catholics, and saw religion as a stabilizing force which could be useful to him. He observed, 'If you take away faith from the people, you're going to end up with nothing but highway robbers.' He wanted to make the Roman Church a buttress of the régime he planned – just as he had used the mullahs in Egypt. By doing so he would deal the royalist cause a mortal blow; everyone was convinced that Catholicism could only return with the monarchy, and the devout were all supporters of Bourbons. He knew that Pius VII and his advisers were badly shaken, that it might be possible to transform them into pliant instruments of government. In July 1801 he signed a concordat with Pius; France was to have ten archbishops and fifty bishops nominated by the First Consul, and be paid salaries by the State. In April the following year the concordat was approved by a plebiscite, Bonaparte attending a Mass of thanksgiving at Notre-Dame on Easter Sunday; a canopy was carried over him, just as formerly one had been carried over the Kings of France on similar occasions. Many republican officers disapproved; General Delmas grumbled, 'All that was missing was those hundred thousand Frenchmen who died to be rid of all this.' Nevertheless, Napoleon had his way. For the moment Pope and clergy were profoundly thankful, amazed at being rescued by a son of the Revolution.

It is too easily forgotten that the Consulate was a police state from the very beginning. On 26 Brumaire, a week after the coup, 59 Jacobins were proscribed; 22 were sent to a species of concentration camp on the Ile d'Oléron, and 37 were transported to the living hell of Guiana. The machinery of repression was constantly reinforced. Admittedly, Bonaparte had inherited much of it from the Directory, and could not survive without such repression. He was menaced by royalists, the 'Chouan' guerrillas of Brittany and the Vendée against whom he sent troops. The Comte de Frotté was lured into an ambush by the promise of a free pardon, and summarily shot. 'I didn't order it but I can't say that I'm sorry for his execution' was Napoleon's comment. Although most of the Chouan leaders surrendered in 1801, the irreconcilables went underground, posing an even worse threat, since they concentrated on the assassination of the First Consul; among their allies were a whole host of returned émigrés and royalist sympathizers, while they included some leaders of real distinction – notably Georges Cadoudal. There were also many Jacobins, former terrorists, who were no less determined to bring down the régime, which would not be really secure until the victory at Marengo in the summer of 1800. Stendhal believed that Bonaparte hated the Jacobins more than anyone else – though he had once been a Jacobin himself. He survived largely because Fouché ran an extremely efficient security service, employing not only police but a swarm of spies, informers and secret agents. He used money, free pardons and countless other inducements, just as he did midnight arrests, brutal interrogation and the threat of transportation, the guillotine or the firing squad. He had two gifted assistants in the ex-Jacobins Charles Desmarets, a former seminarian who was his police chief, and Pierre-François Réal; both had a genius for extracting confessions, the former by blandly questioning, the latter by less gentle means. The First Consul had a very high opinion of Réal in particular.

Joseph Fouché, the Minister of Police, was a most dangerous instrument. He had been educated by the clergy (like Voltaire!) but even his appearance was sinister; eyes of terrifying penetration in a passionless yellow face with bony, reptilian features – a filthy tongue did not improve him. A regicide who had voted for Louis XVI's death, a former terrorist popularly known as the Butcher of Lyons (on account of having executed sixty royalists in one batch with cannon-fire), he had betrayed the Girondins, the Jacobins and the Directory in turn; one day he would desert Bonaparte too. He inspired as much revulsion as fear – 'a monster begotten in the Revolutionary stew-pond by anarchy mating with despotism' is Chateaubriand's comment.

'Intrigue was as necessary to Fouché as his daily bread', said his master. 'He intrigued at all times, everywhere, in all ways and with everybody.' While the First Consul valued his ruthless efficiency in co-ordinating the work of his ministry with that of the High Police, half a dozen other police forces and a vast, omnipresent espionage network, he always distrusted and feared him.

He employed Fouché's assistant and successor, Réné Savary, to keep an eye on him, as far as was possible. Savary was a tall and strikingly handsome cavalryman, still in his twenties; once Bonaparte's ADC, he was appointed Colonel of the Gendarmerie d'Elite, a crack force of mounted military police used only for the most dangerous assignments. According to Bonaparte, Savary 'loved him as a father'. Blindly loyal, brutally energetic and a little stupid, he constantly sent in reports on Fouché – once to the effect that he was in league with the Chouans. He would play a key role in the murder of the Duc d'Enghien. (Savary's later achievements included forging Austrian banknotes for the campaign of 1809 and Russian notes for that of 1812, and making a clockwork time-bomb to dispose of the Bourbons in 1814.)

Both Jacobins and Royalists decided that their only hope lay in assassination. In October 1800 a band of the former, armed with pistols and stilettos, lay in wait for the First Consul at the Opéra but

Napoleon in 1814. By Paul Delaroche. (*Mary Evans Picture Library*)

Hitler ten days before his death. (*Popperfoto*)

The Emperor's army in 1814. By Auguste Raffet.

The Führer's army in 1945.

The Emperor supervises the burning of his Eagles during the Retreat from Moscow.
By A. von Kossak.

Soldiers of the Wehrmacht on the Russian front in 1944. Hitler had claimed in 1942
that 'We have mastered a destiny which broke another man 130 years ago.'

The Führer visits the Emperor's tomb at the Invalides, June 1940.

Napoleon in 1810, ruler of Europe. By Robert Lefèvre.

Napoleon as First Consul, not yet ready to conquer Europe. By Gérard.

Adolf Hitler as Führer and Reich Chancellor in 1935. By B. Jacobs. (*Mary Evans Picture Library*)

The Führer hoping to avoid war in the West – despite appearances.

Generalmajor Carl Philipp Gottlieb von Clausewitz, the Prussian strategist who was on Kutuzov's staff in 1812 and believed that Napoleon had been right to invade Russia. By Wilhelm Wach.

Napoleon as a Roman Emperor.
By Canova, (*Woodmansterne*)

Hitler (aided by Mussolini) saving
the world from Marxism in 1933.
(*Mary Evans Picture Library*)

The pre-war Führer at home at Berchtesgaden (*Popperfoto*)

Napoleon crossing the St Bernard Pass on the way to Marengo. By Paul Delaroche. (*Mary Evans Picture Library*)

were betrayed, arrested and guillotined; they had been under police observation from the beginning. On Christmas Eve the same year, when Bonaparte was driving to the Théâtre Française (to hear a Haydn oratorio) he fell asleep in his carriage, to be woken by a terrible explosion only half a minute after passing a cart. It had been laden with barrels of gunpowder, scrap-iron and broken glass. Many bystanders were hurled into the air, 35 being killed or maimed. Only the accident of his coachman being drunk and driving too fast had saved him. He blamed the Jacobins – 'men of mud and blood'.

Fouché knew perfectly well that the Jacobins were not responsible, but he arrested their leaders. It was a heaven-sent chance to break what remained of the hard-line Terrorists of the Revolution by eliminating their 'general staff'. No less than 129 were transported to the swamps of Cayenne and to the Seychelles; among them were General Rossignol, a former *sans-culotte*, and René Vatar, once editor of the *Journal des Hommes Libres*, with many other extremists who had been members of revolutionary committees or army officers in the days of Danton and Robespierre. By the time they were shipped off the Consul too knew they were innocent. The real perpetrators were a group of royalist fanatics, all save a handful of whom were tracked down and executed. (The forensic methods employed were astonishingly modern, the single intact horseshoe of the animal which had drawn the cart being identified by a blacksmith.) But it was the end of Jacobinism.

Bonaparte's obsession with power grew stronger every day. 'I have no ambition', he told Roederer. 'Well, if I do, it is so natural to me, so much part of my being, that it's like the blood flowing in my veins, like the air I breathe.' On another occasion he informed Roederer 'I've only one passion, one mistress, which is France. I make love to her and she never fails me, lavishing her blood and treasure on me. If I ask her for half a million men, she gives them.'

He soon found the Constitution of 1799 far too liberal. Sieyès and his friends were powerless to stop him, and he grew more like a monarch every day. Court dress reappeared, with knee-breeches and cocked hats for men who had only recently affected the trousers of *sans-culottes*. However, he wanted the substance as well as the trimmings of authority. In 1801 the legislative chambers opposed a bill against 'anarchists' which would have enabled him to arrest anyone he chose. Even after new elections had been rigged to make them more biddable, they refused to appoint him First Consul for life, offering ten years instead. Although it had no constitutional right to do so, the régime held a plebiscite – 'Is Napoleon Bonaparte to be made Consul for life?' After a well-organized vote in favour – and not uninfluenced by the sight of grenadiers ringing the Luxembourg – the Senate surrendered; in addition it gave him the right to appoint his fellow-Consuls and to nominate his successor, together with machinery for suspending the Constitution and overturning legal rulings by the courts. He now possessed absolute power, civil and military, and was above the law.

Bonaparte's greatest mistake was not to restore the monarchy, the real alternative to the Directory. Although the French would never have accepted a return of the *ancien régime* or given up the freedoms won by the Revolution, a constitutional monarchy like that of 1791-2 might well have been viable. Even Sieyès toyed with the idea. Among the candidates for the throne was the Duke of Brunswick, who had commanded the Austrian and Prussian armies in 1792 when they had tried unsuccessfully to invade France; during the Consulate Roederer told Joseph Bonaparte, 'In 1792 people had Brunswick in mind.' He received the reply, 'People still thought of him at the time Bonaparte returned from Egypt – Talleyrand spoke of him to me as our last hope in the circumstances, and so did Sieyès.' Another was the sister of the Dauphin ('Louis XVII') who had died in the Temple; Sieyès seems to have taken her quite seriously. There was also the young Duke of Orléans, Philip, Égalité's son, who had Talleyrand's support. And there was Louis XVIII, the late King's brother, with whom Barras had negotiated. As early as 1797 Louis offered to make Napoleon a Marshal of France and Viceroy of Corsica if he would restore him.

But in Italy that year General Bonaparte confided in Miot de Meliot, 'I most certainly don't want to play the role of Monk. I don't want to play it and I don't want anyone else to play it.' In 1800 Louis wrote, 'You are taking a long time to give me back my throne; there is a danger you may lose the chance. Without me you cannot make France happy while without you I can do nothing for France. So hasten to let me know what positions and dignities will satisfy you and your friends.' Josephine would have been only too happy for her husband to be a Marshal-Duke. He wrote back, 'You must not think of returning to France – you could not do so without marching over a hundred thousand dead bodies.' This was untrue. With the army solidly behind him, he could have restored Louis without bloodshed. Bourrienne tells us that the Consul was obsessed by the exiled royal family, saying that he must build 'a wall of brass' between it and the French. Yet a restoration would have regained the legitimacy whose lack has been the bane of every French régime since 1792. However, Bonaparte, as Sieyès discerned after Brumaire, was determined to rule France himself.

In February 1804 another plot to assassinate 'the tyrant' was discovered. Its leaders were unusually dangerous: General Moreau, the victor of Hohenlinden; General Pichegru (Bonaparte's mathematics tutor at Brienne), who had been deported after the coup of Fructidor in 1797; and Georges Cadoudal, the Vendéen hero who was the most unrelenting of all the First Consul's enemies. Moreau and Pichegru were soon caught, but Cadoudal could not be traced, although he was known to be in Paris. Fouché was deeply concerned, warning Bonaparte that 'The air is full of daggers.' However, on 9 March Cadoudal was hunted down at last. Moreau was sentenced to two years imprisonment, then banished; his victories were too much admired for him to punished more severely; Pichegru was found dead in his cell, officially from 'self-strangulation'; many people believed he had been murdered on Napoleon's orders. Cadoudal was guillotined. It is only fair to record an act of mercy. Among many other conspirators involved were two brothers, Armand and Jules de Polignac; when the former was condemned to death Jules offered to take his place, whereupon the sentence was altered to life imprisonment.

Bonaparte grew angrier and angrier. 'Am I a dog to be killed in the streets?' he shouted. As a Corsican accustomed to vendetta he decided to respond in kind, encouraged by Fouché and Talleyrand. The Duc d'Enghien, the ablest member of the exiled royal family, lived just over the French frontier in Baden. He had commanded a corps of émigrés with distinction during the Revolutionary wars, and was wrongly suspected of having taken part in the plot. On the night of 14 March a squadron of dragoons surrounded his hunting lodge. He was taken back over the border to the military fortress of Vincennes, just outside Paris. Here, a week later, he was tried illegally at midnight by a military tribunal presided over by General Murat, without counsel to defend him, condemned to death, denied a priest and at 2.30 a.m. – immediately after the trial – shot in the moat, where a grave had already been dug. His death had been decided before his abduction; it was murder, and not even legal murder. Murat, Governor of Paris and the First Consul's brother-in-law, a man whose conscience was not exactly delicate, had had to be bullied into signing the order for the court-martial; shortly after, he received a grant of 100,000 francs from the Civil List. The comment (usually attributed to Fouché or Talleyrand) is famous: 'It was worse than a crime – it was a mistake.'[9] All that can be said in extenuation is that Bonaparte genuinely believed Enghien had been plotting against him. Later he tried to excuse himself. 'I was threatened on all sides by enemies employed against me by the Bourbons; menaced by air-guns, infernal-machines and devices of every sort. There was no court I could petition for protection, so I had to protect myself. In putting to death one of the men whose followers were threatening my life I was entitled to strike healthy terror into the rest of them.' He added, 'I am the French Revolution. I say so, and I intend to maintain it.' He had done more than strike at the Bourbons; he had made it clear that under no circumstances would he restore the pre-1789 monarchy. Mme de Rémusat records that 'the Jacobin leaders said "He belongs to us now".' By Jacobins she did not mean extremists but 'Jacobins grown rich' – *Notables*. (Two years later, not less than 21 prefects and 42 magistrates were regicides who had voted for Louis XVI's death.) She also tells us that the popular view of Napoleon changed abruptly, many believing the murder to be 'the beginning of a blood-stained reign'. She considered that it marked his abandonment of moderation, an increasing disregard for moral values.

In order to impress France with a sense of his semi-royal position Bonaparte held frequent parades on the Carrousel outside the Tuileries, or the Champs-Élysées. Surrounded by a glittering staff and wearing his red velvet uniform of First Consul, he reviewed the Consular Guard from his charger. They marched or trotted past in dazzling yellow uniforms to stirring military music, massed bands playing *Partant pour le Syrie* or the *Chant du Départ* (both written by his stepdaughter Hortense de Beauharnais) – though not the *Marseillaise*, nowadays considered Jacobin and seditious. These men, hand-picked, were fanatically loyal. They were deeply admired by the vast majority of their fellow-countrymen.

The man who had once been a starving half-pay officer living in a seedy lodging-house quickly acquired expensive habits, if not perhaps those of luxury. Even though he dressed plainly, his pistols were chased with gold, his sword-hilt set with diamonds. His valet Constant described him approvingly as 'a man for men servants', and it took three of them to prepare him for the day. (Admittedly such dependence was not unusual for the period; at his most poverty-stricken Mozart never went without a valet.) He liked to linger in his bath, sometimes for hours, though dictating to secretaries. He was then rubbed down with eau-de-cologne from head to foot, after which he allowed himself to be dressed like a child. He ate abstemiously (until he married Marie-Louise), his favourite meal being a roast chicken preceded by soup and washed down by a glass of Chambertin and a cup of coffee. He also took the occasional glass of Madeira. He does not seem to have touched brandy.

When he had time he read. One of his Ministers for the Interior, Count Chaptal, who observed him closely, thought he was very poorly educated:

> He knew almost nothing of Greek and Latin authors. He had skimmed through the works of some historians and remembered a few details . . . He said Tacitus was the ancient world's worst historian, perhaps because he based his view on the author's portrait of Tiberius. Horace was only for lovers of luxury. He approved of Homer alone. Among modern writers he had no great opinion of Voltaire, Racine or Rousseau. His favourite French poet was Corneille.

This is not quite fair. He himself said on St Helena, 'The more I read of Voltaire the better I like him . . . I even like his historical works.' However, he certainly lost his taste for Rousseau, the hero of his youth. 'Since I have seen the East I find Rousseau repellent – the wild man without morals is a dog.' He kept his taste for Ossian's verse and enjoyed modern novels. Mme de Rémusat, a conventional and indeed puritanical lady, was shocked at his presenting Marie Louise with Restif de la Bretonne's *Les Contemporains*, a choice which would nowadays be considered imaginative.

His sole languages were French and Italian. According to Chaptal, who is borne out by Mme de Rémusat, he spoke neither well – 'When he was talking French one could easily see that he was a foreigner! His secretaries read extracts from the British and German newspapers to him, but he was unable to pronounce properly a single word of English or German. When he met Goethe he called him Monsieur Goet.'

His most unpleasant indulgence was his temper. Bourrienne tells us, however, that even at the beginning of the Consulate his insults, epithets and outbursts of rage were all carefully calculated. Yet he often lost control of himself, as when during the same period he kicked the senator Volney – a trusted friend from Corsican days – in the stomach, knocking him to the ground. (Volney had to stay in bed for a few days.) The worshipping Baron Méneval has to admit that his face 'grew terrible' when he was angry. He could lose his temper with the humblest people, such as Josephine's unfortunate milliner, Mlle Despeaux, at whom he is recorded as 'yelling like a maniac'. (Though the fact she was a notorious lesbian may have been partly responsible.) When he quarrelled with his wife he would smash the bedroom furniture. Giuseppina Grassini, who had also shared a bedroom with him, says he could 'pass abruptly from the intoxication of love to that of wrath and fury – it was volcanic, Etna roaring while covered in flowers'. These fits of fury made dangerous enemies, such as the row when he called Talleyrand 'shit in a silk stocking' or at the crucial meeting with Metternich at the Marcolini Palace in 1813 at Dresden in which by Metternich's own account he grossly insulted him. He was capable of publicly hitting a general in the face, as he did during the German campaign of that year.

'I have very irritable nerves,' he once confessed. 'In such moods, but for my low blood pressure I would run the risk of going

103

mad.' He could sob for a quarter of an hour on end and sometimes suffered from stomach cramps or fits of vomiting. His rages were so ungovernable as to indicate a minor form of epilepsy – the *petit mal.*

Josephine, an amiable if frivolous and not very intelligent consort, led a miserable life despite spending far more money on clothes and pleasure than Marie-Antoinette. She was always insecure, terrified that one of her husband's mistresses might suddenly bear a child to prove that she herself was now barren, and that he would then divorce her – in order to marry a more fertile wife – which was exactly what happened. It made his countless infidelities a constant nightmare, let alone a betrayal. In any case, his treatment of Josephine was scarcely sensitive. When she was suffering from an excruciating migraine he would force her to ride in a jolting barouche, making her scream with pain. At other times he would shoot at the swans in the park to torment her. It must be admitted that Eva Braun never knew such wretchedness and humiliation.

On St Helena Napoleon boasted, 'I found the crown of France lying in the gutter and picked it up on the point of my sword.' Yet he felt his way very carefully before assuming it. 'Talleyrand wanted me to make myself king but the title "King" is worn out,' he informed La Rémusat. Lazare Carnot courageously told the Tribunate that he would have preferred an American-style President – 'abuse of despotism has far worse consequences than abuse of democracy', he warned. He also rebuked Bonaparte personally, 'You should have stayed First Consul. You were the only one in Europe and look at the company you're in now!' On 2 December 1804 Napoleon was crowned Emperor of the French by Pope Pius VII. He had made the Church bestow its blessing on his régime, and abandon the Holy Roman Empire, which was dissolved the following year.

He took the ceremony very seriously indeed. While he was planning it his brother Joseph infuriated him by insisting on a right to

succeed him if he died. 'It's something I can never forget,' he confided to Roederer. 'It's as though he told a lover he had slept with
his mistress or hoped to. Power is my mistress.'

'For the last two years power stayed in my hands so naturally
that people began to think I was not going to assume it formally',
he explained more calmly to Mme de Rémusat and her husband a
few days after the coronation. 'I decided it was my duty to exploit
the situation in order to end the Revolution legally. Why I chose to
be Emperor instead of dictator is that one acquires legitimacy by
occupying familiar ground.' He wanted every European sovereign
to build a palace in Paris, to attend the crowning of future French
Emperors. 'Men like the Abbé Sieyès', he went on, laughing,
'may complain of despotism but my government will always be
popular. The army and the people are on my side and with that sort
of support a man would have to be an absolute fool not to be able to
reign.'

Nevertheless, he was not popular with everybody. A jingle circulated in Paris at this time:

> On loans and alms I long supported life,
> I fawned on Barras, took his drab to wife;
> I strangled Pichegru, shot Enghien down,
> And for so many crimes received a crown.'

There was an opposition, however crushed and disunited, and this
was what it thought of the saviour of France. On the other hand, a
sycophantic Norman prefect could tell his officials, apparently in all
seriousness, 'God created Bonaparte and rested.'

For all his self-confidence, the Emperor used every means
available to bolster up his régime and discourage dissent. The
Church was forced into yet more humiliating compliance. (Cardinal Caprara, the Papal Nuncio, was sweetened by the gift of a palace
in his diocese of Bologna.) A servile catechism taught French

Catholics that they owed Napoleon 'love, respect, loyalty, military service and the taxes specified for the maintenance of the Emperor and his throne', that those failing to do so 'resist the order laid down by God and render themselves worthy of eternal damnation'. The feast-day of St Napoleon, a 'Roman officer and martyr' who never existed, was introduced into the liturgical calendar.

Despite deep respect for blue blood and ancient lineage, he resented privilege of the sort which had threatened to block his career as a young man. It had given him real pleasure to evict the Knights of Malta, a brotherhood which he himself could never have hoped to enter, from their island home; he described the order as 'an institution designed to support in idleness the younger sons of certain privileged families'. It gave him no less pleasure to confiscate the commanderies of the Teutonic Knights.

Napoleon established a new nobility of princes, dukes, counts, barons and knights – not to mention chevaliers of the Legion of Honour. In 1810 all prefects were made counts or barons and told to assume coats-of-arms. 'I act as a monarch in creating hereditary rank but in a Revolutionary spirit since my nobility is not exclusive.' He was building 'an intermediate caste . . . between himself and France's vast democracy' while he had to have a Court like every other European sovereign. Admittedly, 'I created princes and dukes, gave them fortunes and estates, but because of their humble origins I could not make noblemen of them. So I tried as far as possible to marry them into the old families.' On St Helena General Gourgaud noted resentfully, 'His Majesty has a weakness for the [old] nobility.'

He ensured that as many people as possible had a stake in the Empire. The great fortunes acquired by the members of the Bonaparte family, besides their kingdoms, are notorious. So too are those of men like Fouché and Talleyrand, the latter taking huge bribes from foreign powers to insert clauses in treaties. It is less well known how much the marshals profited; Berthier's estate was worth over 1,300,000 francs a year, Davout's nearly a million, Ney's 728,000 and Masséna's 638,000. (Their magnificent hôtels in Paris and the great châteaux of their country estates were filled with masterpieces; Davout owned a Breughel, a Poussin, a Rubens and a Van Dyck, while Soult had countless works by Murillo, Ribera and Zurbaran – looted in Spain.) It is even less appreciated how many others benefited. Every Imperial title was accompanied by a *hereditary* endowment – 200,000 francs for a dukedom and 3,000 for each of over two thousand knighthoods. There were also cash gratuities; on one occasion General de Lasalle received a million francs. There were highly paid careers in administration. And there were enormous opportunities for government contractors.

Much as Napoleon had employed Gaudin, an *ancien régime* financial official, so Hitler depended to a large extent on Hjalmar Schacht, President of the Reich Bank. A different economic mood came swiftly into being after the *Gleichschaltung*. Schacht's measures were what would later be termed Keynesian. They had first been tried in Germany during the Great War (when they were called 'war socialism') and were far from novel; other European countries implemented them during the 1930s, but none with such vigour or success as in Hitler's Reich – he supported Schacht with ruthless thoroughness. The first step was the Four-Year Plan to End Unemployment drawn up by Georg-Hans Reinhardt, which began in June 1933. Industrial expansion was encouraged by tax-exemption for profits ploughed back into industry or technology. Similar incentives were offered to landowners and farmers. Financial reserves did not exist, so Schacht simply printed the money, backing his notes with the vague security of future tax receipts. Public works were begun on a large scale to provide jobs; they included the construction of *autobahnen* (motorways), which were Hitler's own idea and partly financed by a general tax on transport. The labour service, engaged on other public works such as railways, provided employment too. There were tax rewards for employing women as domestic servants, to stop them competing for jobs with the men. The Second Four-Year Plan, the Hermann Goering Plan (again drawn up by Reinhardt) offered long-term contracts with built-in profits to firms if they would concentrate on new technology and extracting raw materials in order to make Germany less dependent on foreign imports; this resulted in the production of such new substances as coal, oil, artificial rubber and aluminium alloys. State factories were founded. Rearmament, the introduction of military service and the expansion of the bureaucracy also helped. The national income doubled in four years, the national debt disappeared. Whereas unemployment had been 6 million in 1933, there was full employment and genuine job security by 1938. There were huge new housing estates for workers, sports facilities and State-financed holidays; 6 million people went on such holidays in 1936. It was a very far cry from the terrible misery of recent years. Adolf Hitler became the most popular man ever to rule Germany. The Olympic Games of 1936, brilliantly stage-managed, seemed like a species of coronation or jubilee.

Once it was generally believed by (non-Nazi) observers that this economic miracle was entirely due to rearmament, even that economic collapse was only averted by the outbreak of war in 1939. There is still considerable debate. What is indisputable is that for all her bluster, Germany was inferior in armaments to her opponents in 1939. It is coming to be believed increasingly that, in Norman Stone's phrase, 'Hitler had seemingly stumbled on modern economics.' But he could not have done so without Schacht and Reinhardt.

Confidence surged through Germany, which recovered that conviction of superiority over all other nations it had enjoyed in 1914. Every recruit who joined the army – renamed Wehrmacht instead of Reichswehr – felt that he was no less a member of the nation-in-arms than Napoleon's troops had done, was aware that it was re-arming to make it stronger than any other European army, and wore his uniform with pride. Uniforms were not confined to the Wehrmacht; the SS (or Schutzstaffel), SA (or Sturmabteilung), Labour Corps, Hitler Youth and many other organizations had them. The régime's racial policies induced a feeling of superiority, consciousness of Aryan blood giving a gratifying sense of aristocracy to the humblest. Fear of a Bolshevik revolution became merely an unpleasant memory. Everyone faced the future with confidence – save for Jews, political opponents and those antipathetic to rule by a despot. Naturally inclined to like firm rule, Germans were ill prepared to resist. Moreover, Hitler's success, both at home and abroad, seemed uncanny when contrasted with the inept performance of the Weimar régime.

One of the few academics to meet Hitler and leave a description was Professor Schramm of Göttingen University (and also of Harvard). Schramm, a major in the Wehrmacht who was responsible for keeping the High Command's War Diary in 1943-4, had many opportunities of watching Hitler, and as an historian his account is peculiarly interesting. When Schramm first saw him close to, the Führer was in his mid-fifties. He was of medium height, but 'The man's head seemed to dominate his entire body; torso, arms, legs – all seemed to hang down from it . . . He strode on his heels and, keeping his knees straight, walked quickly. His other movements were quite deliberate.' His nose was ugly, 'having something of the shape of a pyramid', which was why he

109

trimmed his moustache to minimize his broad nostrils. He concealed his high forehead by a hanging forelock. Schramm insists that Hitler 'fascinated people with his deep blue, slightly protruding, almost radiant eyes. Many who met him were unable to stand up to his gaze; knowing this, Hitler looked people straight in the eye without blinking.' Describing his own first meeting with Hitler in June 1932, Papen tells us 'He was wearing a dark blue suit and seemed the complete *petit-bourgeois*. He had an unhealthy complexion and with his little moustache and curious hair style had an indefinably Bohemian quality.' Just as Bonaparte had studiously appeared in a plain uniform, he normally wore the simplest Party uniform, though this did not make him any the more impressive; at Berchtesgaden the British Foreign Secretary, Lord Halifax, was to mistake him for a footman.

None the less, he impressed deeply everyone who worked with him. Von Papen refers to his 'extraordinary gifts and will power'. Schramm emphasizes his 'amazing ability to judge people to the extent that he was able to sense immediately whether the person standing in front of him was for him, could be won over, or would be immune to his personal dynamism. In this respect he had a sort of "sixth sense".'

He was capable of deceiving the shrewdest observers. In 1931 Group Captain Malcolm Christie of MI6 gave him a lift in his car for some three hundred miles, after which he told friends that his passenger had an uncanny resemblance to another European statesman – Eamonn de Valera.[10] During the spring of 1933 the young Prince of Pless went to see him at the Chancery in the Wilhelmstrasse on behalf of some mining directors who had been arrested in Lower Silesia. He recalled 'a very polite, agreeable, middle class Austrian addressing me. He was very sympathetic, polite. There was no peculiar aura around him and I could not detect anything hypnotic about his eyes, which I afterwards heard of. I found him a pleasant man with whom I might have discussed any subject.' He told the Prince (who later fought against him in the British army) that he would look into the matter, 'but one had to remember in times like these that where there was a strong light, there was also bound to be a dark shadow'. The directors were released a few days later.[11]

Indeed, Albert Speer went so far as to state in his memoirs 'Hitler possessed many likeable personal qualities.' Schramm concludes:

> Whenever anyone tries to understand Hitler the final result somehow never adds up correctly. His contact with children and dogs, his joy in flowers and culture, his appreciation of lovely women, his relationship to music were all quite genuine. But no less genuine was the ferocity – morally inhibited, ruthless, "ice-cold" – with which Hitler annihilated not only real but even potential opponents.

Many other writers have commented on his Janus-like character, on his two faces – one charming and seemingly kindly, the other diabolically cruel and evil.[12] Behind all the joking, comradeship and sensitive friendship lay a mind always prepared to kill, to kill not just a close comrade like Röhm but millions, proud of its readiness to kill. Schramm comments that, like Medusa's, the Führer's true face would have turned even the most loyal member of his circle to stone had he glimpsed it. Trevor-Roper (writing of Hermann Rauschning, a Danzig Nazi, who saw through Hitler early on) says, 'Above the crunch of the cakes and the tinkle of tea cups he heard, if not the cry of the tortured in the prison camps, at least the blood curdling paean of universal destruction.'

Like the Emperor, the Führer was extremely nervous. Rauschning speaks of 'convulsions of weeping at all emotional crises', claiming that Hitler would weep if one of his canaries died. (Goering once said, before a difficult political meeting, 'We can always send Adolf to cry.') He suffered from frightful insomnia and nightmares, like some tyrant of legend. Such nerves made for uncontrollable rages which verged on frenzy – he would yell for hours on end, screaming abuse, stamping, banging on the table or the walls, his face purple and distorted. Sir Eric Phipps, the British Ambassador, reported in 1935 how Konstantin von Neurath had confided in him that 'Herr Hitler . . . raved at him for five hours without, I hear, stopping to eat or drink.' Bewilderingly, he would suddenly re-establish complete control over himself. Rauschning observes, 'Dostoyevsky might well have invented him, with the morbid derangement and pseudo-creativeness of his hysteria.'[13]

Nevertheless, his gift for inspiring devotion and hero-worship was extraordinary. There seemed to be an almost orgiastic element in his relationship with the vast crowds whom he whipped up into a frenzy. Josef Goebbels writes about him like a woman in love.

If we have little information about the Führer's sex-life, we possess a good deal about his views on women. They are far more complex than might be thought, even though he said, 'A man has to be able to stamp his imprint on any woman.' Like Napoleon, he regarded them as an inferior species whose job was to bear children, be good mothers and make homes for men. (*Kinder, Kirche, Küche* was one of the Nazi slogans.) In his opinion there was 'no worse disaster than to see them grappling with ideas'. 'Women who have no children finally go off their heads.' On the other hand, unlike the Emperor, his personal relationships with them were based on more than physical gratification. 'What I like best is to dine with a pretty woman,' he told Bormann. Beyond question he admired feminine beauty and enjoyed feminine company. He also differed from Napoleon – who was frequently rude and even coarse – in being unfailingly charming and gallant with women, including his female staff. When he explained condescendingly that 'Woman's universe . . . is man' he added, 'She sees nothing else, so to speak, and that's why she's capable of loving so deeply.' He accepted the possibility of partnership between the sexes. 'Marriages that originate only in sensual infatuation are usually somewhat shaky. . . . Separations are particularly painful when there has been a genuine comradeship between man and wife . . . a meeting between two beings who complete one another, who are made for one another, borders already, in my conception, upon a miracle.' His interpretation of much of feminine behaviour was characteristically cynical. 'In the pleasure a woman takes in rigging herself out, there is always an admixture of some trouble-making element, something treacherous – to awaken another woman's jealousy by displaying something that the latter doesn't possess. Women have the talent, which is unknown to us males, for giving a kiss to a woman-friend and at the same time piercing her heart with a well-sharpened stiletto.' He justified female possessiveness by his own brutal criteria. 'The gentlest woman is transformed into a wild beast when another woman tries to take away her man . . . Must one regard this innate savagery as a fault? Is it not rather a virtue?'

His relationship with the wretched Eva Braun was almost banal in its domesticity except that he would not marry her. She suited him perfectly. As he told Albert Speer, in her presence, 'A highly intelligent man should take a primitive and stupid woman.' Yet he was undoubtedly fond of the colourless little blonde photographer's assistant, whose father worked for a baby food firm, although not in the same fashion he had loved Geli Raubal; some observers thought she looked uncannily like his poor mousy mother. Over twenty years younger, fond of dancing and skiing, with no interests in common, she was none the less deeply attached to him, and on two occasions tried to commit suicide when he neglected her – much to his irritation. Although there were no children, their physical relations appear to have been normal enough. Even so, he gave the impression of treating her as a pet rather than a fellow human being. Speer, who liked her, felt sorry for Eva Braun. What is so strange is the way Hitler made her avoid publicity, allowing her to meet only his intimate circle. He seems to have felt that, as the embodiment of Germany, he must appear to be alone. He loved her in his own weird way – as he would show by his marriage to her just before their joint suicide – but he had no desire for the Third Reich to have a First Lady in emulation of Napoleon's Empresses.

Oddly, the Führer expressed admiration for 'the lovely Josephine . . . the woman who, at Napoleon's side, had climbed the rungs leading to the highest post in the State'. He considered that the Emperor had made a serious mistake in casting her off to make room for a Habsburg alliance. In his eccentric opinion, Josephine had been 'the model of the strictly Republican French-woman'. (One wonders if her contemporaries would have recognized this description of the Empress.)

Meanwhile he was tirelessly consolidating his régime. It is hard to exaggerate how powerful German Catholicism seemed at the beginning of 1933. A third of the population was Catholic. It was fifty years since the Church had defeated Bismarck's attempt to shackle it in the struggle known as the *Kulturkampf*, while its political party, the Zentrum, was influential and well supported. Rome had misgivings about the NSDAP, yet many priests were attracted to a party opposed to communists and freemasons, and which (in theory), supported 'the old moral values'. This confusion enabled Hitler to secure a considerable triumph by negotiating a concordat with the Vatican – something which had eluded the Weimar Republic. The man who did the bargaining in Rome was von Papen, a practising Catholic and a Knight of Malta, who acted in all good faith. The Church gained protection for its schools and the continuation of State subsidies; no doubt it was encouraged by the concordat with Mussolini only four years before. In reality Hitler detested Catholicism and all forms of Christianity. Despite his pious mother's example, and although he is said to have taken Communion in the 1914-18 war, he had totally abandoned Catholic belief as well as practice if only, as he himself admitted, 'after a hard struggle'. While admiring Christ's gifts as a propagandist, he disliked intensely what he termed the 'Jewish Christ-creed with its effeminate pity ethic'. (His religion was very like the Emperor's deism; whereas the former had believed in a supreme intelligence, the latter was a monist, acknowledging a single ultimate reality which he called Providence.) He particularly resented the Catholic Church's natural hostility to his racial theories; to be a practising Catholic in Nazi Germany was to incur automatic suspicion of 'political unreliability'. Nevertheless, he feared the Church's hold over the consciences of millions of Germans, and like Napoleon, he hoped to harness it in the service of his new society. Indeed, he instructed Goebbels to remain a Catholic – so Speer informs us.

On 2 May 1933 trade unions were declared illegal in Germany. On 7 July Social Democrats were deprived of seats in the Reichstag and on 14 July the NSDAP became Germany's only political party. The first concentration camp had been set up even before the Enabling Act, in a disused munitions factory at Dachau, while in April a purge of Jewish civil servants and a boycott of Jewish shops was imposed. On 26 April the Geheime Staatspolizei – better known as the Gestapo – was founded by Goering in Berlin. The country swarmed with informers. Not only political opponents were arrested but gypsies, homosexuals and those who tried to leave the country. By 1937 the camps held over 35,000 prisoners.

Hitler's principal policeman was Heinrich Himmler, who by 1936 had outmanoeuvred Goering to become head of the security forces throughout Germany, including Prussia. This unimpressive figure, pale and bespectacled, half crank, half demon, was the régime's Fouché, and in his own way even more sinister. A

Bavarian and a lapsed Catholic of lower middle class origin, he had been born in 1900, joining the Party just before the 1923 Putsch as a protégé of Röhm. Like his leader, in ordinary life he was a total failure, supporting himself by marriage to a chicken farmer eight years older than himself. He worshipped Hitler, modelling himself on 'the hardest man for centuries', but was known to faint at the sight of blood. However inadequate as a human being, he was a genius as a secret policeman. His tools were the SS, the SD Intelligence Service (or Sicherheitsdienst) and the Gestapo. By 1935 there were forty separate Gestapo offices in Germany, while in the following year they ceased to be answerable to the law of the land.

Himmler's deputy was Reinhard Heydrich – 'the Hangman'. Tall and icily handsome, this archetypal Aryan 'blond beast' was a quarter Jewish. Cashiered from the Navy in 1930 after a scandal over a girl, he was a bitter and twisted if brilliant young man, ferociously cruel, totally without humanity. Even his chief feared him.

Hitler indulged his taste for martial pomp. Not only were there frequent parades in every city by the Wehrmacht in their field-grey but his own SS lifeguards, the Leibstandarte Adolf Hitler in black and silver, goose-stepped through the streets of Berlin or Munich to the strains of his favourite march, the *Badenweiler*. (A surprisingly frivolous tune, something from a third-rate operetta, today it is banned in Germany.) The marching song was the raucous *Horst Wessel Lied*. More sonorous was *Wenn alle untreu werden*, an old German chorus sung by the massed SS as a touching hymn of Nazi loyalty – 'If everyone were to be untrue.' Like Napoleon's Imperial Guard, these undeniably superb troops knew themselves to be invincible, as did the cheering crowds who watched them swagger past. Here was another vivid testimony to the *Dolchstoss*, that shameful stab in the back which in 1918 had so unjustly deprived Germany's magnificent troops of their victory over inferior foes.

A comparison of the SS and the French Imperial Guard may

perhaps seem as far-fetched as the Führer's own comparison (in a conversation with Lord Halifax) of the former to the Salvation Army. Yet no less than the Guard, the SS provided its master with Praetorians on whom he could depend. Like the Guard, too, it was the ultimate, savage symbol of the new régime.

Hitler could certainly have restored the German Empire. In Italy the King reigned with Mussolini as his Prime Minister. Most of the Right (probably including most of those who voted for the NSDAP, if a minority in the the Party) hoped for a restoration. As has been seen, many in the centre, such as Brüning, wanted it. In 1932 Papen and Schleicher assured Crown Prince Wilhelm that in the political climate which was developing it was only logical to expect the return of a Kaiser; they were convinced that after Hindenburg's death the nation would feel the need for some permanent repository of authority.' In March 1934 Papen proposed a a restoration, and was agreeably surprised by Hitler's reaction. He told Papen that he did not think the Crown Prince suitable but that his sons would do better – he was seemingly impressed by Prince Louis Ferdinand's taking a job in the Ford works at Detroit. Such a move would have been enormously popular, especially among the predominantly monarchist officer corps, without diminishing his control over Germany. He was on excellent terms with the Hohenzollern family; not only did Crown Prince Wilhelm support him, but two Hohenzollerns had joined the NSDAP. Secretly he hated the idea of a restoration: during the War he was to send a message to a former Social Democrat saying how grateful he was to his party for having rid the country of monarchy. (Members of former ruling families were to be forbidden to serve in the armed forces after 50,000 Berliners had flocked to the funeral of a Hohenzollern killed on active service in 1940.) He wanted to be Kaiser himself, in his own way.

Some observers expected that attempts to rearm would run into difficulty. It was too easily forgotten that Germany had been planning to rearm, even rearming secretly on a very small scale, ever since the Versailles peace treaty. Gustav Stresemann had wished Weimar to do so, and joint manoeuvres between German troops and the Red Army had taken place discreetly in Russia, providing valuable training in tank management. When in 1928 Horace Findlayson, the Financial Adviser to the British Embassy in Berlin, was replaced after attributing discrepancies in the German budget to concealed expenditure on armament it was rumoured that it was because the Ambassador, Sir Ronald Lindsay, did not wish to upset the British prime minister, Stanley Baldwin.[14]

The Führer not only had to train an army for future conquests but needed rearmament to placate the generals. He knew that if he provoked them they would move against him.

The army was becoming increasingly irritated by the noisy pretensions of Ernst Röhm and the SA, as indeed was Hitler himself. Early in the spring of 1933 Röhm, when the worse for drink, grumbled about that 'ignorant war-time corporal' to Hermann Rauschning, an aristocratic Nazi who was already growing disenchanted with his saviour. 'Adolf is a swine . . . he will give us all away. He only associates with reactionaries now. His old friends aren't good enough for him!' He went on, 'He's bought himself a tail coat now!' Most significantly, he added, 'Adolf knows exactly what I want. I've told him often enough. Not a second edition of the old Imperial Army. Are we revolutionaries or aren't we?'

After all, from the very beginning one of the key points in the NSDAP's programme had been the creation of a 'people's army' – as Röhm put it to Rauschning, 'something must come out of our *élan*, like the mass armies of the French Revolution'. The SA had been invaluable to Hitler, a true army of party militants who had not only spread his gospel but, by their rallies and street-fighting with the communists, had helped polarize the Germans into Left and Right. However, they had more than outlived their usefulness; if anything they were a liability, with their rowdiness and rioting, and their leaders' reputation for homosexuality. Above all, they were announcing openly their intention of taking over and replacing the Reichswehr. While the Führer would occasionally volunteer such soothing remarks as 'It is madness to make revolutionary wars with a reactionary army,' he did not see 'the bowlegged and knock-kneed SA' as material for his new military élite. Moreover, in the SS he now had a reliable instrument with which to break the storm-troopers and to kick down the ladder by which he had climbed. What finally decided him to strike was the growing suspicion – possibly justified – that Röhm intended to kidnap him and set in motion a further 'Brown Revolution', coupled with the generals' increasing anger at the SA's impertinence.

In May he took advantage of the ceremonial launching of the pocket battleship *Deutschland* to reach an agreement with the generals. He would bring the SA to heel if the Wehrmacht would support him as head of state when Hindenburg died – an event which was clearly going to happen fairly soon. Meanwhile Himmler and Goering had been forging a devil's alliance against Röhm, who stood in the way of their ambitions. Finally in June 1934 the Defence Minister, General von Blomberg, informed him that Hindenburg was threatening to call in the army unless he curbed the wild men of the 'Brown Revolution'. On 30 June he struck in what he called 'Operation Kolibri' ('Operation Humming Bird'), usually known as 'The Night of the Long Knives.' The pretext, dreamt up by Himmler and Goering, was that Röhm was planning a putsch, after which he would merge the army with SA under his command and take Papen's place as Vice-Chancellor. Perhaps as many as a thousand people were shot during this one night and on the following day; they included not just Röhm and his henchmen but other political opponents such as General von Schleicher (with his wife) and Gustav von Kahr, who had crushed the 1923 putsch.

119

The world was horrified but also curiously relieved, in the delusion that the Nazi revolution had at last come to an end – just as many Frenchmen had been reassured by the crushing of the last Jacobin terrorists after the Infernal Machine Plot of December 1800.

Less than two months later, in August 1934, Hindenburg died. Hitler now took advantage of his bargain with the military leaders, becoming head of state and commander-in-chief. He assumed the title of Führer and Chancellor, the Presidency being abolished. Moreover, the entire armed forces were required to take a personal oath of loyalty to him.[15]

The significance of the oath has been generally underestimated. The special traditions of pre-1918 Lutheran Germany must be taken into account. Luther had abolished the episcopate, replacing it by the monarch – 'the Godly Prince like unto David'. In consequence the head acquired an almost spiritual aura, the oath of allegiance to him a semi-sacramental quality, especially among army officers. Even in Catholic Bavaria and Austria the officers' oath to be *treue und fest* was taken very seriously indeed. It was this, not merely monarchist nostalgia, which had caused German officers such anguish when the Kaiser and the princes had abdicated in 1918. An oath to a Head of State for life seemed eminently reasonable, filling a void, particularly to Lutheran officers – Lutheranism being the religion of most Prussians. (General von Rundstedt attended service every Sunday.) It also made it correspondingly more difficult to act against the Führer.

Hitler's new status was confirmed by a plebiscite, just as a similar plebiscite had once confirmed Bonaparte's assumption of the Consulate for life.

In his *Table Talk* the Führer condemned Bonaparte for turning himself into a monarch:

It was Napoleon's greatest error and at the same time a proof of bad taste on his part, to have renounced the title of 'First Consul' in order to have himself called 'Emperor' . . . he denied the Jacobins, his former companions in the struggle, and lost their support. At the same stroke he alienated, both at home and abroad, countless partisans who saw in him the personification of the moral resurrection that the French Revolution was to bring with it. To understand the effect produced by this wilful action, it's enough to imagine the effect on the people of Munich, and on the rest of the world, if I had myself carried through the streets of Munich in a gilded coach. In any case Napoleon gained nothing by committing this fault, for the old monarchies did not fail to display the scorn they felt for a self-made man.

He cited Beethoven erasing the Eroica's dedication to Napoleon on hearing he had made himself an Emperor, and exclaiming, 'He's not the extraordinary man I believed, he's only a man!' He criticized him for placing his brothers and sisters on thrones – 'Such illogical behaviour can be explained only by the feeling Corsicans have for their families, a feeling in which they resemble the Scots.'

Nevertheless, Hitler was himself a species of monarch. 'In the National Socialist form of State, the title Führer is the most suitable. It implies, amongst other things, that the Head of State has been chosen by the German people, he considered. 'This title is associated with the very form of the State itself.' He termed the concept of a leader elected by the people 'German democracy' – as distinct from parliamentary democracy – but basically the *Führerprinzip* was not so very different from that of Napoleon's concept of the 'People's King'. Significantly, he felt a certain kinship with the elected Kaisers of the medieval Reich, apparently regarding them as his forerunners.

Like the Emperor, Hitler paid keen attention to the Churches, both as a source of support and as a potential focus of opposition. To some extent he controlled the Protestants by setting up a Lutheran 'Reich Church', appointing a 'Reich Bishop' who with his pastors took an oath of allegiance to the Führer. He chose the pliable Ludwig Müller to be Reich Bishop, while regretting he was not a man of more stature; otherwise 'Through me the Evangelical Protestant Church could have become the Established Church as in England.' Despite the heroic example of the Confessional Church and such noble ministers as Bonhoeffer and Niemöller, Lutheranism was by order and tradition ill equipped to oppose the National Socialist state.

Catholicism posed more of a problem. In 1937 Pope Pius XI issued the encyclical *Mit brennender Sorge* ('With burning heart'), drafted in German instead of Latin, almost certainly by Cardinal Pacelli – the former Nuncio in Germany. It has been described as 'one of the greatest condemnations of a national régime ever pronounced by the Vatican.' It totally rejected the racial theory of *Blut und Boden* ('Blood and Soil') and castigated Hitler for 'aspirations to divinity . . . placing himself on the same level as Christ', calling him 'a mad prophet possessed of repulsive arrogance'. Although infuriated, the Führer was shrewd enough not to launch a full-scale persecution.

In his private life the man whose home had been a tramps' hostel took to luxury with ease, becoming – like Napoleon – dependent on servants, unable to exist without a valet. 'Bourgeois comfort' is perhaps a better description than 'luxury', since his sole indulgence was cream cake; he neither drank nor smoked, living on nut cutlets and vegetable soup. He had a curious relationship with his personal staff, whether valets, chauffeurs, cooks, secretaries, doctors or adjutants, treating them almost as a substitute family. The gentlemanly senior officers of the Wehrmacht referred contemptuously to this entourage as the 'Chauffeureska'.

His friend Hanfstängl has given us a list of the books in the Führer's library. Among these were predictably Ludendorff's *Publikationen über den Krieg*, Stegemann's *Geschichte des Ersten*

Weltkriegs, Treitschke's *Deutsche Geschichte*, Houston Stewart Chamberlain's life of Wagner, Kugler's history of Frederick the Great and, of course, Clausewitz's *Vom Kriege*. Other volumes included Sven Hedin's *Kriegserinnerungen*, detective novels and Westerns, even works on erotic art. He enjoyed *Don Quixote* ('the world's most brilliant parody of a society that was in the process of becoming extinct') and thought *Robinson Crusoe* gathered together in one man the history of all mankind. He considered that 'a great basic idea' was contained in *Gulliver's Travels* and – somewhat surprisingly – in *Uncle Tom's Cabin*. He seems to have read Carlyle's *On Heroes, Hero-Worship and the Heroic in History*. He is known to have read at least twice Ernst Kantorowicz's superb study of the medieval Emperor Frederick II of Hohenstaufen (despite Frederick preferring Italy to Germany). Even during the war he went through a book a day, apparently after going to bed or before he got up. The verdict of Schramm – the finest mind among all his historians – is that if his determination in acquiring knowledge was 'nothing short of amazing', the end result was essentially ramshackle.[16]

The Führer had a slightly greater aptitude for foreign languages than the Emperor, possibly because of his ear for music. He had been taught some French at school, and improved it before picking up a working knowledge of English – largely through watching French and British films. He even read American magazines. However, he seems to have been incapable of holding a conversation in any tongue other than German.

His only relaxation other than reading and the cinema (he was a Garbo fan) was music. Until the war he went to the opera or operettas, his tastes remaining unchanged since his youth – 'When I listen to Wagner, it is like the rhythms of the primeval world.' Before 1939 he always attended the Bayreuth Festival. He had seen *Götterdämmerung* over a hundred times. (During the war he played it constantly on the gramophone.) Weber's *Der Freischütz*

123

was a favourite, as was Eugène (or Eugen) d'Albert's now seldom performed *Tiefland* (whose libretto was described in the 1920s as 'ultra realistic, almost brutal'.) He enjoyed Richard Strauss, Verdi and Puccini – especially *Aïda* and *Madame Butterfly* – and heard Lehar's *Merry Widow* and Johann Strauss's *Fledermaus* over and over again. He was also fond of Bruckner's symphonies.

As a young man the Führer admired the traditional Prussian officer, his deference to Ludendorff verging on the ludicrous, but when mature he disliked 'the monocles'. He detested what he called 'the horse people' who subscribed to the chivalrous ideal of the *Rittmeister* (or cavalry captain) so popular among the German artistocracy of the nineteenth and early twentieth centuries; it was they who provided those officers who made him feel so uncomfortable till the end of his life. Of course there were exceptions, like Gerd von Rundstedt, but on the whole he felt there was no room for such people in the new Germany. They had their own élitist ideals, were almost invariably Christians, and in consequence more or less impervious to the neo-pagan ideals of National Socialism. He loathed everything about them – 'Hunting and horse-racing are the last remnants of a dead feudal world,' he told Speer.[17]

Yet Hitler constructed a society no less hierarchical than the Napoleonic Empire. It had its princes, like the Reichsmarschall (Goering) and the Reichsführer (Himmler), while party office conferred such fiefs as that of a Gauleiter. The humblest party member prided himself on Ayran blood which bestowed a minimal 'nobility'. While 'revolutionary', the SS included many of the old aristocracy.

The Führer was as anxious as Napoleon had been for his supporters to have a financial stake in his régime. They themselves used the phrase 'planned corruption'. Rauschning observes that while it is nothing new for a revolution to help its sons enrich themselves, in Germany it was done with such shameless haste that it made spectators dizzy. 'One, two or four houses, country estates, palaces, pearl necklaces, antiques, valuable tapestries and paintings, dozens of motor cars, champagne, farms, factories – where did all the money come from? Had not all these people been as poor as churchmice, up to their eyes in debt? They all had official posts, three, six, a dozen at a time . . .' It was not just the great who profited (like Goering, who had solid gold tiles in his bathroom) but the humblest Nazi. 'There were posts of all kinds, honorary directorships, and dividends, loans and bonuses' says Rauschning. 'Everyone was anxious to help; every bank and business enterprise required the protection of a party member.' Even non-Nazi supporters of the régime profited – like the Emperor, Hitler rewarded his favourite marshals with country estates.

The most striking difference between Napoleon and Hitler was of course their attitude towards Jews. The Emperor believed sincerely that their religious and social disabilities should be removed, placing them on the same level as Protestants and Catholics; wherever his armies went he abolished ghettos. Nor was his attitude merely negative. He hoped to persuade Jews from all over the world to settle in France and take a full part in the nation's life. On St Helena he wrote:

> I have implemented part of my scheme. Some excellent Jewish soldiers joined the French army, considerable wealth entering the country as a result. Had it not been for the events of the year 1814 many more would have come to France, since eventually every Jew would have wanted to settle in a land where equality before the law was guaranteed and where they could aspire to any honour.

His approach was not as universal as might be thought. During the last years of the Directory there had been a rash of bankruptcies, and in consequence much hatred of the Jewish banking community; every moneylender was described as Jewish in a vicious outbreak of anti-Semitism which swept through the French Press – Jews were accused of being enemies to everyone in France save their co-religionists. No attacks of this sort were allowed under the Consulate and the Empire.[18]

In contrast, Hitler heaped disabilities and humiliations on German Jews from the moment he secured full control of the State in April 1933. They were purged from every profession, while in 1935 they were deprived of German citizenship and forbidden to marry or have sexual relations with 'racially pure' Germans; nor could they attend German schools or universities. During *Reichs-kristallnacht* (Reich Crystal Night, so called from the amount of broken glass), an attack by organized mobs on 7 November 1938, hundreds of synagogues went up in flames and seven thousand Jewish shops were gutted. By the end of that year 30,000 Jews were in concentration camps. There were no exceptions. Those who had fought gallantly during the 1914-18 war and those who were members of the Stahlhelm, all suffered ostracism and persecution.

The only similarity here is that Bonaparte and Hitler were each acting as typical products of their age. In this matter Napoleon was for once a true disciple of the Enlightenment at its most benign, Hitler of nineteenth-century German Romanticism and 'historical science' at their most perverted and evil.

But can peace be made? I think it may.

Charles James Fox to the House of Commons, May 1803

I am sure that some day the Czechs will see that what we did was to save them for a happier future.

Neville Chamberlain to the Archbishop of Canterbury,
letter of 2 October 1938

5

War or Peace?

For the moment the First Consul genuinely wanted peace, while for
some years the Führer was officially averse to war. In 1802 the
Whig statesman Charles James Fox wrote, 'I am obstinate in my
opinion that Bonaparte's wish is peace – nay, that he is afraid of
war to the last degree.' Till 1939 Neville Chamberlain was equally
optimistic about the Führer. The French and German peoples were
desperately anxious to avoid any repetition of the Revolutionary
wars, or of 1914-18. We now know that, no less than Napoleon,
Hitler hoped to avoid war – if only in the west. The careers of both
men had a stage in which each successfully expanded his country's
territory to what was called, with a certain hyperbole, 'natural
frontiers'. Napoleon employed war to secure them,
the Führer's aggressive diplomacy was backed up by the *threat* of
war. In both cases it seemed briefly that they would keep them.

Curiously enough, there were historical precedents. At their
most extended France's 'natural frontiers' included the Low
Countries, the left bank of the Rhine and north-western Italy. The
Low Countries had been under Valois rule as possessions of the
Dukes of Burgundy during the late Middle Ages; Louis XIV had
nearly secured the Palatinate and Savoy, Milan and Genoa had
been under French domination for short periods. One could cite the
Carolingian empire. There were therefore arguments, however

specious, to justify incorporating Belgium and the left bank of the Rhine into France, and for the puppet states known as the Batavian, Ligurian and Cisalpine Republics (Holland, Genoa and Lombardy). But Bonaparte would always feel threatened unless France could dominate Europe by acquiring further puppet states.

To begin with, Hitler's *Lebensraum* was the *Grossdeutschland* envisaged by the Frankfurt Liberals of 1848. They had drawn up maps of a state including every German-speaking land – Germany, Austria and Bohemia together with Prussian Poland – all of which Hitler almost secured without going to war. Only when this Great Germany had been built did he intend to conquer the Slavs in the east. Germans had done so before him, and very recently; early in 1918, at the treaty of Brest-Litovsk, Germany had gained another chunk of Poland together with a chance to set up puppet states in the rump of Poland, in the Ukraine and on the Baltic – there were even plans for annexing the Crimea. Every German schoolboy knew how in an earlier age Teutonic Knights and Baltic barons had conquered Poles and Lithuanians, how Hindenburg and Ludendorff had annihilated the Russian would-be invaders at Tannenberg in 1914.

♔
N

By the end of 1800 there were particularly good reasons for the First Consul to consider peace favourably. He had shown beyond dispute that his armies were a match for any in the world, while he had secured France's 'natural frontiers' and fastened her hold more tightly on the puppet states. Austria was exhausted, mourning her losses in men, treasure and territory. Even Britain had grown tired; for a decade she had been vainly spending enormous sums to subsidize coalitions against the French, and her economy was suffering. There was booming prosperity in France. And the French people wanted peace before anything else.

The Austrians signed a treaty at Lunéville in February 1801. Soon only Britain remained at war with France. In 1800, before Marengo was fought, William Pitt had asked the House of Commons with bitter irony if:

> the jacobinism of Robespierre, of Barère, the jacobinism of the Triumvirate, the jacobinism of the Five Directors . . . has all vanished and disappeared, because it has all been centred and condensed into one man who was reared and nursed in its bosom, whose celebrity was gained under its auspices, who was at once the child and the champion of all its atrocities and horrors?

He added grimly, 'Our security in negotiation is to be this Bonaparte, who is now the sole organ of all that was formerly dangerous and pestiferous in the revolution.' However, Pitt resigned office in the same month as Lunéville. By November 1801 – if with a marked lack of enthusiasm – he was telling the House:

> after the dissolution of the confederacy of the states of Europe . . . It became merely a question of the terms to be obtained for ourselves, and for those of our allies who still remain faithful to us.

Lord Cornwallis (who had surrendered at Yorktown) and Joseph Bonaparte signed the peace treaty at Amiens in March 1802. Egypt was to be given back to the Turkish Sultan, Malta to its Knights. The Peace of Amiens was welcomed with wild enthusiasm in both France and England. Everyone hastened to visit each other's capital.

Among the visitors to France in 1802 was Charles James Fox, who was presented to the First Consul at the Opéra in December. Napoleon had small recollection of the meeting, later pretending he remembered how badly Fox spoke French – in reality he spoke it very well. Fox was not altogether favourably impressed by 'a young man intoxicated with success'. But the First Consul told him,

'The two great nations of Europe require peace; they ought to understand one another.' The great Whig wrote ecstatically, 'I feel morally certain that Bonaparte and all his friends are of the opinion that war with England is the only event that can put his power in peril.' Earlier in the year he had given it as his opinion that 'since there is to be no political liberty in the world, I really believe Bonaparte is the fittest person on earth to be master.' This is not so very far removed from the language of certain 'appeasers' in the 1930s.

There was bound to be friction. The noblemen who constituted Britain's ruling oligarchy had scant respect for their royal family, and were scarcely inclined to admire a pseudo-monarch. Nor was the frozen haughtiness of their formal manners best calculated to soothe a parvenu First Consul. (Even Talleyrand admitted emerging a broken man from an interview with Lord Grenville.) Viscount Whitworth, the British Ambassador, was a prime specimen. Enormously tall, beautifully dressed, a former grenadier who had married the Dowager Duchess of Dorset, his very appearance irritated Bonaparte.

Many British statesmen were fearful of Bonaparte. In the last months of 1802 George Canning, the future Prime Minister, declared it was the First Consul's character, not just his policies, which made him dangerous. Asking the Commons for new military establishments, he added, 'for the purpose of coping with Bonaparte, one great commanding spirit is worth them all'. As yet no British general inspired much confidence. (Canning was to play an important role in discovering Wellington.) 'The destruction of this country is the first vision that breaks on the First Consul through the gleam of the morning', warned Sheridan, 'this is his last prayer at night, to whatever deity he may address it, whether to Jupiter or to Mahomet, to the Goddess of Battles or the Goddess of Reason. Look at the map of Europe, from which France was said to be expunged, and now see nothing but France.' Windham was even more alarmed. 'Buonaparte is the Hannibal who has sworn to devote his life to the destruction of England.'

The annexation of Piedmont had first surprised and alarmed Britain. Worse had followed. Portuguese Guiana was ceded to France, while Spain returned Louisiana to France (see p. 166), General Victor being appointed its Captain-General. Haiti was conquered briefly by a French expeditionary force, its Negro leader Toussaint l'Ouverture dying mysteriously in captivity after surrendering on a promise that his life would be spared. Spain agreed that France might have Parma when its reigning duke died. Civil war broke out in Switzerland; Napoleon sent in Ney with 40,000 men, taking control as 'Grand Mediator of the Swiss Confederation' – Aloys Reding of Berne and his hopelessly outnumbered little army being defeated and imprisoned. Turkey was bullied into giving French merchants unprecedented privileges in the Levant. The last straw was the publication of Colonel Sébastiani's article in the *Moniteur*, the Consular régime's official gazette; he stated that most Egyptians wanted the French back, that only 6,000 troops were needed to recapture the country, that the British had tried to assassinate him when he was in Egypt and that the Ionian Islands wished for French rule. When Britain complained France retorted that she had far more grounds for complaint because of the publication of a book insulting the Consul and his army. (Sir Robert Wilson's *History of the British Expedition to Egypt*). On both sides of the Channel the Press grew more hostile. Communications between the two governments sank into what Fox termed 'reciprocal Billingsgate', a mere exchange of abuse.

Bonaparte insisted that as none of his actions broke the Treaty of Amiens, Britain had no reason to object to what was happening, especially in Europe; the Treaty of Lunéville (by which he had guaranteed the independence of the new Swiss, Dutch and Italian republics) was with Austria and had nothing to do with the British. Similarly, Hitler convinced himself that after the Munich agreement Europe was no concern of Britain or France. Almost certainly the Consul wanted peace but on his terms, just as according to Anthony Eden the Nazis 'would have liked to be friends with us if they could have got their own way'.

Moreover, the British did not like the sound of life under Bonaparte. Tom Paine's opinion of the France of 1802 was 'Republic! do you call this a republic? Why, they are worse off than the slaves of Constantinople!' A Colonel Littlehales noticed how the Legislature and law-courts were ringed by soldiers. The Dean of Christchurch wrote that Parisian society was made wretched from insecurity because of Bonaparte's methods of spreading suspicion everywhere, 'considering it his best hold'.

Even so, the majority of the British had been desperately anxious for peace with the First Consul in 1802, just as they would be in 1938. The former Bourbon minister Calonne reported that British enthusiasm for Bonaparte was well-nigh incredible, that the Court, the city of London, the capital, the provinces, and people of all classes down to the humblest artisan were all singing his praises. When war broke out again, however, everyone believed that he had long been planning it, that he alone was responsible. Admiral Nelson complained, 'It is really shocking that one animal should disturb the peace of Europe', while Fox foresaw 'dreadful things if Bonaparte takes, as is natural with him, violent measures'. There was a genuine dread of war.

If with hindsight one can say war was unavoidable one can also say that those who started it had no intention of an all-embracing conflict. The First Consul was determined to assert the dominance of France, but envisaged a series of small wars, never dreaming of a 'war of nations'. He tried to frighten the British government, aware that Pitt's successor as Prime Minister, Addington, was weak and inept. He warned (in a despatch supposedly written by Talleyrand) that, were she driven to declare war, France would conquer the entire European continent:

> The First Consul is a mere 33 years old; up to now he has only destroyed lesser powers. No one knows how quickly he might change the face of Europe, and restore the Western Empire if he is forced.

He also attempted to intimidate the British by bullying their Ambassador, an unrewarding task.

In February Lord Whitworth was summoned to the Tuileries where Bonaparte raged at him for two hours before allowing him to speak. 'Every gale blowing from England carries enmity,' he shouted, claiming that the British government harboured assassins who were plotting to kill him, that the British Press slandered him. As for suspicions that he had designs on Egypt, 'Egypt must one day belong to France' but he had no wish to fight for it. 'What would I gain from a war? Invasion would be my sole means of doing you harm – and invasion is what you're going to have if you force me!' In a gentler tone he added, 'Together we could rule the world. Why can't we reach an understanding?' Whitworth, that 'calm and high spirited nobleman', replied coolly 'His Britannic Majesty merely wishes to protect his rights and has no wish to join in plunder and oppression.'

There was a further outburst during a reception for the diplomatic corps in March. As soon as he entered the room Bonaparte glared at Whitworth and said at the top of his voice, 'So you want war!' The Ambassador tried to reply, but the Consul shouted him down. 'We've been fighting for fifteen years and you're determined to have fifteen years more of it – you're forcing me on!' He continued, 'Why are you arming? If you arm, I'll arm too. If you fight, I'll fight too. You may be able to destroy France but you can't intimidate her!' Bonaparte then roared, 'Respect treaties – Woe on those who fail to respect them, they shall answer for what happens!' before storming out.

Across the Channel Addington and his government were terrified by any suggestion of war – very like Chamberlain's 135 years later. The anti-French party grew increasingly angry, demanding Pitt's return.

By the spring of 1803 war between Britain and France was inevitable. The British Press had grown vituperative, the *Morning Post* having described the First Consul in February as 'an unclassifiable being, half African, half European, a Mediterranean mulatto' while émigré newspapers alleged that he slept with his step-daughter Hortense. George III, who hated the very idea of peace with a nation which had killed its king, was urging his ministers to go to war. The British had had their breathing-space. They were infuriated that France did not even try to negotiate a trade agreement as promised at Amiens, while French hegemony meant that the markets not only of France and her puppet states but of much of Germany were closed to British goods. They demanded the evacuation of French troops from Holland and Switzerland, and insisted on retaining Malta for ten years – to stop any more French expeditions to Egypt. Bonaparte proposed that it be occupied temporarily by the Russians, but the British refused. On 16 May they seized all French ships in their harbours and the First Consul ordered the internment of some ten thousand British residents and tourists in France. War was declared two days later.

Bonaparte was convinced that if he could cross the Channel he could easily defeat any troops who opposed him, that the island would be conquered in a matter of weeks. He was probably right. Moreover, he might have been able to cross the Channel – with luck. In 1798 he had contemplated Hoche's scheme of invading Ireland (and making the octogenarian Cardinal of York, Prince Charles Edward's brother, its king) but the pro-French United

Irishmen had been put down with merciless severity and the British were firmly in control again. Instead he revived Lazare Carnot's old scheme of invasion, of a landing in Sussex (though not in Yorkshire as well). On St Helena he recalled:

London lies only a few days march from Calais, and the English army scattered in order to protect the coast could not have re-grouped in time to save the capital once a landing had been effected . . . I intended to mass 40 or 50 men-of-war in the harbour at Martinique where they would have sailed from Cadiz, Brest and Ferrol. When assembled they were to make for Boulogne with all speed. I needed to be master of the Channel for 14 days. I had 150,000 troops and 10,000 horses in readiness at the coast, with some 3-4,000 flat bottomed boats. As soon as I received news of my fleet's arrival I meant to land in England and make myself master of London.

During 1803 camps were established all along the coast at Boulogne, Dunkirk and Ostend while large fleets were being fitted at Brest, Rochefort and Toulon. Every coastal dockyard, every river-side wharf in north-western France – including Paris – was busy building over 1,200 flat-bottomed gunboats and transports, while 150,000 men were widening the harbours. To prevent British bombardment or landing-parties, 500 heavy guns were placed in cliff-top batteries; there were also 'submarine batteries', submerged at high tide, emerging to fire at low tide if necessary. The north-western coast of France became known in consequence as 'The Iron Coast'. These preparations went on for over two years. Bonaparte's spies brought him reports that no less numerous camps were being set up in Kent and Sussex, in particular at Dover and Deal.

The British response to the threat of the Grande Armée and the 'Boulogne Flotilla' was to bring back William Pitt as Prime Minister in March 1804, in place of Addington, and recruit volunteers and militia. Despite much boasting – 'One Englishman could thrash three Frenchmen' – there was considerable apprehension. The caricatures by Gillray and others grew more savage and grotesque than ever, reflecting – together with such pamphlets as *Atrocities of the Corsican Demon* – an increasingly nervous popular hatred. Many believed openly that the French invasion would succeed; some feared that the poorer classes might rise in support of the First Consul as 'Robespierre on horseback', others that he would land in Ireland and be joined by its peasantry. In general people – though not all – were in agreement with Southey's view (written a few years later) that Bonaparte's ultimate aim was to 'ensnare, degrade and brutalize mankind'. What frightened the more reflective was the knowledge that the French had beaten almost every army in Europe. Meanwhile, in Napoleon's words, 'The rival armies watched each other silently, divided only by the Channel, which swarmed with British ships.'

The First Consul was prepared to wait for his chance, his strategy being that the British could not be sure of co-ordinating their naval resources with the weather and the tides to stop him taking control of the Channel for ten hours. He was gambling on long but not impossible odds. He needed 3,000 transports to bring over 200,000 troops under Davout, Ney, Soult, Victor and of course himself, though he never succeeded in assembling more than 2,000. Nevertheless, Spain's entry into the war on France's side in 1803 gave him the use of many more valuable men-o'-war with which to threaten the West Indies and lure British warships away from the Channel.

In 1805 the French fleet seemed, momentarily, to have a chance of wresting control of the Channel from the British. Napoleon – now Emperor – produced a plan which was certainly worth trying. On his instructions Admiral Villeneuve sailed from Toulon to Cadiz to join Admiral Gravina. The combined Franco-Spanish fleets then made for the Caribbean, pursued – as intended – by Nelson as far as the

Gulf of Mexico. Suddenly they put about, returning under full sail in the hope of seizing command of the Channel. However, after an engagement with Sir Robert Calder's comparatively small flotilla off Cape Finisterre, Villeneuve lost his nerve, putting in to refit at Cadiz. Nelson soon arrived to blockade him.

British diplomacy (and subsidies) built an alliance against Napoleon in the summer of 1805 – Austria, Russia, Sweden and Naples. An Austrian army was to advance on the Emperor in Lombardy, an Austro-Russian army down the Danube valley, a Swedish-Russian army through Hanover and a British-Russian-Neapolitan army from southern Italy. The Emperor concentrated on the threats in Lombardy and from the Danube valley. He sent an army to hold Archduke Charles on the Adige while he himself dealt with the Danube sector. The Austrian General Mack led 60,000 troops into Bavaria, occupying the Upper Danube in order to stop any French attempt to advance through the Black Forest. Napoleon pretended to attack through it but instead went round – placing himself between Mack and Vienna. Mack surrendered Ulm on 19 October, although it could have held out for months. An army of 60,000 men had been eliminated in three weeks.

Two days later all French hope of invading Britain vanished at Trafalgar. Goaded by his master's taunts, and references to 'infamous Villeneuve', the French Admiral had sailed out of Cadiz, to be intercepted off Cape Trafalgar by Nelson, who blocked his escape back into Cadiz. The French ships and sailors were excellent, but not their officers; the noblemen who had sometimes proved more than a match for the British during the American War of Independence had all been murdered or chased into exile in the Revolution. Villeneuve and his captains were outmanoeuvred and then annihilated. Nelson was killed, but a French fleet would never again challenge the British Navy.

Although so much effort and planning had been wasted, there

was some reason for the Emperor Napoleon's dismissal of Trafalgar – 'storms have deprived us a few vessels following a battle in which they were imprudently engaged'. On 13 November he rode into Vienna, the Holy Roman Emperor's capital which had never before been entered by a conqueror. He was about to win the greatest of his battles, Austerlitz.

During the autumn of 1805 Britain could scarcely credit that Napoleon was going to triumph yet again. On hearing rumours of his victory at Ulm, William Pitt snapped, 'Don't believe a word of it! It is all fiction.' Disappointment grew steadily as still grimmer news seemed likely. Nevertheless, with the security won by Trafalgar, the British were no more inclined to make peace. Apart from the illusory reconciliation of 1802-3, save for such wilful optimists as Charles James Fox they had always hated both the Jacobin and the dictator in the Emperor. A Whig, not a Tory, wrote of him in 1805 that while cowing the French – 'Corrupt, divide and terrify are the three great pillars of his throne' – his ultimate aim was the conquest of all Europe; the writer adds that 'General Bonaparte's principal characteristics are 'duplicity and violence'. The descendants of such men would see very much the same evil menace in Hitler, and in much the same way.

Sir Basil Liddell Hart has argued persuasively that misconceived interpretations of the teachings of Clausewitz influenced both the causes and the character of the First and Second World Wars.[19] Yet before hostilities broke out Hitler could be most un-Clausewitzian; in the early 1930s he explained to Hermann Rauschning what he then regarded as the best method of aggrandisement:

How to achieve the moral breakdown of the enemy before the war has started – that is the problem that interests me. Whoever has experienced war at the front will want to refrain from all avoidable bloodshed.

But when war came the Führer would be an extreme Clausewitzian in the most simplistic sense, echoing the master's view that 'only great and general battles can produce great results'.

Clausewitz is best known for his hackneyed dictum that war is a continuation of politics by other means. What is less familiar, although implicit in such a belief, is his contempt for international law: 'Violence arms itself with the inventions of Art and Science in order to contend against violence. Self-imposed restrictions, almost imperceptible and hardly worth mentioning, termed usages of International Law, accompany it without essentially impairing its power.' Like the Emperor, Hitler applied this approach to peace as well as to war.

While the Führer hoped to avoid a war in the West, he certainly anticipated one in the East. His stealthy preparations were an almost text-book application of Clausewitzian principles, as any reader of *Vom Kriege* will recognize immediately. In Clausewitz's words:

> In order to ascertain the real scale of the means which we must put forth for War, we must think over the political object both on our own side and on the enemy's side; we must consider the power and position of the enemy's State as well as of our own, the character of his Government and of his people, and the capacities of both, and all that again on our own side, and the political connections with other States, and the effect which the War will produce on those States . . .
> it is the true flash of genius which discovers in a moment what is right.

From the very beginning the Führer made it perfectly clear that he intended to rearm Germany. Yet he was genuinely astonished by Churchill's warning that Hitler would become a threat to all

Europe. He had no quarrel with the British, whom to some extent he even admired, nor with anyone else in the West – not excepting the French whom he despised and hated, like Bismarck before him – so long as they let him build his *Grossdeutschland* and gave him a free hand in Eastern Europe. Moreover, on taking power he felt himself dangerously weak, with an army of only 100,000 men, no planes, no tanks and almost no navy. The armed might of Facist Italy could inspire him with real fear in 1934.

Indeed, his first diplomatic moves were concerned with securing peace and parity. If Germany withdrew from the League of Nations and the Disarmament Conference in October 1933 it was on the grounds that she was not being treated as an equal. The Führer was surprisingly well disposed towards the British. In *Mein Kampf* he had written that they were Germany's only possible ally in the East. They had been hostile to Russia for most of the nineteenth century, and besides detesting the new Soviet régime – they had helped its enemies in 1918-20 – they feared it might revive Tsarist imperialism and threaten India. He had a very friendly meeting with the British minister Anthony Eden in February 1934, impressing him by his 'sincerity'. (Eden reported to Baldwin, 'He is a surprise. In conversation quiet, almost shy, with a pleasant smile. Without doubt the man has charm.') When Britain fell out with Italy during the same year over the latter's designs on Abyssinia – seen by the Führer as bare-faced cynicism on Britain's part – he took the opportunity to negotiate an agreement which allowed him to increase his navy to one-third the size of the British but no more. He responded to the Franco-Soviet pact of 1935 by a speech to the Reichstag in which he denounced war, offering a non-aggression pact to every country in Europe.

Privately he was noticeably receptive to new ideas in military technology, welcoming General Guderian's book *Achtung Panzer*. This advocated the use of armour and mechanized infantry in over-

142

whelming strength on a narrow front so as to punch a hole in the enemy's defences and achieve a decisive breakthrough. He also gave a sympathetic hearing to Luftwaffe officers who had taken up the theories of Giulio Douhet, in particular the breaking of civilian morale by air-raids on cities. The combination of Guderian's ideas with those of Douhet would produce what was to be known as *blitzkrieg* – lightning war. (This method boded well for the Clausewitzian *Hauptschlacht* – the decisive battle which Napoleon had always sought, with which he had won so many campaigns in a matter of weeks.)

Hitler's first aggressive move was in 1936. Versailles had stipulated that German troops should never be stationed in the Rhineland, as a strategic guarantee to France. In 1936 France had a weak government together with a notably defeatist chief-of-staff in General Gamelin. In March Hitler ordered the reoccupation of the Rhineland, sending in two divisions. His generals were appalled, since the Wehrmacht was still too weak to think of confronting the French army. But Gamelin's imagination magnified 22,000 German troops into 265,000, terrifying his government, who were easily persuaded by Britain to fall back on negotiation – which needless to say proved futile. For years after the Führer described the crisis as the most nerve-racking of his life. 'If the French had marched into the Rhineland we would have had to withdraw with our tails between our legs', he admitted frankly.

His triumph alarmed all Europe, demonstrating that the French would only consider fighting a defensive war. In consequence every French ally was at risk, even if France remained ostensibly the greatest military power in the world. The system which had kept the peace since 1918 was no longer in working order.

Hitler and the British leaders of the 1930s had no more in common than Napoleon and the Whigs. Chamberlain and Halifax and the luminaries of the Third Reich found each other incomprehen-

143

sible. When Goering arrived late for dinner at the British Embassy, explaining, 'I have been shooting', the Ambassador, Sir Eric Phipps, inquired 'Animals, I hope?' Quivering with inferiority, Goebbels thought the aristocratic Eden 'a horrible fop'. Such Englishmen had no hope whatever of understanding the Führer, staying convinced to the end that he preferred peace to war. Confident of his ability to outmanoeuvre them diplomatically, Hitler simply could not grasp that in the last resort they would fight. In this he was abetted by Ribbentrop, whose arrogance when Ambassador in London made him a laughing-stock. Relations with Britain might have been very different had Goering with his bonhomie and cunning led a mission there.

During the closing years of the 1930s British statesmen and diplomatists feared Hitler's paranoia and aggressive, unpredictable nature far more than his unimaginative policies – Churchill had done so since the moment Hitler became Reichskanzler in 1933. Even though he was mistaken in his estimate of the real strength and capability of the Wehrmacht and the Luftwaffe, Churchill's wild exaggerations alerted the British to the fact that danger lay ahead.

Hitler was convinced that North America would never again take part in a European war. Undoubtedly 'Isolationism' contributed to this delusion. His reaction to Franklin D. Roosevelt and the New Deal was bizarre to say the least, if one may believe Hermann Rauschning – 'the last disgusting death rattle of a corrupt and outworn system'. (Rauschning, an East Prussian magnate and Nazi who later left the party and fled to Switzerland and then America from Germany, recorded a number of conversations which he had with the Führer between 1932 and 1934; they are even more revealing than *Mein Kampf* about his real objectives and plans.) 'Since the Civil War, in which the Southern States were conquered against all historical logic and sound sense, the Americans have been in a condition of political and popular decay', the Führer believed. 'The beginnings of a great new social order based on the principle of slavery and inequality were destroyed by that war, and with them also the embryo of a future truly great America that would not have been ruled by a corrupt caste of tradesmen, but by a real *Herren*-class that would have swept away all the falsities of liberty and equality.'

Nevertheless, he did not despair of the United States. The country was on the brink of a revolution from which he alone could save her, and he intended to do so; soon there would be an American SA. Moreover, he told Rauschning, 'I am firmly convinced that in a certain section of the American middle class and the farmers, the sound fighting spirit of colonial days has not been extinguished.' He was encouraged by a 'wholesome aversion for the negroes and the coloured races in general, including the Jews'. Such traits were 'an assurance that the sound elements of the United States will one day awaken as they have awakened in Germany'. He added, 'I guarantee, gentlemen, that at the right moment a new America will exist as our strongest supporter.' However, he did not have a high opinion of American troops. One day all these misconceptions would contribute decisively to his total ruin.

Roosevelt never made the mistake of underestimating 'this wild man'. He suspected 'Brother Hitler' from the beginning, although trying without much hope to discourage Germany from rearming. By 1935 he was convinced that war would come in Europe, and by the end of the year was only too willing to sign the Neutrality Act – designed to prevent United States involvement. But by 1937 he had realized that America could not hope to escape it.

In 1936 the diplomatic situation changed radically. Nazi Germany and Fascist Italy grew increasingly close, to be joined by Falangist Spain when the Spanish Civil War broke out in July. By the end of the year an 'Axis' – Mussolini's term – had come into being. During 1937 France and Britain began to grow fearful of

Germany's increasing might – even those who had hitherto derided Churchill. Yet Hitler may well have been sincere when in 1937 he told Lord Lothian 'another Anglo-German quarrel would mean the departure of both countries from the stage of history'.

Curiously enough, in Hitler's case there were probably less real grounds for mistrust on both sides than there had been in Napoleon's day. In June 1935, when the Anglo-German naval agreement was signed, he had said, 'Politically I see the future only in alliance with the British.' There is no reason to disbelieve him. But when, after he had started to rearm, France and Britain did so too he began to race them, though not very much faster. Churchill exaggerated consistently, having been supplied with incorrect statistics; in 1936 he claimed that Germany was spending 12,000 million marks a year on rearmament – we now know that the figure was under 5,000 million. To some extent Hitler was to blame. In March 1935 he told Eden that his new Luftwaffe already had as many planes as the RAF, a lie which caused panic in Britain.

Churchill for one never doubted that war with Hitler would come. In March 1933 he told the House of Commons: We watch with surprise and distress the tumultuous insurgence of ferocity and war spirit [in Germany]; in 1934 'That mighty Power is now equipping itself once again, 70,000,000 of people, with the technical apparatus of modern war, and at the same time is instilling into the hearts of its youth and manhood the most extreme patriotic, nationalist and militaristic conceptions . . . Beware, Germany is a country fertile in military surprises'; and in April 1937 'we seem to be moving, drifting, steadily, against our will, against the will of every race and every people and every class towards some hideous catastrophe.'

Yet we now know that the Führer did not want war in the West, if he could avoid it.

Even Winston Churchill was not immune to the man's spell.

'One may dislike Hitler's system and yet admire his patriotic achievement', he pronounced in 1937. 'If our country were defeated, I hope we should find a champion as indomitable to restore our courage and lead us back to our place among the nations.' In those days he saw the Führer as one of those 'whose lives have enriched the story of mankind'.

Foreign observers overestimated Hitler's strength. In October 1935 Churchill warned the Commons:

> The incredible figure of more than £800,000,000 sterling is being spent in the currency of the present year on direct and indirect military preparations by Germany. The whole of Germany is an armed camp . . . the industries of Germany are mobilised for war to an extent to which ours were not mobilised even in the year after the Great War had begun. The whole population is being trained from childhood up to war. A mighty army is coming into being. Many submarines are already exercising in the Baltic. Great cannon, tanks, machine guns and poison gas are fast accumulating.

And in 1936:

> Do not forget that all the time those remorseless hammers of which General Goering spoke are descending night and day in Germany, and that the most warlike and, in many ways, the most efficient people in Europe, are becoming welded into a tremendous fighting machine, equipped with the fearful agencies of modern science.

In reality even in 1939 Germany had fewer planes and tanks than France and Britain. It was all a brilliant piece of bluff on the Führer's part.

In July 1934 Austrian Nazis seized the Chancellery in Vienna, murdering the Chancellor, Engelbert Dollfuss. The coup was easily put down. Everyone saw Hitler's hand in the affair, for once unjustly. Dollfuss had been Mussolini's protégé, and the Duce massed several divisions at the Brenner Pass. In 'a state of tremendous agitation' the Führer told Papen hysterically, 'We are facing a second Sarajevo', sending him to Vienna to placate the Austrians and Italians. (At this date Mussolini considered Hitler a ranting buffoon, and referred to him as 'that horrible sexual degenerate' while in lighter moments the latter would give a spirited impersonation of the Duce delivering a speech.)

Despite his army's inferiority, the Führer did not introduce conscription until March 1935. His demands for a renegotiation of the Versailles settlement seemed not unreasonable. Most foreign observers conceded that the division of Europe into the winners and losers of 1918 could not go on for ever.

On 10 November 1937 Colonel Friedrich Hossbach noted down what he remembered of a meeting which Hitler had summoned five days earlier at the Chancery in Berlin. Those present included the Führer, Goering (chief of the Luftwaffe), Field Marshal von Blomberg (Defence Minister), Colonel-General von Fritsch (Wehrmacht commander-in-chief), Admiral Raeder (Naval chief) and Konstantin von Neurath (Foreign Minister). They were asked to consider three possible scenarios. First, a war situation in 1943-5. Second, if civil war broke out in France in 1938-40 (far from impossible), in which case Germany should invade Czechoslovakia. Third, if war broke out between France and Italy, there would be an opportunity for overrunning not merely Czechoslovakia but Austria as well. Hitler argued that Germany could have what she wanted without a 'great war'. Nevertheless, there was no programme of aggression. The meeting's real aim seems to have been to bully Schacht into providing more money for rearmament. Far from being a blueprint for war, the 'Hossbach Memorandum' shows that the Führer expected to get what he wanted without a European war, let alone a world war.

German and Italian collaboration in the Spanish Civil War drew Hitler and Mussolini closer together. The latter urged the new

Austrian Chancellor, Kurt von Schuschnigg, to co-operate with Germany, which he did by an agreement signed in July 1936. In February 1938 Schuschnigg set off a fatal crisis by visiting Berchtesgaden; he asked for economic assistance and help in dealing with Austria's violent Nazis. The Führer bludgeoned him into an agreement by which the NSDAP was to be legalized in Austria and a Nationalist, Seyss-Inquart (an old school friend of Schuschnigg, but a secret Nazi), to become Minister of the Interior. When Schuschnigg returned to Vienna he tried to evade the agreement by a plebiscite – 'Do you want a Free, Christian, German Austria?' But by rigging the voting he enabled Austrian Nazis to appeal to Hitler for 'constitutional justice'. German tanks crossed the frontier on 11 March, swiftly occupying Vienna. Schuschnigg resigned, Seyss-Inquart taking his place as Chancellor. The following day a message came to the Führer from the Duce, stating that he 'had no interest in Austria'. An emotional Hitler cried, 'Tell Mussolini I will never forget this . . .If he should ever need any help or be in any danger, he can be convinced that I shall stick to him, whatever may happen, even if the whole world be against him.' It was one of the promises which that extraordinary man kept. (Yet Count Ciano – Mussolini's son-in-law and Foreign Minister – had written in his diary three weeks earlier that Italian intervention would have been impossible. 'At the first shot we fired every Austrian, without exception, would fall in behind the Germans against us.') Until now the Führer had always declared that he envisaged an independent Austrian Nazi state allied with Germany. However, on 13 March, at Linz – the big city of his boyhood – he announced most unexpectedly that Austria would become part of the Reich. His decision was ratified by a plebiscite of 99 per cent in favour on 10 April.

Churchill pointed out the strategic implications:

A long stretch of the Danube is now in German hands. This mastery of Vienna gives to Nazi Germany military and economic control of the whole of the communications of south-eastern Europe, by road, by river and by rail.

Yet although disturbed, and although still much more powerful militarily, the French and British government took no action. They could not believe that the Führer wanted to start a war with them. Nor did he.

Because of its geographical position between Austria and what is now East Germany, Czechoslovakia was a very real threat to the Reich – 'a revolver stuck in Germany's ribs'. Hitler called it 'a French aircraft carrier'. The most industrialized of the countries carved out of the Habsburg Empire, it was also the most heavily armed. Yet Czechoslovakia was a multinational state – while supposedly founded on national identity. Czech rule was resented not merely by Germans but by Slovaks, Ruthenes, Poles and Hungarians, all hoping for independence or else incorporation into Poland or Hungary.

Czechoslovakia's greatest weakness was its German minority in the Sudetenland. Well over 3 million, it was situated on the German border. Many *Sudetendeutsche* had joined an extremely active local NSDAP under a leader, Konrad Henlein, who was subsidized from Berlin – and whom Hitler had impertinently appointed as his 'Viceroy' at the end of March 1938. They disliked being ruled by Czechs in Prague instead of from Vienna, as they had been before 1918. The *Anschluss* made them eager to follow the Austrians into the Führer's fold.

There were other weaknesses. The Czechs' neighbours all coveted large chunks of their territory, while their only ally was France. Yet they had some strengths as well. Their army numbered 34 divisions, compared with the Wehrmacht's 28 during the spring of 1938, and the mighty Skoda steel works ensured an adequate supply of munitions. In President Beneš Hitler faced one of his most skilful diplomatic opponents, a tough, negotiator who welcomed rather than feared a crisis. Even so, the Führer knew that his own army would expand to 55 divisions by October. His original aims were probably limited to annexing the Sudetenland and neutralizing Czechoslovakia's military potential.

It was the Czechs, not Hitler, who started the confrontation. When he returned from a State visit to Italy in May it was to find that Beneš had accused him, without justification, of mobilizing and had moved troops up to the border to warn the western powers that a crisis was brewing. The Führer was forced to withdraw his own troops from the Czech frontier. At the end of the month he told General von Brauchitsch, 'It is my unalterable decision to smash Czechoslovakia by military action in the near future', ordering an invasion to be planned for 1 October. (Some Wehrmacht officers were so horrified that they began to plan a coup.) Yet at this stage he almost certainly hoped to avoid a war. He encouraged Henlein's men to beat up Czechs, provoking retaliation so that he could claim Sudeten Germans were being persecuted. In September he shouted over the microphone at the Nuremberg Rally, 'Germans in Czecho-slovakia are neither defenceless nor deserted . . . One can never reconcile so uncompromising an enemy as the Czech.' The rising by the Sudeten NSDAP which ensued was a fiasco. But he had suc-ceeded in frightening everyone into believing he wanted war.

On 15 September the British prime minister, Neville Chamberlain, flew to Munich – his first flight – proposing that he should try to per-suade the French to make the Czechs cede the Sudetenland. 'I'm determined to settle it', Hitler yelled at the 69-year-old premier, 'I don't care if there's a world war or not!' Chamberlain returned a week later, announcing that Czechoslovakia was ready to cede the Sudetenland – to be told that 'regrettably' it was not enough, that Germany was going to march in straight away without formalities.

In response the Czechs and French mobilized, while the British Home Fleet was put on the alert. Hitler backed down. 'Despite this unheard-of provocation I shall of course keep my promise not to proceed against Czechoslovakia while negotiations are taking place.' He kept up the pressure by raging at British and French envoys. 'Germans are being treated like niggers – no one dares to treat even Turkey like this', he bellowed at Sir Horace Wilson. I'll have Czechoslovakia where I want her on 1 October.' Then Mussolini proposed a four-Power conference at Munich, which he chaired. Britain and France gave way. On his return from Munich, Chamberlain was applauded rapturously when he told a crowd in Downing Street, 'I believe it is peace in our time.' Every British newspaper save *Reynolds' News* welcomed the agreement with frantic enthusiasm.

On 1 October German troops occupied the Sudetenland, keeping to the Führer's deadline. Shortly afterwards the Poles annexed the Teschen and the Hungarians took southern Slovakia. During the crisis Hitler declared more than once 'We want no Czechs!' Yet he had always regarded Bohemia and Moravia as part of 'Greater Germany' (they had been part of the Germanic Confederation from 1815 to 1866). After Munich Czechoslovakia could not hope to survive – if Germany did not take more territory. Hungary certainly would. Early in 1939 Slovaks began to complain loudly about 'Czech repression'. On 13 March their leader, Monsignor Josef Tiso, read out at Bratislava a declaration of Slovakia's independence under German protectorship. The declaration had been drafted in Berlin.

On 13 March Emil Hácha, the new President of what was now 'Czechia' (Bohemia and Moravia), insisted on going to the German capital to beg Hitler to let the Czechs remain independent. Hitler and Goering bullied the man till he had a minor heart-attack; on recovering he signed a document by which 'Czechia' became the

German Protectorate of Bohemia. As soon as Hácha had left the Führer ran into his secretaries' room and told the girls to kiss him – 'I shall be known as the greatest German in history!' The next day he entered Prague, proclaiming 'Czechoslovakia has ceased to exist!' He thought it would be possible to Germanize the Czechs since, judging from their faces, he believed that they were not Slavs but descendants of Mongol colonists.

A week later German troops landed in Memel, a German-speaking port in Lithuania, on the border of East Prussia. Although Hitler claimed it, he had no plans for its annexation. However, the Lithuanians were so terrified that they handed it over without further delay.

These additions to the Fuhrer's 'empire' precipitated a dramatic shift in British public opinion. He had moved too fast, instead of waiting for the rump of Czechoslovakia to fall into his hands. The appeasers were discredited, while Winston Churchill's prophecies of war were heard with new interest. On 24 March he begged the House of Commons to consider stopping the 'German Dictator' by forming a European coalition:

> Do not let anyone suppose that this is a mere question of hardening one's heart and keeping a stiff upper lip, and standing by to see Czechoslovakia poleaxed and tortured as Austria has been . . . Is it not possible that decided action by France and Great Britain would rally the whole of these five states [of the Danube Basin] as well as Czechoslovakia, all of whom have powerful armies?'

Yet the Führer had convinced himself that the British would never go to war. 'The day of Britain's might at sea is past', he had told Rauschning in 1934. 'Aircraft and the U-boat have turned surface fleets into the obsolete playthings of the wealthy democracies. They are no longer a serious weapon in decisive warfare.' He was encouraged in this delusion by both Right and Left – by Mosleyites and Anglo-German friendship societies on the one hand and by pacifists on the other. His impressions were extraordinary. 'The English are incomparably insolent, but I admire them none the less. We still have a lot to learn from them.' Because of their colonial empire they had become 'a nation of rulers'. However, his qualified admiration was restricted to the British aristocracy, believing that their ancestors had come from Lower Saxony. He seems to have thought the 'masses' were racially inferior, 'unaware of the state of servitude in which they live' and that a socialist Britain must founder in poverty. Chamberlain did not possess the virtues he admired, the prime minister being dismissed as 'a crawling little worm'.[20]

By early 1939 the Führer had secured all Greater Germany save for Danzig and that part of Prussia lost in 1919. The 'Free City of Danzig' had had an exclusively German-speaking population since its foundation in the Middle Ages, and in 1919 had protested so vigorously against incorporation into Poland that the Allies had given it special status. What Hitler now demanded was the reincorporation of Danzig into the Reich, together with a small strip of territory linking East and West Prussia, the 'Polish Corridor'; he did not ask for all former German territory. In February 1939 he even offered the Poles a military alliance with a 'common policy' in the Ukraine; far from wanting to fight them, he hoped that they would help him in his conquest of the East.

In the spring of 1939 Britain and France guaranteed Poland's territorial integrity. This merely angered Hitler, who ordered plans to be prepared to invade Poland in the autumn. In April Chamberlain considered and dismissed the possibility of an alliance with the Soviet Union, the one step which might have saved the Poles.

President Roosevelt's letter of 14 April 1939, urging disarmament, gave the Führer an opportunity to tell the world just how much he had achieved for Germany. He claimed that, because the

Germans had gone unarmed to the Versailles peace talks in 1919, they had been subjected to 'the vilest oppression which peoples and human beings have ever had to bear', that they had suffered 'even greater degradation than can ever have been inflicted on the chieftains of the Sioux tribes'. (No doubt he was partly inspired by Karl May's home-grown German 'Westerns'.) Ironically, he emphasized his triumph in restoring full employment in his country, belittling the New Deal by implication – 'You, Mr Roosevelt, have a much easier task in comparison.' The President's letter also helped to delude him into thinking that Isolationism would always prevent the Americans from fighting.

Roosevelt had not shared the general European optimism about the Munich agreement. In September 1938 he had written (to the American Ambassador in Rome): 'Chamberlain's visit to Hitler today may bring things to a head or may result in a temporary postponement of what looks to me like an inevitable conflict within the next five years.' By January 1939, even before the seizure of the Czech rump, he had begun to fear Hitler's designs on Central and South America, and 'the gradual encirclement of the United States by the removal of first lines of defence'. He warned the Military Affairs Committee of the Senate:

Now, do not say it is chimerical, do not say it is just a pipe dream. Would any of you have said six years ago, when this man Hitler came into control of the German Government, Germany busted, Germany a complete and utter failure, a nation that owes everybody, disorganised, not worth considering as a force in this world, would any of you have said that in six years Germany would dominate Europe, completely and absolutely?

No European leader apart from Churchill saw the situation with such clarity.[21]

On 23 August Ribbentrop signed a non-aggression pact with the Soviet Union, including a secret clause to divide Poland. A week later, on 1 September. Deutscherrundfunk announced that its radio station at Gleiwitz on the border had been attacked by Polish troops, several of whom had been killed. (The latter were Germans under sentence of death, who had been drugged, dressed in Polish uniforms and shot.) To 'defend the Fatherland' German troops hurtled into Poland. Guessing that France and Britain would react only slowly, Hitler deployed all his strength, confident in his superiority in planes and tanks. He was not mistaken. Unlike Czechoslovakia, Poland had not modernized her army, her lancers facing motorized columns, dive bombers and flame-throwers. The Poles knew they could not win; their plan was to hold the Germans for a fortnight so that the western powers would have time to come to their rescue by striking across the Rhine. As the Führer had foreseen, the French and British did little beyond declaring war. After two weeks, by arrangement with their Nazi allies, the Russians invaded eastern Poland. After four weeks the Führer reviewed a victory parade in a Warsaw bombed into surrender.

Mussolini had shaken the Führer badly by informing him on 25 August that 'Italy is not ready for war.' Hitler had no real desire to fight Britain as well as France. He proclaimed on 6 October that the Western Powers should accept Poland's defeat and work out with him a lasting European peace, that he would guarantee the British Empire's survival if Britain would co-operate. We know from his interpreter Paul Schmidt that when the British declaration of war reached him on 3 September he sat silent and unmoving for a time, then glared savagely at his dumbstruck Foreign Minister Ribbentrop, inquiring, 'What now?' Goering muttered, 'If we lose this war, then may God have mercy on us!'

'We are here faced with phenomena that show an unmistakable relationship,' Pieter Geyl pointed out in 1944. While admitting that the principles of the French and the 'Brown' revolutions were radically different, and in some ways diametrically opposed, Geyl argues that they were dangerous for the same reasons. Each was bringing a new order into being, and rejected the standards of the existing order, regarding all opposition as criminal. Napoleon, in Geyl's words, was 'a conqueror with whom it was impossible to live; who could not help turning an ally into a vassal, or at least interpreting the relationship to his own exclusive advantage'. These were the colours in which Hitler showed himself unmistakably in 1939-40.

Nevertheless, in October 1939 the Führer appealed to the Allies to negotiate, stating, 'I believe even today that there can only be real peace in Europe and throughout the world if Germany and England come to an understanding.' Although he later told his generals that this was only a ruse, and that his 'unalterable aim' was to defeat his enemies, there is little doubt he would have preferred peace with Britain and France on condition they let him have a free hand in the East. Throughout the 'Phoney War' of 1939-40 curious rumours circulated among the Allied forces that soon Britain and France would be fighting by Germany's side against the Soviet Union. However, the British, while they did not share the ingrained French hatred of the Boche, saw Hitler in much the same light as they had once seen Bonaparte. Moreover, Churchill, that latter-day Pitt, had by now joined the Cabinet.

Napoleon may genuinely have wanted peace but he had small hope of getting it, principally because the British distrusted him. They were fearful that one day he would build a fleet larger than the British Navy, and were deeply alarmed by his revival of pre-1789 French colonial policy – his acquisition of Louisiana, his sending expeditions to India and the Caribbean. In any case they suspected, rightly or wrongly, that he intended to conquer all Europe. 'The favourite plan of Bonaparte', Lord Minto wrote in February 1802, 'is for our total exclusion from the Continent.' They saw the Peace of Amiens as a mere lull in hostilities; Whitworth suggested cynic-ally, 'By peace we can wage a more dangerous and, I trust, more decisive warfare against his Government.' Only a few weeks after it had been signed, Lord Folkestone denounced it as 'a treaty built on Jacobin principles and confirming Jacobin power'.

In contrast, Hitler had a very real chance of securing peace. For all his bullying bluster, he never anticipated a world-wide conflict; Speer was convinced that he was thunderstruck by Britain and France declaring war in 1939, and had expected to acquire Poland without any real opposition from them. As A. J. P. Taylor puts it, 'He wanted the fruits of total victory without total war; and thanks to the stupidity of others he nearly got them.'[22]

All methods formerly usual were upset by Bonaparte's luck and boldness, and first rate powers almost wiped out at a blow.

Clausewitz, Vom Kriege

Before the war, and still more during the conquest of the West, Hitler came to appear a gigantic figure, combining the strategy of a Napoleon with the cunning of a Machiavelli and the fanatical fervour of a Mahomet.

Sir Basil Liddell Hart, The Other Side of the Hill

6

The Conquest of Europe

Napoleon conquered what was later Germany in 1805, Hitler over-ran France in 1940. Both smashed coalitions whose armies had appeared to have overwhelming superiority. These unexpectedly complete victories made the Emperor and the Führer masters of Europe. Each was intoxicated by his success, yielding to unbridled ambition.

Marshal Alexandre Berthier, the son of an engineer who had been ennobled by Louis XV and himself a sapper, is recognized as one of the greatest staff officers in history. He was both a genius and a dogsbody. While Napoleon was his own chief military planner – crouched over or even lying on his maps with a pair of dividers (spaced to cover 22 to 25 miles, the distance infantry could march in a day), marking his divisions by coloured pins which he moved so as to know where they would be at any given moment, only issuing orders after the most meticulous calculations – the provider of maps and everything else was Berthier, who knew the strength and position of every unit. During one campaign he is said to have gone without sleep for nearly a fortnight. He was so much under his master's spell, that guilty at having deserted in 1814 and not daring to rejoin him, he eventually threw himself out of a window.

General Alfred Jodl and the future Marshal Wilhelm Keitel together constituted a species of joint Berthier. Jodl, originally an artilleryman, was a Bavarian of bourgeois background with intellectual tastes. Too intelligent not to question Hitler's wilder fantasies, he was totally dominated by him, often cynically agreeing for the sake of peace and quiet. Nevertheless, he could plan anything. (He was to plan the brilliantly successful invasion and conquest of Yugoslavia.) Keitel, a Hanoverian country gentleman (whose family had fought against the Prussians in 1866), was also a gunner but not so clever as Jodl. 'From an honourable, soldierly respectable general he had developed in the course of years into a servile flatterer,' comments Speer. 'Basically Keitel hated his own weaknesses; but the hopelessness of any dispute with Hitler had ultimately brought him to the point of not even trying to form his own opinion.' So enslaved was he that when his master staggered to his feet after the bomb attempt of 1944 he embraced him, crying, 'My Führer, my Führer, you're alive!' (It was Keitel who gave Hitler the title *Grösster Feldherr aller Zeiten* – 'Greatest War Lord of All Time'; abbreviated to 'Gröfaz', it became a sarcastic nickname at Wehrmacht head-quarters during the war's later stages.) Together Jodl and Keitel enabled the Führer to function as a commander.

The basic difference is that the Emperor was his own best strategist and tactician, as well as a leader in the field. Hitler, on the other hand, was at this phase of the war – in contrast to later phases – prepared to listen to ideas on strategy and tactics; the defeat of France was undoubtedly due to his readiness to listen to an officer with a plan rejected by the High Command. Modern warfare made it impossible for him to be up at the front like Napoleon.

♔
N

In 1805 the French were opposed by 100,000 fresh Austrian and Russian troops under the Holy Roman Emperor and the Tsar of

Russia. Napoleon had 60,000 men who had marched nearly 1,500 miles during the last three months. On 1 December 1805 the French bivouacked near the Austro-Russian positions around Austerlitz (Slavkov) between Brno and Morava in what is now Czechoslovakia, but deliberately left the Pratzen plateau unoccupied. The Austrians and Russians hastened to seize it, since the plateau commanded the entire area. They saw that the French right was surprisingly weak, and they planned to turn it, though to do so they would have to weaken their centre on the plateau in order to strengthen their left – which was just what the French Emperor wanted. Kutuzov (the future hero of 1812) feared a trap, but his warnings were ignored. On the following morning the battlefield was shrouded by dense fog, enabling Napoleon to mass below the plateau, without being observed, the troops which he had withdrawn from his right, together with those of his centre. On the other hand, the plateau was free from fog, so that the French could see exactly what their opponents were doing. At 9.00 a.m., after three Russian divisions had come down to attack the French right – meeting a ferocious resistance from Marshal Davout – the Emperor promptly hurled 25,000 men up the slopes, overwhelming the Russian Imperial Guard which defended the plateau, cutting the Allied army neatly in two. The battle continued fiercely all along the front for seven hours. The Allies tried desperately to retake the Pratzen, the last Russian attempt to do so failing at about 1.30 p.m. The French then advanced across the plateau to fire down on the Allies' left wing. Bewildered Austro-Russian troops fled in panic across frozen lakes on the plains below, many of them drowning when the ice was broken by French cannon-balls. The Emperor killed 15,000 men, took 10,000 prisoners, and captured 180 guns with 40 colours.

While Tsar Alexander took refuge farther east the Emperor Francis II demanded an interview with Napoleon. Almost his first

words to his vanquisher were a bitter reference to British subsidies –
'The English are dealers in human flesh.' He was given an armistice which resulted in the Treaty of Pressburg three weeks later.
Despite Talleyrand cautioning his master that he was asking too
much, Austria had to surrender Venice, Istria and Dalmatia to the
Emperor, with Swabia and the Tyrol going to his Württemberger
and Bavarian allies. Besides being driven out of her German and
Italian possessions, Austria had to pay a huge indemnity, with 8
million gold francs as a first instalment. Hanover was given to
Prussia, to ensure she did not ally with Britain. As for Naples, the
Emperor announced that its dynasty no longer reigned, its new king
being his brother Joseph; French troops occupied it early in 1806.
Holland became a kingdom under Louis Bonaparte.

In addition a confederation of German client states was set up
under French control. This *Rheinbund* ('Confederation of the
Rhine'), designed to replace the 'Holy Roman Empire of the
German Nation', included all Charlemagne's territory; as he had
threatened in 1802, Napoleon was reviving the Western Empire.
To assert his primacy he promoted the Electors of Bavaria and
Württemberg to kings. The Emperor Francis formally renounced
the title Holy Roman Emperor in August 1806, taking that of
Emperor of Austria in its place.

Always biased in Napoleon's favour, Charles James Fox guessed
from the outset how his campaign would end. Otherwise even the
stoutest heart of oak was shaken. A grim Canning compared Bonaparte to Alexander the Great, Julius Caesar and Frederick the
Great, a general unhampered by constitutional control. William
Hazlitt discerned 'a spirit of unbounded ambition, the insolence of
almost unexampled success, resentment for supposed injuries and
the most consummate military skill'. The British were especially
alarmed by the Confederation of the Rhine. 'There is nothing to
break the gloom,' wrote Lord Addington (the former prime

minister), 'Europe is France.' Sheridan commented 'Bonaparte is surrounding France not with the iron frontier which distinguished the childish ambition of Louis XIV, but with kingdoms of his own creation.'

Britain was still at war. After Trafalgar, invasion was out of the question, but there were other ways of bringing her to her knees. Later in 1806, when he had knocked out Prussia, Napoleon used his control of Germany to cut Britain off from the markets of northern Europe. By the Decree of Berlin in November that year he would introduce the 'Continental Blockade', or 'Continental System'. All trade and communications with the British Isles were forbidden, and any British merchandise, whether from Britain or her colonies, was declared forfeit. The governments of Spain, Holland, Etruria and Naples as well as those in Germany were ordered to enforce the blockade. The Emperor explained, 'I am going to conquer sea-power with land-power.'

Indirectly, the *Blocus Continental* affected the United States. Britain forebade Americans to trade with Napoleonic Europe, allowing direct trade with Sweden alone. American vessels were intercepted by British warships, their cargoes seized and their crews press-ganged. At the end of 1807 President Jefferson steered an Embargo Act through Congress, forbidding trade with both Britain and France; his object was to starve Britain into changing her policy without war. Relations continued to deteriorate, and in 1812 President Madison declared war on Britain. John Randolph of Roanoke warned that such a war meant allying with forces opposed to civilization; privately Madison agreed. Most informed Americans detested Napoleon.[23] During the crisis of 1807 Jefferson admitted, 'It is really mortifying that we should wish success to Bonaparte and look to his victims as our salvation.' In 1816 he wrote, 'I considered him the very worst of human beings, and as having inflicted more misery on mankind than any other who had ever lived'; in

1823, 'He wanted totally the sense of right and wrong', had destroyed 'millions of human lives' and 'must have been a moral monster, against whom every hand should have been lifted to slay him'.

Despite its hostility, the Emperor was fascinated by America, by the speed of its development and constant expansion. (On St Helena he would read all he could about it.) He prophesied that 'The Americans will not become a great people at once but gradually', that one day they would be the 'avengers of the sea' and cause the British serious anxiety.

In 1801 in exchange for creating 'Etruria' (by adding formerly Habsburg Tuscany to Bourbon Parma) he obtained from Spain the former French territory of Louisiana, which had been under Spanish rule since 1763. For a moment he toyed with the old dream of a French transatlantic empire and tried to secure Florida as well. However, he was too much of a realist not to realize the difficulties. In the event of a renewed war the British fleet would at once sail into New Orleans; on the other hand, if he sent French troops to garrison it, the Americans would immediately ally with Britain – as Thomas Jefferson observed, if French soldiers arrived 'We must marry ourselves to the British fleet and nation.' Accordingly he sold the entire territory to the United States in 1803 for the paltry sum of 60 million francs. He secured by this more than money, preventing an Anglo-American rapproachement. His own comment on the Louisiana Purchase was that, by making the United States a truly continental power, 'I have just given to England a maritime rival that sooner or later will humble her pride. He did not regret surrendering Louisiana because, as he said, 'with war on the way I could not have kept it and then the English would have taken it.' Even so he always wanted to visit Louisiana.

As it was, the French were causing the British quite enough anxiety already. Fox was certain Napoleon had mastered Europe.

He would have agreed with him when he wrote to Josephine after Austerlitz: 'The English won't be able to stand up to us now.' Pitt despaired, and the failure of his foreign policy killed him. On 23 January 1806, broken by gout, overwork and alcoholism – he was rumoured to need twenty glasses of wine at dinner before making a speech in the House – the Prime Minister died at forty-six 'like a candle burning out'. His government was succeeded by a coalition of 'All the Talents', from both Whigs and Tories, in which Fox was Foreign Secretary. He sent Lord Yarmouth to Paris in June 1806 to explore the possiblity of a general peace.

In France public opinion, nervous about reopening a full-scale European war, was delighted by the Treaty of Pressburg, which it hoped meant lasting peace. Yet even the least warlike Frenchmen felt pleasure at what seemed to be final victory over the Habsburgs. Few save Talleyrand realized that Austria would seek revenge. In vain he advised his master to give her Moldavia and Wallachia so she would look east, but Napoleon had ambitions of his own in that direction.

Talleyrand considered the sheer brilliance of Napoleon's intellect the principal cause of his ultimate ruin. In his view the Emperor made plans for too many contingencies, anticipating the most un-likely dangers from his neighbours – a state of mind which led inevitably to war. Before Austerlitz his foreign policy had been essentially defensive, more or less content with the 'natural frontiers' of the Alps and the Rhine. But his amazing victory intoxicated him, convinced him he was invincible, made him wish to rule all Europe.

Yet this was not immediately apparent after Austerlitz. Many in Britain as well as in France believed that peace was possible now that Charles James Fox was in charge of British foreign policy. The Emperor offered Malta and in secret Hanover – George III's former electorate – although he had just given it to Prussia. He insisted that in return Britain must let him occupy Bourbon Sicily. But this was unacceptable, and negotiations broke down. Then Fox died in September after only a few months in office. Napoleon wrote years later that had Fox lived his career might have been very different – 'we would have arranged a new order in Europe'. It was wishful thinking.

Britain informed Prussia that she had been offered Hanover, promising to subsidize the Prussian army if it fought the French. Tsar Alexander visited Berlin to persuade King Frederick William III to declare war. A wave of anti-French sentiment swept through Prussia. Despite the French victories of recent years, the Prussians were convinced that their own rigidly drilled troops were still the best in Europe, as they had been under Frederick the Great. When war was declared on 1 October 1806, instead of waiting for the Emperor to invade and for Russian reinforcements, 160,000 Prussians advanced into Saxony on too wide a front, taking up positions on the river Saale, with their main supply depot at Naumburg dangerously exposed on their right. From the very beginning their campaign was disastrous. On 10 October Prince Louis of Prussia was killed shortly before the French turned his army's flank and seized Naumburg, blowing up the magazines and cutting their opponents off from fresh ammunition. On 15 October, having crossed the river Saale at Jena, Napoleon routed Prince Hohenlohe, inflicting 12,000 casualties and taking 25,000 prisoners and 200 guns. On the same day Marshal Davout, guarding one of the crossings of the Saale with 26,000 men, was attacked at Auerstadt by the Duke of Brunswick with 60,000. The Prussians relied on their cavalry to break the French squares, charging again and again, only to be mowed down. Davout then formed his squares into columns and charged the Prussian infantry, which broke; Brunswick and his two senior officers were mortally wounded, 10,000 Prussians lay dead or dying and 115 guns were captured. The Prussians were dazed; one of their officers described the French as small, pitiful creatures who under fire become 'super-human'. Murat's cavalry pursued relentlessly, making it impossible for the Prussians to rally. Hohenlohe surrendered with another 20,000 men. On 27 October the Emperor entered Berlin to the strains of the *Marseillaise,* chosen for its anti-royal sentiment. Frederick William fled to Memel, on the eastern-most border of his realm. By 8 November the Prussian army no longer existed. Besides Memel only Königsberg and a few towns held out.

It has often been said that on this occasion Prussia had treated her army like some family heirloom credited with miraculous powers, taken down from its glass case and dusted. Her generals followed blindly the strategy of fifty years before.

Among prisoners of the French were Prince August of Prussia and his 26-year-old ADC, Captain Carl von Clausewitz. They would spend the next two years in captivity in France. Clausewitz wrote bitterly in after years of the defeat at Jena that the Prussian generals had together thrown 'themselves into the open jaws of destruction with the oblique order of Frederick the Great, and managed to ruin Hohenlohe's army in a way that no army was ever ruined, even on a field of battle. All this was done through a manner which had outlived its day, together with the most down-right stupidity.' Elsewhere he writes that 'the stain of a cowardly submission can never be effaced' – words that would be quoted in *Mein Kampf.*

Napoleon took the opportunity to visit the tomb of a soldier whom he genuinely admired – Frederick the Great. Indeed, to some extent he had modelled himself on the grim old King, whose example inspired his plain grey uniform and small unbraided hat. He sent back to Paris not only 340 Prussian standards to hang up in the Invalides but Frederick's sword which he took from the tomb at Potsdam. (*Der Alte Fritz* was even more a hero of the Führer. 'Despite all

Napoleon's genius, Frederick the Great was the most outstanding man of the eighteenth century', he declared. 'When seeking to find a solution for essential problems concerning the conduct of affairs of State, he refrained from all illogicality' – presumably a reference to the King's notorious lack of scruple. In particular Hitler considered him the Emperor's superior because of the latter's nepotism: 'When Napoleon set the interests of his family clique above all, Frederick the Great looked around him for *men*, and, at need, trained them himself.')

The years 1806 and 1807 represent the peak of the Emperor's achievement as a soldier. He did not invent his tactics. His genius lay in improving on them. They are the brain-children of officers of the old pre-1789 French army – Bourcet, Guibert and to a lesser extent Montalembert. Bourcet's contribution was manoeuvring an opponent into dispersing his troop concentrations and then concentrating one's own forces. Guibert was the advocate of mobility and fluidity, of self-contained divisions operating autonomously, and of the rear attack – a Napoleonic speciality. Montalembert was the creator of a complete new system of fortification. However, the Emperor applied these innovations under totally changed conditions. As Clausewitz observes, the wars which preceded the French Revolution had been on a small scale, restricted by generally observed conventions and with limited objectives; plundering and devastating were looked on as barbarous and counter-productive. Then came the Revolution, and war suddenly turned into 'an affair of the people, and that of a people numbering nearly thirty millions', while 'energy in the conduct of war was immensely increased; the object of an action was the downfall of the foe; and not until the enemy lay prostrate on the ground was it supposed to be possible to stop'. The new Revolutionary warfare was perfected by Napoleon – 'this military power, based on the strength of the whole nation, marched over Europe, smashing everything in pieces, so surely and certainly, that where it only encountered the old fashioned armies the result was not doubtful for a moment'. One day the Führer's revolution would inspire the German army to very similar achievements.

Where the Emperor did not resemble Hitler was in his complete lack of interest in technical innovation. His cannon were those introduced by the great artilleryman Guibert, who had died in 1789, weapons with which he had first become familiar as a young officer in the regiment of La Fère; they remained unchanged, apart from slight modifications in 1803 and a new 24-inch howitzer. The standard musket carried by the Imperial army was the model of 1777. He rejected rockets and the percussion cap, together with observation balloons, submarines and the telegraph.

The British did not despair at the Prussian collapse, though they were deeply depressed by it. Wordsworth wrote:

> Another year! – another deadly blow!
> Another mighty Empire overthrown!
> And We are left, or shall be left, alone;
> The last that dare to struggle with the Foe.[24]

But Russia had not given up the fight.

Marshal Murat rode into Warsaw on 28 November 1806, the Emperor a fortnight later. He did not give the Poles back the independence they had lost ten years before, as they had expected; he was nervous that Austria might fight for the Polish provinces, while he would need a bargaining counter when dealing with the Russians after their defeat. It was a bad mistake, since although many Poles fought for him he never gained the entire support of that fanatically patriotic nation. Despite terrible winter weather, and ignoring their disaster at Austerlitz, 120,000 Russians advanced into Poland and East Prussia. There were a series of minor if bloody engagements at the end of December, brought to a halt by an unexpected thaw turning the ground into a sea of mud. Napoleon sited his men's winter quarters on the far side of the Vistula to tempt the Russians into attacking. Their new commander-in-chief, Bennigsen, swallowed the bait. The Emperor was waiting, and eventually caught up with him at Eylau on 7 February 1807, the battle being fought the next day. Bennigsen's batteries, concealed by a snowstorm, blew Augereau's corps into red ruin, the Cossacks finishing them off, whereupon the Russians surged forward at the French centre and nearly took the Emperor prisoner. He was saved by Murat charging at the head of 10,000 sabres, though when the French cavalry pressed on it was mown down in turn by cannon masked by snow. Davout almost broke the Russian left, but was beaten off. Both sides charged again and again, all along the line, neither gaining any advantage. It was Napoleon's longest and bloodiest battle so far. In the end Bennigsen decided to withdraw, 30,000 of his men being casualties or prisoners. But the French were in no condition to pursue him, with 3,000 dead and 7,000 wounded. Even the Emperor was shaken by the butchery, which had gained him no advantage. He spent the rest of the winter mopping up what remained of Prussia.

On 14 June Napoleon again caught up with Bennigsen at Friedland in East Prussia. Marshal Lannes had intercepted him, barring his retreat with 26,000 men against more than 80,000 from 3.00 a.m. until midday when the Emperor arrived. He feigned attack on all fronts while concentrating his strength on the right, eventually driving the Russians into the river Alle; 25,000 were killed or drowned, and the rest fled, abandoning 80 guns. It was the anniversary of Marengo.

Tsar Alexander asked for an armistice. The two emperors met near Tilsit on 8 July in a pavilion constructed on a raft in the middle of the river Niemen. The Tsar's first words were: 'I hate the English even more than you do.' 'If that's the case, then peace has been made' was Napoleon's reply. Both fascinated each other. Alexander commented, 'I have never loved anything more than that man', while Napoleon thought the Tsar 'a very handsome, very fine young emperor'. He had brought the Comédie Française with him, and when an actor declaimed, 'A great man's friendship is like a gift from the Gods' Alexander seized his hand. Yet in secret the Tsar listened to Talleyrand, who warned him not to join in schemes which might destroy Europe.

By the Treaty of Tilsit Russia entered on an alliance with France, stipulating that she might be allowed to wrest Finland from Sweden if she enforced the Continental Blockade. Prussia had to surrender half her territory and five million subjects – lands west of the Elbe being joined to Hesse-Cassel to make the Kingdom of Westphalia for Napoleon's brother Jerome; her Polish provinces became the Grand Duchy of Warsaw, with the King of Saxony as Grand Duke. In addition, besides enforcing the Continental Blockade she had to pay indemnities beyond her power, ensuring French occupation.

The Emperor was now the undisputed master of Europe. In addition to France, territories directly under his rule included Belgium, northern and much of central Italy, and Dalmatia. The German lands, Holland, Switzerland, Naples, and the Grand Duchy of Warsaw were client states, while Russia, Denmark and – in theory – Spain were his allies. The *leitmotif* of his 'new Western Empire' was the Continental Blockade. He knew that to impose a lasting hegemony over Europe he must eventually break Britain's will to defy him. It became an obsession which caused him to demand even tighter control over satellites and neighbours in order to see that they enforced the blockade, which ultimately drove him to annexation and fresh wars.

Napoleon's next great enterprise was the destruction of Portugal, Britain's last ally in Europe. (Her loyalty had been assured by preferential tariffs for her port wine and wool.) It was intended to be a first step in the subjection of the Iberian peninsula. Even Hitler never quite surpassed the sheer duplicity of what ensued. It was agreed (in the secret Treaty of Fontainebleau) that Portugal should be divided in three, one-third going to the Spanish minister Godoy and another to the King of Spain's sister (in exchange for her kingdom of Etruria), while the remaining third would become a French puppet state. In November 1807 General Junot entered Lisbon after a gruelling march across Spain; the Portuguese did not even try to fight, their royal family fleeing to Brazil. The tiny French army had to be reinforced, the Spaniards allowing the French to concentrate vast numbers of troops in northern Spain. In February 1808 Murat was given sealed orders and appointed Lieutenant General in Spain.

In 1795 Spain had accepted that the French Revolution was there to stay, and since then had fought by the side of France against Britain, her traditional enemy. Some Spaniards with 'enlightened' views were happy with the alliance. Most, however, detested being ruled by Godoy, the Queen's lover, whom the French controlled with bribes and threats, and despised Charles IV. Opposition to Godoy and Charles, opposition largely hostile to France, centred round the boorish Ferdinand, Prince of the Asturias, who hoped to replace his father on the throne. In March 1808 Godoy was overthrown and Charles forced to abdicate. The new King, the insecure Ferdinand VII, asked France for a dynastic alliance. A pretence was made of considering an Imperial niece but finding her unsuitable.

Murat and a French 'Army of Observation' installed themselves in Madrid on 23 March. He had been instructed by the Emperor to 'treat the King and the Prince of the Asturias well and everybody else. Tell them you know nothing and are awaiting my orders.' Murat told Ferdinand that he had no authority to recognize him as King, he sympathized with Charles IV and the Queen, and advised them to go to France and seek Napoleon's arbitration. Hopefully, they travelled to Bayonne. Here the Emperor was at first most amiable, persuading Ferdinand to return his father's crown, but then bullied Charles into abdicating; the three were sent into semi-captivity in France. (Napoleon had already offered Spain to his brother.) The Spanish expressed their disapproval, regardless of 50,000 French troops outside Madrid. On 2 May the Madrileños killed 700 Frenchmen. Murat crushed them with grapeshot and the bayonet, slaughtering 1,200 and shooting 200 more who had been taken prisoner.

All Spain now rose, French soldiers being murdered everywhere. Marshal Bessières routed the main Spanish army at Riosecco on 14 July, killing 20,000 and securing Madrid for 'King José' – Joseph Bonaparte – with whom Napoleon had replaced the Bourbons. But General Dupont was cut off and forced to surrender at Baylen with 20,000 men, while Saragossa held out heroically. A British expeditionary force under Sir Arthur Wellesley (the future Duke of Wellington), quickly defeated Junot and occupied Lisbon. By September 1808 the French had been driven back into the Spanish provinces north of the Ebro.

The news infuriated Napoleon. He hastened to Paris, then to Spain, bringing 150,000 men with him. He broke the Spaniards at Burgos, Espinosa and Tudela, battering his way to Madrid with a superb charge through the Somosierra Pass by his Polish lancers, entering the capital on 4 December. The British under Sir John Moore fled before him over the Sierra de Guadarrama in atrocious weather; the Emperor heard his own troops cursing him during the snowstorms. Undeterred, he pressed on after the British. However, at Astorga, convinced he had subdued the peninsula, he handed over command to Marshal Soult and rushed back to Paris.

He had good reason to hurry back from Spain. He suspected Talleyrand of plotting against him, though he could discover nothing. He had fallen out with the Pope; his troops had occupied Rome in April 1808, while Pius VII was to be imprisoned in 1809; he had refused to recognize Joseph Bonaparte first as King of Naples and then as King of Spain and would not enforce the Continental Blockade against the British in the Papal States – the cornerstone of Imperial foreign policy. Moreover, Austria was rearming and preparing to attack him once again.

Austria declared war on 6 April 1809. The Archduke Karl, a formidable commander, marched on Bavaria with 175,000 men. Davout had 50,000 troops at Ratisbon, Masséna 60,000 at Augsburg; the Austrian plan was to get between them and destroy each separately. The Emperor hurled himself into the gap with 40,000 troops, his two marshals linking up with him. On 22 April he inflicted a crushing defeat on his opponents at Eckmühl. On 10 May he entered Vienna once more. But on 21 May at Aspern the Archduke cut Napoleon off from Davout and his reserves by destroying the bridges over the Danube with fire-boats, bottling him up on the island of Lobau. It was his first serious reverse. However, the Austrians had suffered too many casualties to destroy him and he escaped from the fortifications with which they had encircled him. On 6 July at Wagram, after Masséna had blocked an attempt to turn the French left, Karl extended his front too far, enabling the Emperor to overwhelm his centre. The Archduke retreated, having suffered 24,000 casualties, a further 12,000 of his men being taken prisoner. The French had 18,000 killed or wounded. At the Treaty of Vienna in October 1809 Austria surrendered nearly 4 million subjects, ceding territory to France, Russia, Saxony-Warsaw and Bavaria.

Napoleon was growing tired of war, and decided that a dynastic alliance would strengthen his position. Although the Tsar had not intervened to help him during the recent campaign, he would have liked a Russian Grand Duchess, but Josephine's gossip lost him his Romanov bride. Fearful of being divorced, she told the Prince of Mecklenburg-Schwerin that her husband was impotent. (She had long been spreading rumours that *'Bonaparte est bon-à-faire-rien'*.) The Prince informed the Dowager Tsarina, who refused to let her daughter make so humiliating a marriage. The Emperor turned to the Habsburgs instead.

Looking back, he thought he had made a bad mistake in not insisting on the division of the Austrian Empire into its three major states – Austria, Hungary and Bohemia. If this was wisdom with hindsight, he was correct in believing that Austria had been left much too strong for France's safety and would be able to join in destroying her. It is probable, however, that he was already contemplating making the Austrian Empire his junior partner instead of Russia. At the back of his mind there may have been an unwilling acceptance of Talleyrand's opinion, that if Austria did not exist she would have to be invented.

In his own words, 'The [Napoleonic] monarchy, the well being and best interests of my people, which have always dictated my actions required me to leave the throne on which Providence had placed me to legitimately begotten children.' At the end of 1809 he divorced Josephine in order to marry Francis II's daughter, the Archduchess Marie Louise – Marie Antoinette's niece – in March 1810 at a proxy wedding in Vienna. Afterwards he spoke of his grief at having to abandon Josephine, 'my beloved wife', giving a curious insight into her character – she loved luxury and was a consummate liar but was none the less devoted to him and possessed an extraordinary knowledge of the way in which his mind worked.

Far from making him more secure, the marriage ensured that France and Russia would soon be at war. Not only did Tsar Alexander mutter, 'The next thing will be to drive us back into our forests', but he genuinely believed it. At the state banquet which followed the formal wedding in Paris, Prince Metternich, the Austrian Emperor's special envoy, drank ostentatiously to 'The

King of Rome' – a title very like that once borne by the heirs of Holy Roman Emperors. For the moment even Metternich thought that the Napoleonic hegemony looked likely to last.

Nevertheless, bad news was again coming out of the peninsula. Sir Arthur Wellesley had beaten the French at Talavera in 1809, while Masséna had failed to drive him out of the lines of Torres Vedras. In Holland Louis Bonaparte proved so independent-minded that he had to abdicate, his kingdom being incorporated into the French Empire in 1810. Both the Confederation of the Rhine and occupied Prussia hated the French; there was no proper commissariat, so they fed and paid themselves by plunder. Even the Emperor was uneasy about occupying the Papal States, anxious to come to an understanding with the imprisoned pontiff. In 1810 too Marshal Bernadotte, whom Napoleon sometimes suspected of being a secret enemy, became the King of Sweden's adopted heir. The Continental Blockade was becoming harder and harder to enforce, imposing an ever-increasing strain on the Russian alliance.

Even so, Napoleon's confidence knew no bounds. His marriage to an Austrian Archduchess and the birth of a son and heir in June 1811 induced something like euphoria. 'Up to the time of her marriage Marie Louise possessed but one social talent, on which she prided herself not a little', says the great Napoleonic historian Frédéric Masson, 'the power of moving her ears without stirring a muscle of her face. It proved a somewhat insufficient means of amusement, and was neglected in favour of billiards.' The Emperor had to take lessons from a chamberlain to play with her. She loathed warm rooms, while he detested cold. Yet he was in love with her, and although she was over twenty years younger, she seems to have returned his affection. A strongly sensual streak in her nature contributed, but it also made her vulnerable to other men. (In 1814 General von Neipperg would seduce her away from the Emperor.) He allowed her to sponge him in his bath and ate his meals with her, interminable courses in rich cream sauces which increased his obesity. As Masson points out, 'It was not so much the woman he desired as the princess.' She was a status symbol, a token of his acceptance by other monarchs. The existence of a future Napoleon II, 'King of Rome', heightened his illusions. His judgment of Austrians, especially of his wife's relations, suffered; as he said himself, he 'gorged them with diamonds'. In Hitler's opinion, the arrival of an Austrian Empress in France 'irremediably wounded the national pride of the French'. Politically if not domestically, the Habsburg marriage turned out to be a disastrous mistake.

Fouché came out of retirement to warn against a war with Russia while Spain remained unconquered. He thought it unwise to fight beyond the Pyrenees and the Niemen at the same time. The Emperor brushed his objections aside, without even reading the memorandum he had presented. 'There is no crisis. This is a political war,' he told the horrified Fouché. 'Spain will fall as soon as I destroy the English influence at St Petersburg. I need 800,000 troops and I've got them. I can drag all Europe along with me, and nowadays Europe is only a rotten old whore who has to do just what I want when I have 800,000 men.' 'Don't you worry,' he continued. 'Regard the Russian war as a war of common sense, for everyone's good and peace of mind, for everyone's security.' He added, 'How can I help it when all this power is sweeping me on to world dictatorship?' Then he revealed his real plans. 'I'm going to finish what is so far only on the drawing-board. We want a European legal code, a European appeal court, a single currency, a single system of weights and measures. I shall make the European nations into one nation and Paris the world capital.'

Fouché's account is borne out by the Abbé Pradt's record of a conversation with the Emperor in November 1811. 'In five years I shall be master of the world. Only Russia is left, but I'm going to crush her.' Paris, the centre of the universe, would reach as far as Saint-Cloud. 'I want to make it a city of two, three or even four million people, something fabulous, something colossal, something unknown before our time. Its public buildings will be in proportion to the population.' He regretted that it was not possible to transport St Peter's from Rome for re-erection on the bank of the Seine.

While there are indications that even Napoleon had his nervous moments about so vast an enterprise, he had decided that war with Russia was inevitable. He would have preferred a peaceful solution, for the Tsar to obey him. However, he did not doubt for a moment that he would be victorious. He contemplated annexing a large area of territory to the Grand Duchy of Warsaw, while the remainder of the western half of the Russian Empire might be replaced by a puppet Grand Duchy of Smolensk. Sweden could be bribed into attacking St Petersburg with the promise of Finland and the Baltic.

The western powers were aghast at the seemingly effortless way in which the Wehrmacht had subdued a people whom Chamberlain called 'that great virile nation'. Foreign observers did not take into account Polish inferiority in equipment. The Führer and his army appeared invincible. The notably un-Napoleonic French General Staff adopted a supinely defensive strategy, their slogan being 'We're going to win because we're stronger' ('Nous gagnerons parce que nous sommes le plus fort').

The Allies made no move of any sort until April 1940. A Franco-British expeditionary force then landed at Narvik in Norway, with the objective of blocking German imports of iron ore from Sweden. However, they were forestalled, 2,000 crack Austrian mountain troops under the Nazi General Dietl (one of Hitler's favourite officers) holding Narvik against 20,000 British, while an even smaller German force seized Oslo. At the same time Denmark was overrun by a single Wehrmacht battalion. Within a matter of weeks a mere 10,000 German troops had conquered all Norway, despite being heavily outnumbered by the French and British. Although initially the Führer had been reluctant to move, showing considerable nervousness, this remarkable campaign was largely due to his inspiration.

On 10 May 1940 General von Bock invaded Holland and Belgium, the Dutch surrendering almost immediately. The Allies had expected the main thrust to come from this direction, since plans for such a campaign had been captured; it was very like the old Schlieffen plan of 1914, to strike at Paris through Belgium. The French and British advanced into Belgium to meet the invaders, with a third of their entire joint strength. But the real German thrust was to be at the Allied centre, through the hills and woods of the Ardennes and over the river Meuse, between the main Belgian redoubt near Liège and the Maginot Line. No one expected the Wehrmacht to come that way, since the terrain was thought unsuitable for armoured vehicles; it was guarded by only a few poor-quality troops, most of them cavalry. General Gerd von Rundstedt and 50 German divisions struck here on 13 May. Once through they raced towards the Channel ports, sweeping as intended like a sharp scythe round the right and rear of the Allied armies to the north, 1,500 tanks refuelling at roadside petrol pumps. They were almost unopposed, those French troops they met surrendering in droves. By 20 May German tanks had reached to sea. The British were cut off in Belgium, together with France's best fighting divisions.

None the less, 338,000 British and French troops were evacuated from Dunkirk, in what Churchill called 'a miracle of deliverance'. If the Wehrmacht had not halted between 24 and 26 May the entire British Expeditionary Force would have been destroyed and Britain almost certainly forced to surrender. The halt, which gave the Allies time to prepare defences around Dunkirk, was ordered by Hitler personally. It has been said that he did so to avoid driving Britain into a last-ditch mentality. In reality there were more practical considerations; during the 1914-18 War advances on the Eastern Front had frequently petered out because of over-worked horses – nearly half the German tanks in France had broken down by 24 May 1940. There was still a danger of a counter-attack by the remaining two-thirds of the French army, while Goering had assured the Führer that his Luftwaffe could deal with the Dunkirk pocket. Finally, Rundstedt advised it would be wise to allow the infantry to catch up with their armour. Hitler's caution would prob-ably have been endorsed by Napoleon, even if some generals argued against it. In the event the RAF were able to give just enough pro-tection and make possible an evacuation by 4 June.

By then nearly half a million Allied troops had been eliminated at a cost to the Wehrmacht of less than 25,000 men. On 10 June German armour crossed the Seine in strength; four days later they took Paris. The Italians invaded from the south. The octagenarian Marshal Pétain who had saved the French army from dissolution in 1917 – and who many had wanted to take power during the 1930s – was appointed Head of State. To avoid what he called the *'Poloni-sation de la France'*, Pétain asked for an armistice. It was signed on 22 June in the same railway carriage, and on the same spot in the forest of Compiègne, in which the Germans had signed the armis-tice of November 1918; outside, bands played *Deutschland über Alles* and the *Horst Wessel Lied*. Pétain's régime kept south-eastern France, with Vichy for a capital, while the north-west, including Paris and the main industrial areas, was to be under German rule, though with French local-government officials and police. The French army was to be disbanded, surrendering all weapons and munitions, and prisoners of war were to stay in German captivity till the end of the war. Hitler presided over the armistice ceremony, though not over the victory parade in Paris – he had no need.

The amazing victory had been won by Hitler's personal decision, against his generals' advice, to strike through the Ardennes. He had rejected their original plan of attacking through Belgium as much too obvious. By a fluke General von Manstein, transferred to Poland in disgrace for producing a plan based on an advance through the Ardennes, managed to meet him and discuss it. The Führer had already suggested an attack on the area, and responded enthusiastically, eventually forcing the Wehrmacht to adopt the Manstein plan. He had not intervened during the Polish campaign in any way, leaving the entire planning and direction to the generals, though it had been his decision to intervene at Narvik.

General Jodl, his chief military planner, attributes the victory entirely to Hitler. 'The man who succeeded in occupying Norway before the very eyes of the British Fleet with its maritime supremacy, and who with numerically inferior forces brought down the feared military power of France . . . had overruled the General Staff's thought of a broad encirclement [through Belgium, as in the Schlieffen Plan] by initially careful but then increasingly tenacious and unhesitating intervention in the military leadership.' Jodl adds, 'First the [enemy] front collapsed; then Holland, Belgium and France collapsed. The soldiers were confronted by a miracle.'

The ascendancy which was established henceforward by the Führer over his commanders is conveyed to some extent by Jodl – 'it was always Hitler whose restless spirit would first cast its spotlight into the dark future, long before the eyes of his military staff were able to perceive anything tangible or threatening in that darkness.' Even so, it is often said that the Führer cannot be considered a true military commander since he never fought at the head of his troops, ignoring the fact that no twentieth-century commander – Haig or Ludendorff, Eisenhower or Montgomery – has done so. Recently John Keegan has published a study of how throughout history great commanders have persuaded their troops that their struggle is a common one by giving them the impression they are led by a hero. Keegan (who omits Napoleon from his survey) describes how until the second half of the nineteenth century generals stayed reasonably near the 'killing zone', but that with the coming of modern weaponry they had to command from the rear. There was an instinctive popular revulsion against this style of leadership after the 1914-18 War, during which commanders like Haig had sent vast numbers of men to their deaths without having to risk their own lives. Keegan argues that Hitler cast himself as both a First World War hero and a Titan engaged in mortal combat with the evil forces of the world, convincing his troops that the latter was 'the moral equivalent of their physical ordeal'. Through Goebbels's skilful propaganda *Ministerium* he succeeded to such effect that his armies accepted the myth totally and fought 'until five minutes past midnight'. There is a good deal to be said for this argument, not least because the Führer believed in the myth himself.

Moreover, in Clausewitz's words: 'To conduct a whole war, or its great acts, which we call campaigns, to a successful termination, there must be an intimate knowledge of State policy in its higher relations. The conduct of the war, and the policy of the State, here coincide; and the general becomes at the same time the statesman.' In the Führer's case the statesman became the general, combining, as Liddell Hart points out, strategy and policy in one person – 'Thus he enjoyed the same advantages as Alexander or Caesar in the ancient world, or Frederick the Great and Napoleon in later times. This gave him an unlimited opportunity, such as no pure strategist would enjoy, to prepare and develop his means for the end he had in view.'

General Jodl, when in prison at Nuremburg, made much the same comment as Liddell Hart. 'Strategy is the supreme leadership activity in war,' he wrote. 'It comprehends foreign and domestic policy, military operations and economic mobilization, propaganda and popular leadership, and must harmonize these vital aspects of the war effort in terms of the purposes and the political goal of the war.' He emphasizes that the Führer really did lead the war, that for all the German senior commanders 'the strategic remained for them a veiled secret'.

Jodl also claims that the Führer's early victories gave him overweening self-confidence, because he had always refused to allow the High Command to overrule any of his decisions. If he increasingly lost touch with reality during the later stages of the war, one can only agree with Jodl that his early victories seemed to verge on the miraculous. (This had been no less true of Napoleon's military career.)

After the war Liddell Hart gained the definite impression from German generals whom he interviewed that most of them considered 'Hitler had a natural flair for strategy and tactics of an original kind.' However, his chief-of-staff General Franz Halder held a very different opinion of him. Halder's diary is full of unflattering entries. 'His underestimation of the enemy's potentialities, always his weakness, is beginning to assume grotesque forms,' he wrote in 1942. 'Morbid over-reaction to the impression of the moment and a total inability to understand the apparatus of leadership and its opportunities characterize this so-called "leadership".' The disillusioned General von Tippelskirch thought the Halt Order before Moscow in 1941 'his one achievement'. According to another fighting commander, General of Panzers Hasso von Manteuffel – who saw more of the Führer than any other front-line soldier during 1944, when the situation was growing desperate – 'Hitler had a magnetic and indeed hypnotic personality', though he himself stood up to him. The Führer 'had read a lot of military literature, and was also fond of listening to military lectures . . . coupled with his personal experience of the last war as an ordinary soldier, he had gained a very good knowledge of the lower level of warfare,' the General told Liddell Hart. 'He was particularly good in gauging how the troops felt.' On the other hand, 'he had no idea of the higher strategical and tactical combinations . . . he did not understand how armies operated'. Yet Manteuffel concedes that he would listen to soldiers who had fighting experience and practical ideas. By contrast, a staff general like Alfred Jodl – who practically never left Hitler's side during the war – while agreeing (in a memorandum of 1946) that he 'resented any form of counsel regarding the major decisions of the war', regarded him as a great warlord who 'acted as all heroes in history have acted and will always act'.

We have already noted how, unlike the Emperor, the Führer was fascinated by new technology. Jodl was not only impressed by the way he watched the production of weapons and munitions down to the last detail but, in Jodl's words by:

> his astounding technical and tactical vision [which] led him also to become the creator of modern weaponry for the army. It was due to him personally that the 75-mm anti-tank gun replaced the 37-mm and 50-mm tank guns in time, and that the short guns mounted on the tanks were replaced by the long 75-mm and 88-mm guns. The *Panther*, the *Tiger*, and the *Königstiger* [i.e. *Tiger II*] were developed as modern tanks at Hitler's own initiative.

This applied also to the psychological aspect of weaponry: the terrifying sirens attached to the wing-tips of Stuka dive-bombers were the Führer's suggestion. Field Marshal von Manstein confirms Jodl: Hitler 'could display a staggering grasp of the effectiveness even of new enemy weapons as well as of our own and enemy production figures'.

During a brief visit to Paris three days after the armistice the Führer visited Napoleon's shrine at the Invalides, standing in silence for a long time. Later he commented that his own tomb would have to be raised so that pilgrims would gaze up at it instead of looking down, as they did on the Emperor's. He did more than visit. 'L'Aiglon', Napoleon's son – in theory Napoleon II – had been buried with the Habsburgs in Vienna. At one o'clock on the morning of 15 December 1940 his coffin, escorted through the snowy darkness by German motor-cyclists, arrived at the Invalides, where it was handed over to the Garde Républicaine for reinterment near his father.

The British were horrified by the collapse of France, and of what had been the world's most formidable army. Their chiefs of staff warned, 'Should the Germans succeed in establishing a force with its vehicles in this country, our Army forces have not got the offensive power to drive them out.' But Churchill had succeeded Chamberlain as Prime Minister in May. He admitted that many 'have feared for our survival when they saw so many states and kingdoms torn to pieces in a few weeks or even a few days by the force of the Nazi war machine.' Fortunately, Britain was protected by sea, had strong economic resources and – as it had shown in 1914-18 – was capable of turning civilians into soldiers at short notice. Hitler declared publicly he did not want war with Britain, guaranteeing the survival of the British Empire which accorded with his own racial and historical philosophy. His aims remained unaltered – the destruction of Bolshevism and Judaism, the conquest and colonization of western Russia.

On 16 July 1940 the Führer issued Directive No 16. 'As England in spite of her hopeless military situation shows no sign of wishing to reach an understanding, I have decided to prepare a landing operation against England and, *if necessary*, to implement it.' He envisaged occupying the whole country. 'Operation Sea-

Lion' was based around a wide front from Ramsgate to an area west of the Isle of Wight.

Even at the time many German officers supposed that Hitler had no intention of launching such an operation. After the war Rundstedt recalled: 'We looked upon the whole thing as a sort of game because it was obvious that no invasion was possible when our Navy was not in a position to cover a crossing of the Channel or carry reinforcements. Nor was the German Air Force capable of taking on these functions.' He himself had always been sceptical. 'I have a feeling that the Führer never really wanted to invade England. He never had sufficient courage. He used to say, "On land I am a hero but on water I am a coward." Hitler definitely hoped that the English would make peace overtures to him.' During 1940 Rundstedt is known to have referred to 'Sea-Lion rubbish', and he is borne out by General Blumentritt, who informed Liddell Hart that among themselves senior German officers talked about it as bluff to frighten the British.

Yet Rundstedt admits that 'serious preparations were made'. Hitler had issued Directive No 16 in deadly earnest, if reluctantly. However, he had not hitherto examined the feasibility of an invasion. Only later in the year did he begin to realize fully the immense difficulties. Nevertheless, both he and a number of his commanders definitely considered for some weeks at least that Sea-Lion had a good chance.

Since France had fallen so miraculously, the Wehrmacht were confident of success, according to Jodl. He comments, 'Eight weeks earlier they would have regarded this order as the vagary of a madman.' The General explains, however, that Hitler was ill at ease with 'nautical imponderables' and allowed himself to be swayed by professional advice – for perhaps the only time during the war – and abandoned the invasion. 'The warnings of the Commander-in-Chief of the Navy [Admiral Raeder] together with an evaluation of the situation that I had prepared for him decided the issue.'

One can see with hindsight that Hitler's invasion had even less chance of success than the Emperor's. Yet neither was entirely unfeasible. Immediately after Dunkirk, Churchill cautioned the British people that there was no absolute guarantee against invasion:

In the days of Napoleon the same wind which would have carried his transports across the Channel might have driven away the blockading fleet. There was always the chance, and it is that chance which has excited and befooled the imagination of many continental tyrants.

He reminded the House of Commons of when the Emperor 'Lay at Boulogne for a year with his flat-bottomed boats and his Grand Army'. In September he informed the nation that there were clusters of ships or barges in harbours all the way from Hamburg to Brest, behind which immense numbers of German troops were waiting to embark. As late as October he warned the House that the enemy had enough shipping to send over 'half a million men in a single night', though conceding that autumn weather was ill suited for such a crossing, and that 'over our own island we have the mastery of the air'.

In the Führer's view there were other ways of bringing down Britain. As early as November 1939 he had issued Directive No 9, imposing a 'Continental Blockade'. At first he hoped to cripple the British economy simply by attacking ports and merchant shipping. Then in May 1940 on his instructions Keitel sent an addendum ordering both the destruction of British industry and an attack on food imports to 'break the will to resist', This replaced Operation Sea-Lion, which was discreetly forgotten. Like the Emperor before him, he recognized Britain's refusal to surrender was a very dangerous obstacle. In the words of Liddell Hart, 'It is evident that

Hitler's thoughts ran so closely in Napoleon's groove that he imagined a conspiracy between England and Russia when nothing of the sort existed.' However, unlike the Emperor – who fought Russia to get at Britain – the Führer saw the Soviet Union as his ultimate enemy.

He decided to strike at Britain by taking control of the Mediterranean. In Directive No 18 he explained that political measures to bring Spain into the war had begun, with the object of capturing Gibraltar and closing the Straits. He was confident of securing General Franco's permission to send his troops through Spain, since he had helped him so much during the Civil War. 'Operation Felix' was timed for 10 January 1941, the assault on Gibraltar for a month later. Most unexpectedly, Franco refused to co-operate despite a meeting with the Führer in October 1940 on the Spanish border which the latter rated worse than a lengthy visit to the dentist. Shortly after, Keitel announced that Operation Felix would not take place since 'The necessary political situation no longer exists.'

Hitler was forced to fight on more than one new front because of Italian incapacity. By February 1941 General Wavell had thrown an invading Italian army out of Egypt, advancing 500 miles into Libya; ten Italian divisions disintegrated, 130,000 men being taken prisoner. The British naval presence in the Mediterranean was growing alarmingly – in November 1940 the Italian fleet had suffered severely in a raid on Taranto. It was necessary to send General Rommel and his Afrika Korps to Africa.

By spring 1941 Hitler's hegemony over Europe stretched from Scandinavia to the Pyrenees, from the Atlantic to the Balkans. In November Romania allied with him; although she had had to give half Transylvania to Hungary and some coastal towns to Bulgaria, her *Conducator* or Leader, Marshal Antonescu – who had recently replaced King Carol with the boy king Michael – needed support for his semi-fascist state. The Romanian alliance was of great value to Germany because of the country's oil-wells, though the value of its army was doubtful. Hungary joined reluctantly the same month, despite the grave reservations of its Prime Minister Count Teleki, as did Slovakia, which had no choice. Yugoslavia joined in March, though its regent, Prince Paul, was far from pro-Nazi (as asserted mistakenly), and like Teleki had serious misgivings. Bulgaria also joined in March, its extremely able ruler King Boris seeing no alternative. In the Balkans only Greece remained hostile, because of Italy's onslaught. If Spain remained uncommitted, many of Franco's ministers were sympathetic, while Finland would soon become an ally. Sweden and Turkey seemed friendly enough. And the Axis was now world-wide; in September 1940 Germany, Italy and Japan had signed a Tripartite Pact, promising to assist each other in their programmes of expansion.

Hitler found himself sending troops to a front in which he had small interest. After Mussolini had conquered Albania in 1938, inspired by the Führer's successes, he had invaded Greece in October 1940. It was scarcely blitzkrieg. Within days the Italians had been thrown back into Albania; by December 1940 they were contemplating an armistice. In January Hitler agreed to bail them out, partly because the British were helping the Greeks, partly because of an oddly quixotic attitude towards Mussolini – in a letter he assured him that he was 'A man who feels bound to you in good times and in bad alike.'

Before intervening in Greece the Führer was involved on yet another front. Anti-German officers in Yugoslavia overthrew Prince Paul's government at the end of March 1941. Hitler reacted with savage speed, bullying the Hungarians into allowing his troops to pass through their territory. The invasion began on 6 April, Yugoslavia surrendering eleven days later after a lightning campaign conducted, on Hitler's instructions, with 'merciless brutality'.

191

With the disintegration of the formal Yugoslav resistance the Germans could attack Greece from the north. The Greeks surrendered on 24 April, the British being driven out from even Crete at the end of May. Liddell Hart was secretly convinced that his country could not win the war.

Hitler was equally confident of a lightning victory in Russia. As he explained in Directive 32, 'After the destruction of the Soviet Armed Forces Germany and Italy will be military masters of the European continent – with the temporary exception of the Iberian Peninsula. No serious threat to Europe by land will then remain.' In consequence it would be possible to bring about 'a final collapse through a landing in England'. He saw war with Russia as the logical outcome of his 'philosophy', the final triumph of Teuton over Slav and the beginning of a new German empire. He also saw it as a clash between two systems – National Socialism and the Bolshevism which had betrayed his country in 1918. He did not foresee much difficulty – 'We'll kick the front door in and the whole rotten structure will come crashing down.' Further, the war would demonstrate Germany's leadership of Europe. When it was in full swing he boasted in a speech in October 1941, 'In the ranks of our German soldiers, making common cause with them, march the Italians, the Finns, the Hungarians, the Romanians, the Slovaks and the Croats; the Spaniards are joining the combat; the Belgians, the Dutch, the Danes, the Norwegians and even the French are fighting on the same front. Many people in the nations he had conquered or bullied into submission hated communism more than Nazism – like the men of France's SS Charlemagne Division.

Like Metternich in 1811-2, informed observers agreed in 1941 that Russia was doomed. She had liquidated most of her senior officers in 1937-8 – everyone had seen how easily Finland had at first routed her forces during the recent Winter War. Stalin himself was clearly terrified of Germany, acceding slavishly to every German demand for supplies. American Intelligence estimated that in the event of war the Soviet Union could not hold out for more than three months. The British estimate was still gloomier – six weeks.

The motives of Emperor and Führer for invading Russia were somewhat different. As Napoleon made plain, he did so to enforce the Continental Blockade; in attacking Russia he was above all attacking Britain. Hitler's principal aim was to carve out a new German Empire. Yet both intended to attack British India after the success of their invasions.

Originally neither man had intended to conquer Europe, whatever contemporaries may have suspected. The Emperor came to do so gradually, because it would accept neither him nor his hegemony, the Führer for much the same reason, though also because it stood in the way of his plans for expansion in the East. Both had wanted peace with Britain, in the almost certainly sincere if mistaken belief that 'the two most powerful nations in the world' had no cause to quarrel. One can understand their reasons for thinking so. An unending war with an apparently invincible Bonaparte could well have meant Britain's economic ruin; as it was she had to spend vast sums on her Navy and on subsidizing Continental allies, while her trade and industry suffered grievously – British statesmen like Fox questioned the need for conflict. Similarly there was a case (of sorts) for Britain leaving Hitler to destroy Communist Russia and, hopefully, perhaps himself as well, instead of pouring out her resources and undermining her Empire in a struggle to the death.

Had anyone other than Winston Churchill been prime minister it is quite possible that Britain would have made peace in 1940. In the event Napoleon and the Führer chose to play the same fatal card. Ironically, what prompted their decision was the desire to avoid a war on two fronts.

Why Hitler invaded Russia is, in my opinion, that he found himself in exactly the same situation as Napoleon. Both men looked upon Britain as their strongest and most dangerous adversary. Both could not persuade themselves to attempt the overthrow of England by invading the British Isles. Both believed, however, that Great Britain could be forced to come to terms with the dominating continental power, if the prospect vanished for the British to gain an armoured arm as an ally on the Continent. Both of them suspected Russia of becoming this ally of Britain's.

General Walther Warlimont

Most of the commanders were now asking: 'When are we going to stop?' They remembered what had happened to Napoleon's army. Many of them began to re-read Caulaincourt's grim account of 1812. That book had a weighty influence at this critical time in 1941. I can still see von Kluge trudging through the mud from his sleeping quarters to his office, and there standing before the map with Caulaincourt's book in his hand. That went on day after day.

General Günther Blumentritt

7

The Russian Fronts of 1812 and 1941

Napoleon and Hitler destroyed themselves in attempting to conquer Russia. While the former did so in response to new political circumstances, the latter had always planned such a conquest – it was essential for the realization of the Nazi dream. Nevertheless, secretly both men were nervous at such an enterprise yet emboldened by previous military successes and increasing megalomania.

Each invaded Russia in what appeared to be overwhelming strength, with better equipment and commanders than their opponents. Their armies came from all over Europe. Each planned to attack Moscow and St Petersburg-Leningrad; the latter with the aid of the Swedes in the Emperor's case, with that of the Finns in the Führer's. Each opened their offensives too late in the year, Napoleon delaying because he thought the Tsar might come to heel, Hitler because he had to deal unexpectedly with Greece and Yugoslavia, and each having to contend with unusually severe winters. Each invaded over too wide a front, the former's troops so spread out as to deprive him of all control of his lukewarm Austrian allies, the latter with three army groups aiming at three separate objectives, weakening the impact of his overall onslaught.

By 1811 the French had firm evidence that the Continental System was inflicting serious damage on the British economy. Not only had Britain lost her European markets but those in South America were saturated and unable to take any more British goods. The Royal Navy's counter-measures against the blockade infuriated the United States, President Madison's declaration of war against Britain in 1812 depriving her of the North American markets as well. The Thames was full of ships laden with unsold goods. Cotton-mills, iron-foundries and shipyards laid off their hands. There was a run on the pound, paper currency being discounted at 18 per cent, and many banks closed their doors. Widespread un-employment was accompanied by high bread prices as a result of bad harvests in 1809 and 1811. There were riots and mob violence, 'Captain Lud' and his followers smashing the textile machinery which was putting so many men out of work. It was essential that all Europe should co-operate in enforcing the Continental Blockade if the Emperor was to win the victory which appeared to be within his reach.

Yet Russia was suffering almost as much as Britain from the blockade, unable to sell her grain, iron, copper and potassium, her timber, leather, hemp, pitch and tallow, all of which had a British market. The Tsar spoke publicly of the collapse of Russian com-merce. Even so, Napoleon demanded that he seize all neutral ships entering the Baltic ports, which meant commercial ruin. Alexander refused, turning a blind eye to secret trading with Britain – it was rumoured that at Riga it stayed just as it was in normal years.

In any case, a very uneasy relationship had developed between France and Russia. Not only had the Tsar failed to help the Emperor against Austria in 1809 but he had refused to allow Napoleon to marry his sister. On the other hand, he was alarmed by the increase in the Grand Duchy of Warsaw's territory which had been one of the consequences of 1809, fearful that the French might restore the Kingdom of Poland. He was also angered by the Emperor's marriage to Marie Louise and the new Franco-Austrian alliance. The friendship struck up at Tilsit had evaporated. If Napoleon still considered Alexander more intelligent than any other European monarch, he also thought him a decadent Byzantine *(un vrai Grec du Bas-Empire),* so superficial and false that one could never tell if he was sincere or not. For his part the Tsar was deeply apprehensive of his former friend's overweening ambition and dreams of world conquest, listening now to Talleyrand's warnings. In December 1811 Alexander formally withdrew from the Continental System, whereupon the Emperor annexed Oldenburg, whose Grand Duke's consort was the Tsar's sister. The annexation was not, however, intended to provoke Alexander, its real purpose being to close the last weak spot on the German sea-coast.

During 1811 Napoleon moved more and more troops into northern Germany and the Grand Duchy of Warsaw, with concentrations nearer and nearer the Russian frontier. While he dismissed Fouché's warnings about overt hostilities with seeming contempt, he had moments of realism as well as megalomania. Later he claimed he had not wanted war with Russia. 'I knew as well as anyone that Spain was a gnawing cancer which had to be healed before embarking on a such a dreadful war whose first battle would be fought 500 leagues from my frontier . . . I would have been a fool if I'd begun the war of 1812 to get something I could have had by peaceful negotiation.' Yet he was clearly speaking with conviction when he promised Fouché that Spain would collapse once he had stamped out British influence at St Petersburg, or the Comte de Narbonne that a single terrible blow at the heart of the Russian Empire would deliver 'this blindly apathetic mass' (of serfs) into his hands. He also told Narbonne that when Moscow had fallen and the

Tsar had made peace or had been murdered by his subjects, or when a new state had taken the place of the Russian empire, a Franco-Russian army would be able to march out from Tiflis, invade India and destroy British rule – 'It will have to be an expedition on an enormous scale, I admit, but it's feasible in the nineteenth century.' In saner moments he shrank from the conflict. As late as 1812, when the Russians demanded that the French withdraw their troops from Prussia, although he bellowed at the ambassador 'You're behaving just like the Prussians before Jena', he still did not quite dare to declare war, hoping until the very last moment for a peaceful solution.

The Emperor summoned an august assembly to meet him at Dresden in the spring of 1812. Among those who came were the Austrian emperor and the Kings of Prussia, Bavaria and Saxony, together with a host of lesser sovereigns. It was the pinnacle of Napoleonic glory. Yet only the King of Saxony accepted the situation and was truly loyal. Observers at Dresden detected an air of repressed fury at such outlandish dominance, while it was clear that all too many Germans loathed the sight of French troops. But the Russians would not come to heel.

Some Prussian officers were unable to stomach their king's alliance with Napoleon against the Russians, their former allies. Thirty resigned their commissions in disgust and took service with the Tsar. Among them was Major von Clausewitz, whose new employer speedily found him a staff appointment.

Even before Napoleon's Russian campaign two important allies deserted him. Turkey, deeply resentful of his proposal that Russia should take Moldavia and Wallachia, made peace with the Tsar at Bucharest on 28 May, releasing Russian troops for service against the French. Worse still was the defection of the former Marshal Bernadotte, who had been made Crown Prince of Sweden. The Swedes had lost Finland to Russia, their traditional enemy, only in

1809, together with its substantial Swedish ruling class, while the French had marched into Swedish Pomerania in 1811 to enforce the blockade. The Emperor calculated that the Crown Prince would seize any opportunity of ingratiating himself with his future subjects; that in return for regaining Finland, Estonia and Pomerania he would be only too willing to attack Russia from the north, occupying St Petersburg. But Bernadotte, an amalgam of smooth cunning and ruthless ambition, had not only always disliked him, but like Fouché and Talleyrand, foresaw his ruin. At Bucharest, as official arbiter between Russia and Turkey, he reached an understanding with the Russians and the British, who agreed to let him have Norway in place of Finland. In August Bernadotte met the Tsar at Abö in Finland, agreeing that because of the emergency 3,000 Russian troops sent to help him conquer Norway should return to reinforce Wittgenstein. In consequence St Petersburg was saved; Napoleon later claimed that it could have fallen to a single Swedish cavalry patrol.

The 'Grande Armée' which assembled in Germany numbered approximately 675,000 troops. Only a third were French; 50,000 came from the Emperor's Italian kingdom, 30,000 from Naples, over 150,000 from the Confederation of the Rhine, 60,000 from the Grand Duchy of Warsaw, 30,000 from Austria. There were Swiss, Danes and Croats, even Portuguese and Spaniards. (The latter had to be disarmed when they started shooting their French officers.) They were accompanied by 150,000 horses (including cavalry), 30,000 wagons and 1,200 cannon. However, when Napoleon crossed the Niemen on 24 June it was with only 250,000 men. He advanced on a front 50 miles broad, the Austrians to the south-east, where he had little control over them. The invasion was divided into three principal army groups, one under the Emperor himself, another under Eugène de Beauharnais (Josephine's son) and the third under Jerome Bonaparte – supervised by Marshal Davout.

Napoleon had delayed too long at Dresden, hoping that Tsar Alexander would be cowed by news of the spectacle. He compounded his tardiness by spending almost three weeks at Vilno – the Russians had destroyed their supply depots, and he was anxious to replace them.

The Tsar's forces were heavily inferior, consisting of 200,000 men at most, divided into two main groups under commanders scarcely of the same metal as Napoleon's marshals. Barclay de Tolly, defending the road to St Petersburg, was too cautious; Prince Bagration, defending the road to Moscow, too pugnacious. Kutuzov, soon to be appointed overall commander, was even more timid than Barclay, too old for his job at sixty-eight and aptly named 'The Dowager' by the Emperor. With Kutuzov was Carl von Clausewitz. It was a summer of burning heat, and on both sides men began to drop. Clausewitz, in his study of the campaign, says there was so little water that he could not wash for a week on end, and frequently had to drink out of muddy puddles.

When Napoleon recommenced the campaign over a fortnight later his army had dwindled to 182,000 men because of disease, hunger and lack of fodder for the horses. He could have had many more. The Poles assumed he was going to restore their kingdom until he told a delegation from the Diet at Warsaw that while he admired their patriotism, he had guaranteed Austria's occupation of Galicia. The last thing he wanted was a Polish national rising. When this was generally realized countless Poles who would otherwise have sacrificed everything for him stayed at home.

After Bagration had been savaged by Davout he joined forces with Barclay to defend Smolensk. This fell to the French on 17 August, whereupon the Russians set fire to it and retreated towards Moscow, creating a desert as they went. Fearful for his capital, the Tsar replaced Barclay with Kutuzov, 'The Dowager', with orders to fight a battle whatever the cost. Kutuzov chose an extremely strong position at Borodino in the fields in front of the river Moskva, with a huge fortified battery linked to strong redoubts on both flanks and protected by a deep ravine in front. By now the Emperor's troops had dwindled still further to 133,000, while the Russians had 120,000. Both armies had each about 500 cannon. At 4.00 a.m. 7 September in a thick fog the French attacked all along the line. It was a slugging match fought, according to Clausewitz, without finesse and as mere trial of strength, which lasted for twelve hours. During what Napoleon called 'the most terrible of my battles' the Russians were driven from their position in a series of ferocious charges by Murat, Ney and Eugène de Beauharnais, and had their flank turned by the iron Davout. Yet at 4.00 p.m. they still held part of the field. The Emperor might have broken them if he had used the Guard, but he was keeping it for an emergency. By now he had lost 30,000 men – including 40 generals. If he renewed the attack he knew he would suffer still more casualties at the hands of the Russians, who he admitted were very brave soldiers. In Clausewitz's opinion he was justified, Although he had won only a 'half-victory'; with barely 100,000 effectives left, he simply could not afford to lose more men, while his opponents were very unlikely to seek another battle. The way to Moscow, his goal, lay open. He let them withdraw unmolested. They had suffered 50,000 casualties, among them Prince Bagration.

On 14 September the Grande Armée entered Moscow. The same night fires were started, probably on the governor's orders, and within a few days four-fifths of the city burnt to the ground. Most of the population had already been evacuated. Napoleon installed himself in the Kremlin, expecting the Tsar to beg for peace now that he had lost his capital. Alexander simply sat in his other capital of St Petersburg – thanks to his alliance with Sweden – waiting for the winter. On 13 October the first frost set in. A week later the Emperor marched out of Moscow with an army of 80,000 men and 50,000 camp followers. On 24 October Kutuzov tried to bar his way at Malojaroslavets some seventy miles west of Moscow, but was beaten off. Napoleon was withdrawing by the way he had come; it was a desert, but he had adequate provisions in his wagon train. He underestimated the Russian winter. When the Grande Armée staggered into Smolensk on 9 November, expecting to find food and clothing, there were neither, due to sheer administrative incompetence. The nightmare march had to go on. The snow fell unrelentingly and the temperature dropped mercilessly. Not only did this freakishly bitter cold kill countless men, but it destroyed all vegetation, depriving the horses of their fodder so that they died from starvation as well. The wagon trains were abandoned together with their provisions. Kutuzov surrounded Davout at Krasnov and he had to be rescued by the Imperial Guard. (The Russian partisan hero, Davidov, described them as 'passing through our Cossacks like four-decker men-of-war through fishing smacks'.) On 25 November the starving Grande Armée and its pathetic followers reached the Beresina. Napoleon confused the Russians as to where he meant to cross by brilliant feinting; two bridges, each 160 feet long, were built over the frozen river with house timber from the village of Studienka – a heroic feat in which most of the sappers died from cold or drowning. Victor held off Wittgenstein's force on one bank, Ney and Oudinot beating back those of Admiral Tchitchagov on the far side, while the Emperor crossed. Next morning the rearguard and camp followers jammed the bridges attempting to follow him; one bridge collapsed and thousands drowned, Russian cannon continuing to bombard the other – at least 30,000 souls perished. The cold grew even more lethal, killing 20,000 in three days alone. Napoleon abandoned his army at Molodechno on 5 December, returning to France by fast sleighs and carriages; totally unexpected, he reached the Tuileries a fortnight later, telling the

French in a reassuring bulletin, 'The Emperor's health has never been better.' His return had been prompted by a coup in his absence, led by the half-crazy Republican general Malet, who very nearly succeeded in seizing Paris; what alarmed him especially was that no one had rallied to his son's defence, revealing the unpopularity of his régime. (The men behind the plot seem to have been both Republicans and Royalists who hoped to restore first the Republic, then Louis XVIII.) Moreover, he could only hold Austria and Paris in check from Paris. He left Murat in charge of the army with instructions to defend the left bank of the Niemen from Vilno where there was plenty of food, clothing and ammunition. However, Murat lost his nerve and did not stop retreating until he was well inside Germany.

The Grande Armée had suffered 380,000 casualties; the rest were broken men. Jomini rejects Napoleon's claim that he had been beaten only by the burning of Moscow and the cold – 'I have annihilated armies but flames, ice, numbness, death, these I could not conquer' – arguing that the Grande Armée was destroyed by its commander, not by the winter. Certainly he made disastrous mistakes; he should have restored the Kingdom of Poland, he ought not to have lingered for so long at Moscow, he might have halted his retreat at Smolensk. Yet the Emperor himself thought it 'the best, the most skilful, the most cleverly led and most methodical of all the campaigns I have commanded'.

No less an authority than Clausewitz supports him in this opinion in *Vom Kriege*, believing that anyone who admires Bonaparte's earlier campaigns should admire this one too. 'His campaign did not miscarry because he advanced too swiftly, or too far as is generally believed, but because the only means of success failed . . . It was only by reaching Moscow with the force of his blow that Bonaparte could hope to shake the courage of the Government, the loyalty and steadfastness of the people.' It had failed because neither government nor people were shaken by the French onslaught. Although he concedes that Napoleon made a mistake in invading Russia, this greatest of military philosophers thinks he had no choice.

> Instead of burdening himself with an interminable costly defensive war in the east such as he had on his hands in the west. Bonaparte attempted the only means to gain his object: by one bold stroke to extort a peace from his astonished adversary.

Moreover Clausewitz – who, after all, was on Kutuzov's staff – thought that the Emperor had had at least some chance of winning:

> If Bonaparte in the year 1812, either before or after taking Moscow, had been able to give the Russian Army of 120,000 on the Kaluga road a defeat, such as he gave the Austrians in 1805 and the Prussian Army in 1806, then the possession of that capital would most probably have brought about a peace although an enormous tract of country still remained to be conquered.

He also makes the point that 'General Winter' wreaked nearly as much havoc on the Russians as on the French, stating that the army which pursued Napoleon (and in whose ranks he was serving) left Kaluga 120,000 strong and reached Vilno with 30,000 effectives; he comments: 'Everyone knows how few men were lost in actual combats during that period.' Again and again he stresses that the French almost won – 'In the Russian campaign, the complete defeat of the Russian Army was the last blow required: the Emperor Alexander had no other army at hand and, therefore, peace was the certain consequence of victory.'

In February 1945 the Führer confessed to Martin Bormann that before invading Russia he had 'pondered long and anxiously over

Napoleon and his experience'. It is inconceivable that he had not studied Clausewitz's analysis of the 1812 campaign in *Vom Kriege*. Yet while this study could be taken in an encouraging sense, it had to be admitted that the campaign ended in defeat. The great theorist was at his most obscure and ambiguous in dealing with the subject. He had 'acquired a philosophical mode of expression without developing a truly philosophical mind' is Liddell Hart's comment. 'Not one reader in a hundred was likely to follow the subtlety of his logic or to preserve a true balance amid such philosophical jugglery. But every one could catch such ringing phrases as: 'we have only one means in war – the battle.' In the circumstances there could have been no more dangerous authority to follow. Unluckily, no other German military theorist of even remotely comparable calibre had written about 1812.

Hitler also explained to Bormann that, although he had always opposed war on two fronts, there was no hope of invading Britain. Meanwhile time was on Russia's side. The only chance had been to forestall her by taking the initiative. After all, Clausewitz had written of the necessity to bring a conflict 'completely to an issue before the worst time arrives, or of gaining at least in the meantime some advantage'. And if the Russians were no longer apathetic serfs, it was probable that most of them detested Stalinism. However vast their country, it was infinitely more centralized than in 1812, while problems of distance and extended communications could be surmounted by motorized transport, by rail and by air.

In his diary for 16 June 1941 Goebbels explains more fully why the Führer was invading the Soviet Union:

Moscow intends to keep out of the War until Europe is exhausted and bled white. Then Stalin will move to bolshevise Europe . . Russia would attack us if we were weak and we should face a two-front war, which we are avoiding by this pre-emptive strike. Only then

205

shall we have our rear protected. I estimate the fighting capacity of the Russians even lower than does the Führer.

Goebbels adds that the Soviet Union had to be beaten before Germany could begin an all-out assault on Britain, using the Luftwaffe on a massive scale. 'Bolshevism must be destroyed and with it England will lose her last possible ally on the European mainland.'

Despite his long-term plans for the conquest of eastern Europe and his much vaunted contempt for the Soviet Union, Hitler had, like the Emperor, moments of uneasiness. Goebbels describes him just before declaring war on Russia as living 'under an indescribable strain'; on the eve of the declaration he writes: 'The Führer seems to lose his fear as the decision comes near.'

Until he announced them, very few had guessed at Hitler's real intentions about Russia. He let no one into his confidence even if, when provoked by Stalin's foreign policy, he would shout that his life's mission was war with the Soviet Union. Yet, as Goebbels discerned, he was terrified by the prospect of a war on two fronts. There were moments when he thought that the Russians might help him overwhelm Britain, even if it was as early as July 1940 when first he told his military leaders that he meant to attack Russia in spring the following year envisaging a campaign which would destroy the Soviet Union completely. Understandably, Hitler was always nervous about Stalin's long-term intentions. Russia had not only swallowed up eastern Poland but in June 1940 took advantage of German preoccupation with France to seize Bessarabia and the northern Bukovina from Romania, which seriously alarmed the Führer, since it threatened his oil-supplies. Russia also had an eye on Finland, from whence came her nickel. Hitler moved troops into Romania as 'military advisers'; into Finland on the pretext they were in transit to Norway. Then Franco's refusal to allow German forces through Spain stalemated him over Britain. However, an even stronger Axis front might at last frighten

Churchill into making peace, or topple him. In November 1940 he invited the Soviet Union to join with Germany, Italy and Japan, offering Istanbul with the Straits of Gallipoli and Persia. But the Russians demanded too much, far more than was offered; in addition, they insisted on being given bases in Bulgaria, recognition of their interests in Finland, Romania and Turkey, a naval base in Denmark, the Arab oil fields as well as those of Persia, together with the withdrawal of all German troops from Romania and Finland.

Soviet greed made up Hitler's mind. Like Napoleon, he was going to strike at Britain through Russia. On 18 December 1940 he issued Führer Directive No 21, 'Operation Barbarossa' – 'The final objective of the operation is to erect a barrier against Asiatic Russia in the general line Volga-Archangel. The last surviving industrial area of Russia can then, if necessary, be eliminated by the Luftwaffe.' (The Soviet Union beyond the Urals was to become part of the Japanese Empire.) The operation was originally timed for 15 May 1941 but was postponed on account of the Yugoslav and Greek campaigns. (The Führer was very conscious of the Emperor's disastrous delay, ordering 'reputable historians' to state publicly that Napoleon had set out a day later than his own troops.) When they crossed the Russian border on 23 June his armies took the Soviet forces completely by surprise, despite Western attempts to warn Stalin; on being informed by the German ambassador that the two countries were at war, Molotov gasped, 'What have we done to deserve this?' At dawn three German army groups struck along a 1,500-mile front; in the centre Field Marshal von Bock drove towards Moscow with 930 tanks; in the south-east Field Marshal von Rundstedt raced towards Kharkov and Kursk with 750, and in the north-east Field Marshal von Leeb towards Leningrad with 570. Finland was to attack from the north, its army joining up with Leeb.

Hitler had an uneasy relationship with the men who were leading

Operation Barbarossa. The Wehrmacht commander-in-chief Field Marshal von Brauchitsch saw himself as military adviser to the Head of State, while the Führer regarded him as a subordinate officer bound to obey orders. What complicated matters further was Brauchitsch's contradictory character – that of an intelligent soldier who was excessively cautious, a man both weak and stubborn. He was also a product of the Great War, naturally inclined to a defensive outlook. This was an attitude shared by the three army group commanders, Rundstedt, Bock and Leeb, who were all in their sixties. Leeb, a Bavarian nobleman and an expert on defensive strategy – described by Johannes Popitz as 'almost fossilized' – was appalled at the very idea of war with Russia. General Halder, Chief of the General Staff, had even more reservations about Hitler, whom he secretly despised. Icily obstinate, he regarded Moscow as the campaign's primary objective. Ultimately such men (with the partial exception of Rundstedt) were incapable of working with the Führer. Had their places been filled – as they were later to be – by such men as Model and Schörner, who were totally in sympathy with him, the invasion might well have succeeded.

The Field Marshals saw Moscow as the goal. Hitler disagreed. He told Halder, 'Only completely ossified brains, absorbed in the ideas of past centuries, could see any worthwhile objective in taking the capital.' He informed a group of generals in August 1941 that even if they had read Clausewitz, they did not understand wartime economics. 'I too have read Clausewitz and remember his axiom "first destroy the enemy's army and then occupy his capital".' But by itself Moscow was not enough. In the different circumstances of 1941 he must not only capture Leningrad but cut Russia off from its Caucasian oil and Ukrainian grain, and from its industries in the Donets Basin.

The German invaders and their allies numbered 3 million men – 118 infantry divisions, 19 panzer divisions and 15 motorized divisions. They faced 178 divisions, of which 40 were motorized and 20 cavalry. Their 3,550 panzers confronted 10,000 Russian tanks, of which 2,000 were excellent though the rest were obsolete. On paper the Luftwaffe's 3,350 aircraft were outnumbered by 12,000 Soviet planes, but these were unquestionably inferior. The Russians suffered from three crippling disadvantages. First, they had had no proper warning. Second, they were grouped in echelon, three army groups one behind another – the hindmost 250 miles from the frontier. Third, their officer corps was thoroughly demoralized; more generals and colonels had died in the purge of 1936-8 than were to die during the entire war.

German troops were explicitly ordered to use the utmost brutality. The Geneva Convention did not apply in Russia, and captured Russians must not be treated like other prisoners-of-war – commissars were to be 'shot out of hand'. This order was issued by the German High Command on 6 June. A supplement to Führer Directive No. 33 informed the troops that they would only be able to hold down large areas of territory 'by striking such terror into the population that it loses all will to resist'.

At first the invaders drove all before them, capturing 150,000 prisoners, 600 guns and 1,200 tanks in ten days. General Halder, an inveterate pessimist, confided to his diary on 3 July: 'It would probably be no exaggeration to say that the campaign against Russia has been won within the first fortnight.' Rundstedt entered Kharkov in September, while the whole of the Crimea (save Sevastopol) would be in German hands by mid-November.

However, Leeb was held up in Estonia. Hitler had ordered Bock in the centre to send the panzer groups on his flanks south and north to help Rundstedt and Leeb, despite his protests. In consequence Bock was held up at Smolensk for two months. The Führer has been criticized for this, but he was probably justified. Bock needed to overhaul and refit his tanks, while reinforcements enabled Rundstedt to make his spectacular gains – the Russians were taken completely by surprise, attacked from unexpected directions in daunting strength. In the north Leeb was able to make progress, capturing Schlüsselburg (Petrokepost), supposedly the key to Leningrad: however, he was then told to seal off the city instead of capturing it. The panzers were returned to Bock so that he could resume his advance on Moscow at the end of September in 'Operation Typhoon'. He now had 2,000 tanks, and faced little more than infantry.

However, German losses by 8 October were estimated at over half a million men – more than the entire casualty rate between September 1939 and the opening of Operation Barbarossa in June 1941. The autumn rains, which had begun two days earlier, turned the unmetalled Russian roads into rivers of mud, disrupting supplies – as in 1812, Smolensk was the furthest limit for depots – and slowing down the panzers. Yet Bock and his centre army group ground forward, the elimination of two Soviet pockets at Vyazma and Bryansk netting another 600,000 prisoners by the end of October. The Russian government fled from Moscow, where rioting broke out. Nevertheless Stalin stayed, appointing General Zhukov to command the defences. Just as Clausewitz had observed of the Emperor, the Führer and indeed almost everyone else – including probably the majority of informed Russians – thought that Russia would collapse with the centre of its nerve system. Bock began what he believed would be the final push on 15 November, starting from positions sometimes as close as forty miles away. But already there were frosts, and the rain was turning to snow. Bock used his armour recklessly, and too many tanks were knocked out or broke down. Operation Typhoon began to run out of steam, even if some units came within 20 miles of Moscow. Eventually Guderian, directing Bock's panzer onslaught in heavy snow, had only 50 tanks left out of 600. The temperature was 35 degrees below and most of them could not fire their guns. On 5 December he went over to the defensive.

By now the German High Command estimated its casualties at 3 million men, killed, wounded, diseased or frostbitten – the snow killed more than the enemy, the wounded freezing to death in their hospital beds. The troops had no proper winter clothing, Hitler having told them they would be back in Berlin in time for Christmas. The mud of autumn had changed into rock-hard ground, rain into terrible blizzards. In these temperatures oil froze in the sumps, rendering tanks and lorries immobile until fires were lit beneath their engines. Even telescopic sights were unusable. Not only did mechanized transport suffer but as in Napoleon's day vast numbers of horses died from hunger, unable to reach the grazing beneath the snow. (It is seldom appreciated how much the Wehrmacht depended on horsed transport, especially supply wagons, during the first half of the war.)

The Russians, who knew how to handle such conditions, had started to counter-attack. Troops in winter white, many of them Siberians on skis, smashed through the German positions all along the thousand-mile front. Cossacks carrying their own fodder operated just as they had in 1812, cutting communications and supply lines, spreading panic and penetrating almost as far as Smolensk. Often it was impossible to fire rifles or cook food, men losing hands and feet, ears or noses from frostbite.

The three army group commanders were dismissed for withdrawing without permission. In all nearly fifty senior officers lost their commands. Brauschitz, who had had a heart attack from worry, was sacked on 19 December – whereupon Hitler appointed himself operational commander-in-chief of the Wehrmacht. By mid-December Guderian had withdrawn fifty miles, complaining of shockingly high losses, that his men could 'do no more'. He was dismissed immediately. Hitler's orders were that there must be no retreats; the line must be held. General Jodl particularly admired 'Halt-Order', he believed that but for the Führer the Wehrmacht would have suffered the same fate as the Grande Armée. Grouped in 'hedgehogs' – bastion towns such as Kursk, Taganrog and Novgorod – supplied from the air, linked by radio and going to each other's assistance but letting the enemy bypass them, the Wehrmacht managed to hold the Red Army, whose counter-offensive petered out in January 1942. It too lost many thousands of men, just as Kutusov's army had lost three-quarters of its effectives in 1812. Its front now consisted of a long line of exposed salients which would be very vulnerable to counter-attack.

The failure to take Moscow is sometimes attributed to Hitler's meddling. He has been compared to a hysterical back-seat driver. Halder, Chief of the General Staff, complained of his constantly interfering which, as a somewhat pedantic professional, he regarded as a personal insult; after the war, in *Hitler als Feldherr*, he exaggerated Hitler's military shortcomings. On the other hand, the Führer considered that he had been let down by his generals. Liddell Hart apportions the blame equally, commenting that 'the most fatal factor had been the way that Hitler and his top generals had wasted the month of August in arguing as to what should be their next move – there was an amazing state of mental haziness on the topmost level of the German Command'.

Liddell Hart's verdict is that Operation Barbarossa failed to succeed, but only just, because the German army's mobility depended on wheels instead of on tracks. On the muddy roads of a Russian autumn the lorries which carried the petrol, spare ammunition and food could not keep up with the tanks – 'If the panzer forces had been provided with *tracked* transport they could have reached Russia's vital centres by the autumn in spite of the mud.' He stresses that had the Soviet Union possessed roads comparable to those in France or even Yugoslavia it would have been overrun almost as quickly, and it owed its survival to 'continued primitiveness'. A further factor which he cites was that the Germans had underestimated the enormous reserves of Russian manpower, quoting Halder's diary in mid-August – 'we reckoned with 200 divisions, but now we have already identified 360'.

Undoubtedly another contributory cause was the lack of communication at personal level between Hitler and his generals already referred to.

Opinions will always vary about the Führer's military abilities, yet he coped better with the December crisis than his generals. The three army group commanders, all elderly rather than middle-aged, were more susceptible to cold because of their years; they were on the spot, and since they were men not entirely without compassion, they were badly shaken by the appalling temperature and the sufferings of their troops. In Germany (save for one swift visit to Mariupol) the Führer could afford a more detached view. He later told Albert Speer, 'I knew that any retreat would mean the fate of Napoleon.' And, like the Emperor, he was indifferent to the fate of his soldiers.

According to Clausewitz, it is always dangerous to attack experienced troops when they are in a strong position, and would-be attackers should have special equipment. Hitler may have been aware that his troops were padding their tunics and trousers with newspaper, wrapping themselves in sacks, in the absence of winter clothing, but he knew that their weapons were as good as those of the Russians, while he had the Luftwaffe with which to supply the 'hedgehog' bastion-towns. Above all, he trusted in their fighting qualities to repel the counter-attack.

Napoleon insisted that 1812 had been his most brilliant campaign – even though he had cried at the crossing of the Beresina, 'This is

213

what happens when one makes mistake after mistake!' What destroyed him was neither the winter nor the burning of Moscow but the Russian army's survival. If not exactly the Emperor's finest hour, the Russian débâcle was, in many observers' opinion, the Führer's. The otherwise hostile General von Tippelskirch considered it 'his one great achievement'. Tippelskirch continues, 'At that critical moment the troops were remembering what they had heard about Napoleon's retreat from Moscow and living under the shadow of it. If they had once begun a retreat it might have turned into a panic flight.' Hitler was justified in claiming he had saved the German army from the fate of the French 130 years before, even if, unlike the Emperor, he had sometimes been able to supply his troops from the air.

Neither leader was able to bring himself to cut his losses after the failure of his troops, or to accept that he had been defeated. Napoleon stubbornly refused to surrender territory or to withdraw from Germany, while the Führer would never for a moment – not even during 1944 – contemplate restoring Russia's frontier as it was before Operation Barbarossa. Both were incapable of rational compromise, an incapacity which meant their doom.

He began to believe that there was something superhuman in his own faculties, and that he was privileged to deny that any laws were made for him . . . He became a deity to himself; and expected mankind not merely to submit to, but to admire and reverence, the actions of a demon.

Lockhart, The History of Napoleon Buonaparte, 1829

But Germany . . . will be Germany only when it is Europe as well. Without power over Europe we must perish. Germany is Europe.

Hitler to Hermann Rauschning, August 1932

8

Blocus Continental, Festung Europa

A single European state has been a dream since antiquity. Charlemagne restored the Roman Empire, and the Germans maintained a version of it until the nineteenth century. Napoleon and Hitler both united Europe, after a fashion. During the spring of 1945, amidst his nightmare ruin, the Führer described himself as 'Europe's last chance', explaining 'It could not be conquered by charm or persuasion – I had to rape it.'

To some extent the Emperor considered that he was reviving the Western Empire, claiming his sovereignty derived from the people like the Roman Emperors'. His 'Continental System' covered an area corresponding to the heartland of today's European Community. France swallowed up Belgium, Holland, the southern Rhineland, the German North Sea coast, Piedmont, Tuscany, the Papal States and Illyria. Napoleon was also Protector of the Confederation of the Rhine, his kindred ruled Spain and Italy as client kings. Western Poland was likewise a vassal. 'From nothing I soared until I became the mightiest ruler in the world,' he recalled 'Europe lay at my feet.'[25]

Hitler was even more of an admirer of Charlemagne than Napoleon had been, regarding him as a German. In 1942 he told

Himmler that Karl der Grosse was one of the greatest men in history. As for the Carolingian state, 'for centuries the peoples of Europe have regarded it as the successor to the universal empire of the Caesars'. (At the Nuremberg Rally of 1935 he was presented with a replica of Charlemagne's sword.) His own 'Great Germanic Empire of the German Nation' embraced all the lands once ruled by Charlemagne, together with those as far east as the Urals. The Reich proper – territory under his direct rule – stretched westward to the Channel, including Holland, Belgium, Luxembourg; its southern boundary was the line of the Somme, taking in half of Burgundy. In the north he planned to incorporate Denmark and Norway.

Both men were at least realistic enough to seek a junior partner to help them rule Europe. At first Napoleon hoped it might be Russia, but he fell out with the Tsar. He then opted for Habsburg Austria instead, since it was ready to let him have a dynastic alliance – a marriage which he supposed would guarantee his acceptance by the old European monarchies. In return Austria might expect favoured-ally treatment, and new territory at Russia's expense. Hitler too sought a partner to buttress his European hegemony, fascist Italy.

As has been seen, the creators of the Napoleonic and Nazi empires did not rule out the possibility of expansion beyond Europe. Nearly a century ago Emile Bourgeois produced a study of Bonaparte's foreign policy in which he argues, eloquently if not altogether con-vincingly, that it had been inspired by a secret determination to take over the crumbling Ottoman Empire. He dreamt of going even farther than Asia Minor, prophesying that 'India will be lost to the English by foreign invasion'. (In his view the Indians were incap-able of ruling themselves – they 'will not grow up, they always remain children'.) The Führer too indulged in fantasies of this type, though never as seriously as Napoleon; after all, he had not led an army to Egypt. Nevertheless, he opened negotiations with the

Grand Mufti and had designs of a sort on Iraq's oil-fields. As for the sub-continent, 'the Indians are unanimous in their desire to shake off the British yoke. Some of them would like to try Bolshevism for that purpose, others would like to try us.'

☒

The Emperor grew steadily more dictatorial. He was obsessed by power, would not share it, would brook no criticism, let alone opposition. The Tribunate, the last consultative institution to remain from Sieyès's constitution, was reduced to a tame shadow, then finally abolished in 1807. The Senate was too cowed to question Imperial decrees. Ministers were deliberately prevented from working together as a body; to divide them still further, they were encouraged to compete for his favour. Men of genius like Talleyrand, Fouché and Chaptal who expressed reservations about his policies were eventually dismissed. In consequence there was much confusion, with considerable duplication of effort. From the very beginning he set out to create a numbing atmosphere of fear and distrust. Even under the Consulate, during a visit to Paris in 1801, the Rev. Jackson, Dean of Christchurch, received the strong impression that Bonaparte's 'great end is to diffuse suspicion everywhere, considering it his best hold'. Napoleon himself declared, 'I reign only through the fear I inspire.' Not just France but the entire *Grand Empire* became increasingly fearful as the years went by.

'Napoleon was always on his guard against ambitious generals or popular discontent, constantly breaking the former or forestalling the latter,' says Count Chaptal, his Minister of the Interior for five years. He tells us how the Emperor kept his commanders at a distance, barely speaking to them, rarely congratulating them, though loading them with honours and estates to ensure their loyalty. He adds that Napoleon had henchmen whom he neither liked nor trusted. 'Yet by nature distrustful himself, he relished their blind obedience and was able to pretend that his orders were carried out so easily. These men were all the more dangerous since his first reactions [to a threat] were invariably quite terrifying.'

'Virtue, good feeling, religion, enthusiasm – these are in his eyes, to use his favourite expression – "the eternal enemy of the continent",' Mme de Staël informs us. He saw men as 'things, not fellow human beings'. Metternich says the Emperor was convinced that everyone in public life was motivated by self-interest.

'That terrible man enslaved us all,' recalled Decrès, Minister for the Marine. 'He held our imagination in his hand, sometimes a hand of steel, sometimes a hand of velvet; one never knew how it was going to be from day to day, so that there was no means of escaping. Once he fastened his hold over one he never let go.'

If one is attempting a comparison with Hitler, Napoleon's most stimulating interpreter is certainly Hippolyte Adolphe Taine (1828-93). One of the forgotten 'great minds' of nineteenth-century France, he is quoted but seldom read. The Left find him antipathetic, as he rejects the revolution; the Right cannot forgive his condemnation of the Emperor. Admittedly he is eccentric. (In his *Histoire de la Littérature Anglaise* he claims that the English have developed large feet to cope with their country's marshes.) Yet his portrait of Napoleon, in his *Origines de la France contemporaine*, is not implausible. It is of a man possessed by the devil, a foreigner who is an amoral egoist on a vast scale. His dream of ruling Europe brings misery on the French:

> At home he demanded not only undisputed control over all executive and legislative power but, even more, the annihilation of any moral authority other than his own, the silencing of public opinion and the isolation of each individual; and consequently the systematic destruction in advance of any initiative, spiritual,

clerical, educational, charitable, literary, departmental or municipal which whether at the present moment or in the future might unite men against him or even at his side. Being a good tactician he guarded his rear; during his European struggle he ensured that in the France he was dragging with him, no hostile elements were able to join forces.

Commenting on this passage, Geyl says that in the 1940s certain resemblances would occur to readers which Taine could not have foreseen; even so, Taine considered the distinguishing features of the Napoleonic régime to be 'the shattering of individuality and of group, the uprooting of local government, the destruction of all initiative and all conviction in political matters'. (It is only fair to record that on the whole Geyl disagreed with Taine, regarding his Napoleon as a failure.)

The Emperor can at least be exonerated from the appalling 'racial' pseudo-philosophy which was the basic inspiration for Hitler's dreams of empire. His own inspiration was self-aggrandizement, purely and simply. Even so, in certain areas of Europe – such as southern Italy – he undoubtedly contemplated imposing a new nobility of French settlers. He certainly tried to create a new ruling class in France. It was to be constructed by intermarriage between the old French noble families and men of humble origin who had proved their merit by their achievements; the Minister of Police was ordered to supply statistics of suitable girls from the nobility, including physique, intelligence and education, and a number of these were forced to marry 'new men' whom he selected. The great schools such as the Polytechnique and the new *lycées*, together with the Imperial University, were founded to instil Imperialist principles – 'If one does not learn in childhood whether to be a republican or a monarchist, an infidel or a believer, the State will never be formed into a nation.' There was opposition from many parents to sending their children to the new boarding schools, which were run on semi-military lines – Taine comments that the atmosphere was that of 'anterooms to barracks'. In 1808 Napoleon had a register compiled of leading families of the *grande-noblesse* and *haute-bourgeoisie* throughout France, with the intention of forcing them to send their sons to the military academy at Saint-Cyr.

If Taine's interpretation is correct, the purpose of the new educational system anticipated the totalitarianism of the twentieth century to a remarkable degree:

> training at an early age, systematic, continuous, relentless training which concentrates every method – lessons, example, practical application – on indoctrinating young minds with certain principles, moulding them so that they will retain permanently the 'national doctrine', a species of social and political catechism, whose first item is a demand for fanatical obedience, passionate loyalty and total self-sacrifice to the Emperor.[26]

One might almost feel that the Führer read Taine.

Nevertheless, the Napoleonic régime possessed considerable support. For most of its existence it enjoyed great material prosperity, while the French were not averse to being the European master-race. Since the campaigns were far away, they were spared the miseries of war. There was also an element of resignation, at least until 1813. The Emperor had not so much ended the Revolution (which he sometimes claimed) as embraced most of its vast complexities, and the majority of Frenchmen preferred monolithic authority to the nerve-racking uncertainties of the 1790s. No doubt many who accepted the Empire yearned in secret for a Bourbon restoration or for a republic, but they had no wish to see an accompanying civil war – had one been possible.

Imperial France was no less of a police state than Nazi Germany. The title and plot of *Une ténébreuse affaire* ('A Dark Business'), Balzac's novel about political persecution under the Empire, foreshadows the decree *Nacht und Nebel* ('Night and Fog') of 1941 by which those deemed to threaten the State disappeared without trace. The Emperor is widely admired for giving France what is called the Code Napoléon; in reality this was the culmination of over a century's work by legal experts and had been initiated by Louis XIV, who if anyone was its true instigator. The 'modern Justinian' manipulated it as he pleased. There was no need for the Führer to give Germany new laws; it already possessed an excellent legal code, very much the same as that enjoyed by today's Federal Republic.

The Empire was even more heavily policed than the Consulate, Savary proving far heavier-handed than the subtle Fouché. The new administration's efficiency ensured its repressiveness. The only opposition, from the Right, was muted; the royalists were too discouraged to mount any further plots after Georges Cadoudal's death in 1804, their activities being confined to *salon* gossip, although devout Catholics among them grew increasingly restive at Napoleon's ill-treatment of the Pope. The régime's most dangerous if silent opponents were Fouché and Talleyrand when they foresaw it might be destroyed by its creator's ambition, their unease reflecting that of the *Notables*, who began to fear for their wealth. There was no overt defiance until the very end, save for General Malet's tragicomic attempt.

Censorship was stifling. Eventually only four newspapers were allowed to appear in Paris (compared with seventy-three in 1799), every issue being read by the Minister of Police before publication; most of contents were supplied by the authorities, Napoleon himself sometimes contributing pieces. All British newspapers were banned from 1802. 'If the Press weren't censored, I shouldn't stay in power another week,' said the Emperor. Plays were censored from 1800, the number of theatres in the capital being cut to eight in 1807. Booksellers were forbidden to sell any book before it had been with the censors for a week. Bookshops and printing presses came under government control in 1810, the number of shops in Paris being restricted to sixty – regularly inspected by the police – while printers had to take an oath to print nothing contrary to the interests of the State. Letters were systematically intercepted in the post and scruitinized. There was a determined effort to influence the climate of ideas. Napoleon disliked and distrusted intellectuals, whom he described variously as 'metaphysicians', 'ideologists' and 'vermin'; in 1803 the faculty of moral and physical sciences in the Institut de France was closed down. The Emperor's remark that the Minister of the Interior should do something about the decline of literature is only too revealing, and it is hard not to agree with Mme de Staël that his sole interest in writers was as witnesses to his glory. Yet classical French theatre and actors like Talma received his enthusiastic support, while he was the patron of fashionable composers such as Cimarosa and Paesiello. Châteaubriand, a known enemy of the régime, was allowed to publish books so long as they contained nothing political – though he was too widely read to persecute with impunity.

He secured considerable support from the Church, persuading the French hierarchy to tell the peasants not to evade conscription in their pastoral letters. Yet he failed to secure absolute control over it, to make Paris 'the metropolis of Christendom, the centre and guide of the religious as well as the political world', as he put it.

During a disagreement with Pius VII in 1806 Napoleon declared: 'For the Pope's purposes I am Charlemagne – like Charlemagne I join the crown of France with the crown of the Lombards.' Had he conquered Russia and finally subjected Europe he would have enslaved the Church too. He wanted the pontiff to be in constant attendance on him, at his beck and call. 'I would have been master of religion as though I were its sole lord,' he claimed when on St Helena. He planned a Byzantine caesaro-papalism, with the Pope as an obedient patriarch. While Pius was prepared to reconcile Catholics to the revolution, even quoting Rousseau in his sermons, he declined such a role. After he refused to implement the Continental Blockade, in 1808 the Emperor occupied the Papal States, annexing Rome itself in May of the following year on the pretext that it had been part of the Carolingian Empire. The Pope excommunicated him, to be arrested and confined at Savona. In 1811 Pius signed a concordat [dictated by Napoleon] almost certainly as a consequence of morphine administered in the guise of a sedative – though he swiftly repudiated the document. He was brought to Fontainebleau in 1812 but would not submit. A final attempt to break the old pontiff in 1813 was no more successful, if he yielded just enough to save the Papacy from being installed at Paris or Avignon. (Almost incredibly, in 1817 Pius was to ask the Allies to release his tormentor from St Helena.) Understandably, after 1809 many Catholics began to regard Napoleon as anti-Christian. Some clergy even denounced his wars from the pulpit.

Catholic opposition was partly fuelled by a reaction against the *philosophaillerie* of Voltaire and Rousseau. As Bonald had written in 1796, the terror lurked behind all the Enlightenment's elegant verbiage, just as plague so often accompanied cargoes of spices from the Levant. The ideals of the Emperor's youth were going out of fashion.

The régime was undeniably imposing, if marred by a certain flashiness. Among other embellishments Paris was given the Arc de Triomphe, the Bourse, the Madeleine ('Temple de la Gloire') and the Odéon, together with such elegant thoroughfares as the Rue de Rivoli, the Rue de la Paix and the Rue Soufflot. The Louvre was refurbished, the horses of St Mark from Venice placed on top of the gateway of the Tuileries and the column set up in the Place Vendôme. Among less showy edifices were granaries and abattoirs, so that the capital's workers were assured of cheap food. The Emperor intended to build much more, including a vast new 'Palais du Roi de Rome' – which would have been bigger than the Luxembourg – and a new opera house. There were brilliant military reviews and Court spectacles, though the latter had an unmistakably tinsel quality.

The Imperial Guard – the Old Guard, Middle Guard and Young Guard – was the ultimate protector of both the régime and its creator. He chose its men with the utmost care, vetting, promoting, rewarding, cashiering. He rode at its head over countless battlefields and on countless parades, to that stirring if raucous march the *Chant du Départ*. He often hummed it to himself, the Empire's music of triumph.

In its own way Imperial France was surprisingly well organized for war, by the standards of the time, relatively perhaps more so than Nazi Germany. It coped with shortages resulting from the British blockade with considerable ingenuity. Since sugar cane could no longer be had from the West Indies, its place was taken by the cultivation of sugar beet, while since tall Baltic timbers were not available for warships' masts, composite masts were constructed. Understandably, the armaments industry flourished, its workers being exempt for military service; nearly 270,000 cannon and small arms were produced in 1806. If great Atlantic ports such as Nantes and Bordeaux were hit badly by lack of trade there was something of an industrial boom – except in manufactures like cottons, which depended on imports. To some extent shortages were alleviated by widespread smuggling, which received a considerable measure of tolerance from the régime. The steady drain of manpower into the Imperial armies caused difficulty in working the land; peasant women took to ploughing, and in 1809 the Emperor experimented with foreign slave labour in the form of Austrian prisoners of war, though on a very limited scale. One cannot deny that France suffered severely from the straitjacket wrapped around it by the Royal Navy, for all the often heroic efforts of privateers and blockade-runners.

Yet despite relative prosperity, the sense that France was the greatest nation in the world and the gratifying exploits of the Grande Armée which marched into every European capital, there were frenetic, uneasy undertones. It was not just corruption and venality (vast fortunes were made by everyone, from the Imperial family and Talleyrand down to the lowest army contractor, while bribery was a fact of life) but a combination of insecurity and repression. The *Notables* feared increasingly for their new wealth each time Napoleon embarked on a fresh adventure, gambling his entire régime on the fortunes of war. The police were ubiquitous, constantly raiding the most inoffensive gatherings; hunting horns might not be blown in taverns, women had to obtain a licence if they wished to dress like men and a curfew was enforced. There were *agents provocateurs* everywhere, stirring up discontent in order to identify potential enemies of the régime who were then arrested at midnight, brutally interrogated, and imprisoned or executed.

The Parisian working class was deliberately pampered by the Emperor – still nervous of revolution after what he had seen as a young man. Nevertheless, with the country people who formed the great bulk of the French population, they suffered savagely in consequence of conscription – 'the blood tax'. The sons of the rich were allowed to buy themselves out by hiring a replacement, at a price often almost ten times a labourer's annual wage; as many as 9 per cent of the draft did so. Less fortunate young men chopped off thumbs or gouged out eyes to avoid serving. Deserters were hunted down by the gendarmerie, 60,000 being caught during 1812. Many hid in the woods or in cellars, their families having to pay fines for their evasion. Chateaubriand writes of entire villages miserably scanning call-up lists posted at street-corners, of parents arrested as hostages for sons in hiding. He also writes of 'passers-by crowding beneath long lists of those sentenced to death, studying them frantically for the names of children, brothers, friends and neighbours. By 1813 the Emperor was recruiting men over sixty and boys under fifteen (the 'Marie Louises', so called after his Austrian Empress). On one occasion he described the latter as 'only fit for filling up the hospitals and roadsides'.

The country suffered as much from soldiers who followed the colours as it did from deserters. Paris and every major French town was filled with noisy, swaggering, pugnacious troopers. Frequently drunk, they fought each other, attacked civilians, broke into wine-shops and molested women. Not everyone in France was pleased to see the splendidly uniformed soldiers of the Grande Armée.

Needless to say, everything was much worse in the conquered territories than in France. Brute force was used to cow initial opposition to French occupation, calculated atrocities subsequently holding down the population. Napoleon welcomed shows of defiance since it enabled him to identify opponents and break their resistance. The rising in Madrid in 1808 and Murat's savage suppression of it was exactly what he wanted. The same year he informed his brother Joseph, who he had installed as King of Naples, 'I would like the Neapolitan mob to try a rebellion. So long as you haven't set an example you won't be their master. Every conquered country should have its rising.' Spanish resistance was met with savage reprisals, even subjugated areas seeing the ghastly executions of the sort portrayed in Goya's horrible drawings. The French conquerors were scarcely less brutal in southern Italy, hanging, burning and looting even if Napoleon's gauleiters – his brother Joseph and Murat, whom he made kings – did not impose a new French nobility as he wished. Plunder was on a vast scale in Spain, Portugal and Naples, marshals such as Soult anticipating Goering in their greed for works of art.

Among Napoleon's kinsmen, Joseph Bonaparte ruled in Naples and then in Spain, Louis Bonaparte in Holland, Jerome Bonaparte in Westphalia, Joachim Murat in Naples and Eugène de Beauharnais in northern Italy. The first three – appointed solely because they were Napoleon's brothers – were too feeble to be compared with the Führer's gauleiters. The last two were quite as ruthless, even if they too were promoted for family reasons, being respectively the Emperor's brother-in-law and stepson. All found a bare handful of collaborators. In Spain the *Josefinos* were drawn from the liberal, free-thinking element among the nobility, disciples of the Enlightenment who hoped for an end to the bigotry and backwardness of the Spanish Bourbons; if these were genuine enough, there were very few of them, and in any case they were seen as traitors by the vast majority of Spaniards. In Holland Louis Bonaparte tried to fill his Court with Dutchmen, and took the side of new subjects much too enthusiastically for his Imperial brother's taste. He refused to enforce the blockade, and he obstructed French officials, in order to avert the commercial ruin which threatened the Dutch; besides welcoming American ships carrying British goods and encouraging smuggling. In 1810 he abdicated, his kingdom being absorbed into France. At Cassel Jerome Bonaparte proved an unmitigated disaster.

The Emperor has been severely criticized for giving his family crowns. Geyl calls them 'that peculiarly unpleasant set of people' and stresses the contradiction in appointing someone to embody a nation while insisting he stay a Frenchman. Napoleon's explanation is that he 'was dropping anchors' throughout Europe to make his own new monarchy in France more acceptable to the world. On the whole the Bonaparte sovereigns were embarrassingly ineffectual. All save Murat and Eugéne had to have a marshal behind them – notably Davout in Westphalia, Masséna, Marmont, Soult and Suchet in Spain – together with civilian advisers, such as Fréville at Madrid or Count Daure who was Minister for both War and the Marine at Naples. Control was also exerted through ambassadors, not to mention French bayonets and French police.

The most committed Imperial satellite was Frederick Augustus of Saxony. Slavishly grateful for being made a king and Grand Duke of Warsaw, he hoped to wear the Polish crown worn by his grandfather. (He had been accepted as the next King of Poland in the Constitution of 1791.) Other German satellites, such as the Kings of Bavaria and Württemberg, secretly detested their French master and would one day betray him.

The emperor was greeted as a liberator by the Poles. 'We worship you', the Palatine of Gniezno told him in 1807. 'We place all our hopes in you, the man who builds or destroys empires, who humbles the proud – restorer of our country, lawgiver to the world.' In 1812 they felt sure he would bring back their ancient monarchy. Yet he never had any intention of upsetting the Austrians who occupied a third of Polish territory. On St Helena he declared, unconvincingly, 'Circumstances were stronger than my wishes. I had hoped to restore the Kingdom of Poland as a strong and powerful bulwark against the Tsars' insatiable ambition.' In reality Poles – apart from his beautiful and noble mistress, Countess Walewska – meant no more to him than money or cannon-fodder, and he bled their country white.

If not a puppet or a client state, Prussia was very much an occupied country. French garrisons were installed at every strongpoint, maintained by Prussian money (a sum which eventually came to 160 million francs). The Emperor refused to withdraw his troops until a general European peace was settled – a peace which must include Britain.

While the subject lands, whether occupied territory or client states, produced men and money, the system was inefficient at every level, despite the Emperor's attempting to supervise it as much as possible, and devoting considerable attention not only to military but to fiscal and economic problems. In particular there was the difficulty of feeding wretchedly paid troops without a proper commissariat. Outside France they had to live off the country, which meant that food and wine, grain and livestock, were commandeered without compensation, that thatch was torn from roofs to serve as fodder for horses who otherwise grazed in rye or wheat fields – if these had not been flattened by detachments marching or riding over them. There were no military police apart from inadequate provost marshals, so that drunken, swaggering ruffians were able to rob and to rape. The ordinary French police who accompanied them behaved as badly, both treating the population as they did Spaniards. (The traditional German dislike of the French dates not from Louis XIV's devastation of the Palatinate but from the Napoleonic occupation.) There were swingeing levies, grinding taxation, appropriation of raw materials, foodstuffs and luxury goods, confiscation of property, theft of art treasures, and – in Austria and Prussia – extraction of huge indemnities. Another burden was military service. Few of the conscripted came home and those who did brought tales of dreadful suffering.

There were far more resisters than collaborators. In Spain it meant full-scale civil war. In Italy, while northerners and those in the centre stayed cowed, guerrilla warfare proved ineradicable in Calabria. In Germany the situation was more complex.

Although admitting that they hated him, the Emperor afterwards claimed that he had been good to Germans. 'I could have extorted enormous contributions from the Germans to pay for the war and would have been justified. But I took great care not to treat them ruthlessly since I respected them.' Somewhat querulously, he grumbled, 'I was forced to fight on their soil for ten years yet they could neither grasp my aims nor see I was planning to give them very real and very important benefits.' He fascinated the Romantics of the nascent *Sturm und Drang,* but even if he inspired much music together with many plays, German composers and playwrights alike detested him and his army of occupation, which by 1806 stood at 200,000 men. A Naumburg journalist called Palm published anonymously a pamphlet entitled *Germany In Her Deep Humiliation.* Napoleon ordered all booksellers stocking it to be shot; Palm, who lived on neutral territory, was grabbed by a troop of gendarmes and sent before a firing-squad. Andreas Hofer, who led 40,000 mountaineers against the transfer of his native Tyrol from Austria to Bavaria, was hunted down and executed, Colonel Dornberg, trying unsuccessfully to seize Cassel, met a similar fate. The Prussian Colonel Schill – without his King's permission – invaded Westphalia with his regiment but was driven off, cornered at Stralsund and slaughtered with his men.

Yet, to quote Geyl, 'What are the executions of Palm, of Hofer, what are even the severities with which so many villages and towns in Germany and Spain were visited, besides what in our time all occupied territories have had to suffer from Hitler's armies?'

The Europe of Napoleon and Hitler's Europe shared a common insecurity, their rulers being always fearful of attack or invasion. Both men were convinced that they had to win fresh victories to survive. Each despised and mistrusted their own subjects, to an extent, which is seldom appreciated, seeing the role of French or Germans as servants to their overweening ambition. The peoples of the lands they had subjected were even less than this. Each set up surprisingly similar hierarchies.

'Berlin must become the true centre of Europe,' Hitler observed in July 1941, 'a capital that shall be the capital for everyone'. His 'New Europe' was no less of an empire than Napoleon's. If its creator refrained from becoming 'Kaiser Adolf I', he was sufficiently conscious of his monarchical role to consult the speeches of Wilhelm

II, keeping four volumes by him at his headquarters throughout the war. He was not philoprogenitive like the Emperor, and he did not possess presentable relations. He therefore ruled the conquered lands through 'Reich commissars', mainly men whom he had known for many years, 'Old Party Fighters' such as Hans Frank or Alfred Rosenberg. Seyss-Inquart did just what was wanted in Holland, the Führer describing him as 'an extraordinarily clever man, as supple as an eel, amiable – and at the same time thick-skinned and tough'. He was anxious (in Holland, at any rate) to avoid 'a North German martinet' who might 'alienate popularity'. He had no such inhibitions about Poland or Russia. The former Munich lawyer Hans Frank ruled the Polish *General-Gouvernement* from the Royal Castle on the Wawel as a corrupt tyrant, while Erich Koch terrorized an East Prussia incorporating a large slice of Russia with sadistic brutality remarkable even by Nazi standards. Once a citizen of the Russian Empire, Alfred Rosenberg – who was supposed to hold sway over the territories farther east – had a certain sympathy for his 'subjects', but his master would allow nothing but vicious repression or extermination – a policy implemented ruthlessly by the SS. The 'hangman' Reinhard Heydrich proved a surprisingly subtle Deputy Reich-Protector of Bohemia, giving Czech workers such a high standard of living that it alarmed the Allies. The Führer was very pleased with Josef Terboven's performance in Norway, which he thought 'the most difficult commissarship of the Reich'. The Nazis had valuable assistance from arch-collaborators like Vidkun Quisling in Norway, Anton Mussert in Holland, Léon Degrelle in Belgium and Ante Pavelić in Croatia, their followers providing militia recruits for the Waffen SS.

Like Napoleon, Hitler had satellites. He saw not only Italy but Finland, Hungary, Romania and Vichy France — and, marginally, Spain – as part of his 'New Europe', in much the same way that the Emperor had regarded the German states and the Grand Duchy of

Warsaw. After Mussolini he rated General Antonescu, Romania's Conducator, as his most satisfactory ally. He considered Admiral Horthy the Regent of Hungary, to be the least, and he eventually replaced him in 1944 with the bloodthirsty Ferenc Szálasi and his Arrow Cross Party – murdering Horthy's son in the process.

There was an only too recent precedent of a Germany geared to war, that of 1916-18 when General Ludendorff had been virtually a military dictator, with the support of the uncompromisingly nationalist Vaterland Party. Nevertheless, from the consumer point of view, life in Nazi Germany was comfortable enough. Such luxuries as champagne, furs, spirits and scent flooded in from the conquered territories. The nation's economy was surprisingly un-militarized, in contrast to what Ludendorff had imposed by 1918. Women were not made to work in factories (as in Britain), while it was always possible to find servants. The huge bureaucracy which resulted from Hitler's policy of playing off one satrap against another – as Napoleon had done – enabled determined shirkers to evade military service in well-paid and undemanding jobs. Even so, wartime conditions enabled the Führer to fasten his absolutism still more firmly over all Germans.

Everyone lived in dread of the Gestapo. Under the 'Night and Fog' decree of 1941 the security services had powers to remove without warning or trial, and in such a way that they disappeared without trace, anyone who was suspected of disloyalty to the régime. Opposition – apart from espionage – was confined to the Right, mainly to people who trusted each other because of close family or social links. A few officers plotted against the Führer from as early as 1938, and by 1942 were scheming somewhat ineffectually to assassinate him. Himmler was vaguely aware of such activities, that *something* was going on, but for the time being he did not take them very seriously. They stemmed partly from a genuine sense of outrage at the régime's cruelty and immorality, though the only effective plot to overthrow Hitler did not occur until he was seen to be facing defeat. German officers remained cowed till their nation was threatened by cataclysmic ruin in 1944, just as the Emperor's paladins had feared for the destruction of France in 1814.

Hitler's relationship with the Wehrmacht was complicated. Its officers had always kept out of politics, and he made them still more unwilling to intervene by discrediting their leaders; two successive commanders-in-chief were destroyed by scandal – as soon as Field Marshal von Blomberg married a typist from the War Ministry it was revealed that she had posed for pornographic photographs, while General von Fritsch was unjustly branded as a homosexual. In any case, the army was inclined to accept the new régime because of the enormously increased chance for promotion; additional opportunities were provided by the Luftwaffe and the Waffen SS. Yet he never succeeded in subjugating the General Staff, not even in 1941 when he made himself commander-in-chief. It had its own ideas till the last, unshakably traditional; while wanting a strong Germany with the frontiers of 1914, it had no wish for military adventures – let alone to conquer Russia. In the end it tried to kill him, in July 1944. Even after that unhappy failure anyone visiting the army headquarters building beside the Tirpitz Ufer in Berlin was unlikely to hear the greeting 'Heil Hitler'.[27]

After becoming Pope in 1939 Pius XII (the former Cardinal Pacelli) was so well aware of the threat to humanity posed by the Führer that he acted as go-between for a group of German generals and the British government in an abortive plot to remove him the following year. Hitler knew the pontiff for his enemy, remarking that had *he* been the Duce 'I'd have entered the Vatican and thrown everybody out.' Pius was sufficiently apprehensive to dress the Swiss Guard in khaki, arming it with machine-guns for a token resistance. He also wrote a secret letter of provisional abdication, to come into effect should the Gestapo arrest him, with the conscious intention of avoiding the leadership crisis which existed while Pius VII was Napoleon's prisoner. When Mussolini fell in 1943 the Führer seriously contemplated seizing the Pope, but had second thoughts.

Within the Reich itself the German hierarchy dared not be too outspoken, just as in Napoleonic France – though one must not press the comparison too far since, officially , the French empire had been a Christian state. When Count von Galen, Bishop of Münster (the 'Lion') denounced Gestapo activities Hitler refrained from making a martyr of him. Sometimes the Führer echoed Napoleon's view of Catholicism's role: 'The Church is almost certainly necessary for people,' Albert Speer records him as saying, 'It is a strong conservative element.' After the war Hitler planned to impose an emasculated Catholicism which would be the servant of National Socialism.

The Führer made determined attempts to build a new Germanic 'aristocracy'. Special boarding-schools, 'napolas' *Nazional-politische erziehunganstalten,* were established to inculcate National Socialist principles into promising young Aryans. 'The pupils of these schools will consist of a selection of the best elements from the boys and girls of all classes in the German Reich', Hitler declared. 'I aim at forming a *corps d'élite* of fine physique, well-formed character and supple intelligence.' He saw no difficulties in surpassing in every way the British public schools which to a large extent were their model. (Similar academies were set up in Holland and Norway.) The products of these Nordic Etons emerged as fanatical Nazis, but scarcely as an élite – many were rejected as officer material by the SS.

Occupied countries were governed by a Reich Commissioner or a Military Commandant. Everywhere their half-starved populations were cowed by the presence of the Wehrmacht and the Gestapo, who reacted savagely to the resistance movements which sprang up. Just as the Empire had Europeanized the Grande Armée, every country had to provide troops for the Waffen SS, which became a kind of enormous Foreign Legion. There was also forced labour, the press-ganging of men to work in German factories.

Some countries fared worse than others, notably in the East. No doubt the Führer found justification for his decision to wipe Poland off the map in *Vom Kriege*, where Clausewitz describes it as a 'Tartar state' which could not be really regarded as a European state, as a member of the community of European nations. 'For a hundred years this country [Poland] has ceased to play any independent part in European politics, and had only been an apple of discord . . . Poland, if it had not been partitioned, must have become a Russian province.' He also speaks contemptuously of the 'turbulent political condition and unbounded levity' of its leaders, seeing little reason to wonder at 'the noiseless downfall of Poland' at the end of the eighteenth century. In his view he was not writing as a soldier of expansionist Hohenzollern Prussia but merely trying 'to look at things as they really are', an attitude which would have had considerable appeal for his ardent twentieth-century disciple.

Pomerania, Silesia and Posnania (beyond the furthest boundaries of previous German annexations) were incorporated into the Reich. The inhabitants were deported to the territory known as the General-Gouvernement, which was ruled from Warsaw as a German colony, while three-quarters of a million Germans were settled in their place. The Nazi occupation was accompanied by a systematic attempt to exterminate Polish nobility, intelligentsia and clergy, schools and universities being banned. In October 1939 twenty bearers of the nation's most historic names were shot at Koscian. In November the entire faculty of Cracow University was invited to a meeting to discuss academic problems, then taken away and murdered. By October 1941 74 priests had been shot in Posnania alone, while another 450 were in prison camps – not because they were priests but because they were potential leaders who might head a cultural resistance. It was even worse for clergy farther east.

All educated men, whether landowners, lawyers, or school-masters, were liable to be shot. Poles of Jewish origin were herded into ghettos; eventually almost three million were murdered. Still more Poles suffered deportation or press-ganging as slave labour. Any Pole venturing outside the General Gouvernement had to wear a yellow 'P', like the yellow star of the Jews. In the Führer's words, 'There should be one master only for the Poles, the German.' His policy of destroying the Polish nation, so that it became no more than a pool of brutalized serfs, was frustrated by the heroism of the resistance. Ironically, it is conceivable that a Vichy-style régime might have attracted substantial support from Poles eager to free their fellow-countrymen from the Russians. The situation became bewildering in occupied Russia. While Hitler intended to reduce all Slavs to serfdom, many army officers and even some high-ranking Nazi officials sympathized with the Ukrainian nationalists and with White Russian refugees. On the whole, however, both Ukrainians and Russians were treated with indescribable brutality.

Late in 1945 SS Oberführer Günther D'Alquen under interrogation told Colonel Charles Beauclerk of the British Intelligence: 'We could have recruited a million Russian troops and conquered Russia without difficulty', and that he had been charged with organizing such an operation. D'Alquen was a sufficiently influential Nazi for Himmler to have been best man at his wedding. Contact had been made before Operation Barbarossa with Ukrainian nationalists, but after the invasion they were sent to camps only marginally superior to those of other prisoners. The millions of Russians who surrendered in 1941, and indeed many who surrendered much later, did so because they felt no allegiance to Marxist socialism. Alfred Rosenberg, a German Balt born a subject of the Tsar, who was appointed Reich Minister for the East, begged frantically that Russia should be divided into its component nationalities, as the Central Powers had tried to do after the Treaty of Brest-Litovsk in

1918, but in vain. The Führer envisaged four Reich Commis-sariats – Ostland, Ukraine, Caucasia and Moscovia – inhabited by a race of Slav serfs reduced to bestiality and ruled by German settlers. He grudgingly permitted the establishment of General Vlasov's anit-Soviet force, though its members were treated as inferior troops and inadequately equipped. D'Alquen was convinced that if they had received proper treatment, many more might have been recruited, in which case Germany could have won the war even in 1943.[28]

Needless to say, Jews anywhere could expect no mercy. Beyond question this was Hitler's express wish. Until as late as 1941 he may have thought of expelling them from his territory to some far-distant place such as Madagascar instead of murdering them, but the enormous expansion of his empire made this impossible. Schramm says, rightly, 'no one has ever surpassed him in the extent to which he allowed anti-Semitism to grow into so intensive a mania that it almost completely shattered his faculty of reason', that he was 'almost like the medieval person who sensed the Devil everywhere'. He concludes: 'In the end, all attempts to explain the unprecedented and immeasurable intensity of Hitler's anti-Semitism finally founded on the inexplicable.'

There is a theory that the real responsibility for the 'Final Solution' (systematic extermination of the Jews) lies not with the Führer but with Himmler. It argues that he had not thought out the logical consequences of his anti-Semitic 'ideology' as his empire grew, that the Reichsführer introduced the Final Solution without his knowledge, and cites the lack of documentary evidence involving him. Yet exactly the same methods had been applied earlier, and not only to the Polish élite. He had never had any pity for those who did not fit into his ideal racial world; in 1939 Germany had begun to gas the mentally handicapped, thousands dying before protests by religious leaders halted the policy. Another race besides the Jews was systematically exterminated; throughout the Nazi

239

empire gypsies were rounded up and sent to the gas chambers, probably as many as 25 per cent of the entire Romany folk perishing. It is impossible that so all-seeing, so malevolent an eye was unaware of what was happening in his Reich.

The holocaust visited on the Jews by Hitler was not, mercifully, foreshadowed by Napoleon. Apart from being generally well disposed towards Jews, Napoleon would never have given Fouché power of the sort wielded by Himmler, nor did he dominate Fouché in the way the Führer did the Reichsführer. Fouché may have been evil, but he was a formidable personage in his own right – without Hitler, Himmler was nothing.

Both empires constitute a remarkable achievement, however much misery they may have caused the people of Europe. Yet, as will be seen, they soon produced far more problems for their creators than they solved. Constant vigilance, many thousands of troops and a vast apparatus of administration were needed to hold down conquered, resentful nations, to stop unwilling allies deserting. Throughout their existence Blocus Continental and Festung Europa always bore the seeds of their own destruction, even if their eventual overthrow had to be through force of arms.

No conquest can be finished too soon.

Clausewitz, Vom Kriege

It has to be remembered that Napoleon, who was a professional strategist, had been just as badly dazzled by his own success, and made the same fatal mistakes in the same place.

Sir Basil Liddell Hart, The Other Side of the Hill

9

Ulcers

Napoleon and Hitler both fought a war on two fronts, sometimes on more. As has been seen, the former's 'Spanish Ulcer' (together with the continuing threat from Britain) contributed to his decision to strike at Russia in 1812 – in order to avoid just such a dual conflict. Similarly, the Führer hoped that a successful invasion of Russia would enable him to eliminate Britain. Each failed, ensuring his own destruction. A refusal to make peace on at least one front, however brilliant the use of declining resources, proved suicidal. Moreover, each man had further commitments on lesser fronts.

Looking back from St Helena, the Emperor himself admitted that:

> The unfortunate war in Spain ruined me. All my reverses originated there. The Spanish war destroyed my reputation throughout Europe, increased my difficulties and provided the best possible training ground for English troops. I trained the English army myself, in the Peninsula.

For the situation required Napoleon's presence, yet he could not spare the time. Clausewitz considers that he might have overcome Spain in 1808 despite the British intervention, but he dared not ignore Austria. The same observer thinks it remarkable that the French were able to stay in the Peninsula in the circumstances, and could do so only because they had 'great superiority both physically and morally over the Austrians'.

The true venom in Napoleon's 'gnawing cancer' in Spain was not Wellington but the Spanish guerrillas. Clausewitz pinpointed the terrifying potential of guerrilla warfare, which he had seen for himself in Russia: 'the Spaniards by their stubborn resistance have shown what the general arming of a nation and insurgent measures on a great scale can effect'. Hitler seems to have thought that Marxist socialism had destroyed Russian nationalism. It was his most costly mistake. Just as the Emperor had spurned the Poles, so did the Führer reject any thought of enlisting support from Ukrainian or anti-Communist Russians.

The Emperor's brother Joseph – 'Don José Primero'– was not up to the role of King of Spain, while his Marshals were no match for Wellington, who was a superb commander, as brilliant a strategist as he was a tactician. The situation deteriorated steadily. In Clausewitz's words, 'In Spain, the war itself became an affair of the people.' (He comments that in 1812 the example of the Spaniards was an inspiration to the Russians.) Napoleon agreed – 'The Spaniards acted in the mass like a single man of honour.' He recognized the extent of the problem at an early stage, even if he did not extricate himself. 'Vast means are needed to pacify Spain', he lamented, 'and not a single Spaniard supports my cause.' During the Austrian campaign of 1809 the entire Iberian peninsula burst into bloody uproar, with a gun behind every bush. There were countless small campaigns and battles, tying down nearly 300,000 French troops.

The Spanish regulars who opposed the French were led by out-of-date generals. In consequence they were beaten time and again. Yet such successes proved Pyrrhic victories for the French, since the defeated troops joined the countless guerrilla bands led by unconventional though far more formidable commanders. French deaths in spain averaged about a hundred a day between 1809 and 1814, well over 180,000 fatalities in all. Wellington managed to inflict only 45,000 casualties on the French, including prisoners, during this period.

The most important role of the British Expeditionary Force was to support and encourage the guerrillas. Usually Wellington faced French forces of over 100,000 men with scarcely more than 20,000, and to begin with he fought very few battles, content to make the country a desert and demoralize the enemy by starving them. Unluckily for Napoleon, his commanders were incapable of co-ordinating offensives, seeing each other as rivals and competing for the lion's share of money, provisions and troops. As time went by they became too interested in loot and living like satraps. (Pieter Geyl comments that Spain was 'a training ground in disobedience for the marshals'.) It was impossible for him to control them from a thousand miles away. He could not appreciate that his normal method of feeding his troops – living off the country – did not work. Unlike the British, who had proper supply trains carried on the backs of six thousand mules, and were systematically revictualled from the sea, the French had only what they could find to put in their knapsacks. Wellington's policy of cheering on the the guerrillas and scorching the earth proved lethal. He could go where he pleased with his small force while the French had to cope with an enormous area and to guard over-extended communications.

Eventually Wellington began to give battle to the French. In July 1809 he defeated Marshal Victor at Talavera, though he then had to retreat to Portugal, pursued by superior French forces. After defeating Austria the Emperor was able to devote much more time to the Spanish problem – until 1812 – though he did not take command himself. He sent Masséna to drive the British out of their Portuguese base. After a delaying action at Busaco, Wellington withdrew to the lines of Torres Vedras in front of Lisbon. Masséna was baffled by the lines, and after a month had to limp home, his troops decimated by hunger.

Meanwhile the guerrillas became more and more threatening, tying down corps who should have been chasing Wellington – 90,000 alone being needed to protect the road to France. Soult's entire army was required in Andalusia, unable to help Marmont, who had replaced Masséna. By 1811 there were 370,000 French troops in Spain. Yet during the following year Wellington was able to capture Ciudad Rodrigo and then Badajoz, going on to defeat Marmont at Salamanca in July, and then to a brief occupation of Madrid. The French concentrated their forces for once and chased him out, but in doing so they relaxed their hold on too much territory, strengthening the guerrillas enormously. They were further weakened when Napoleon withdrew troops from the Peninsula after the retreat from Moscow. The end in Spain came in the summer of 1813, Marshal Jourdan being totally defeated at Vittoria.

Even Joseph Bonaparte complained about 'the horrible treatment' inflicted on his unwilling 'subjects' by French military governors. The only properly administered regions were the four provinces north of the Ebro which had been annexed to France. Both sides inflicted inhuman atrocities on each other. Even the Emperor gave way to despair; when one of Marmont's officers came to see him early 1812 and described the situation he exclaimed, 'But how will all this end?' He explored the possibility of an armistice with the British in Spain, though he broke off negotiations when London insisted on restoring the Bourbons.

There were lesser ulcers. People forget that Napoleon was threatened on another southern European front. The exiled Bourbons of Naples had taken refuge at Palermo, protected not only by the Royal

Navy but by British troops. The latter might always invade, as they did in the summer of 1806, when an expeditionary force landed to defeat a far larger French force at Maida in Calabria. The situation improved when Murat became King of Naples, recovering Capri from the British. Even so, guerrilla warfare continued, monopolizing 50,000 French troops.

Because Britannia ruled the waves, she could land men when and where she liked. One such landing took place in 1809 during the renewed war between France and Austria. General Lord Chatham – the late William Pitt's cousin – led 40,000 men to seize the island of Walcheren off the Dutch coast, at the mouth of the Scheldt, and then occupied Flushing on the mainland. However, an epidemic broke out, killing thousands, Chatham having to disembark his men. Although the Walcheren expedition was a failure, it demonstrated the vulnerability of Blocus Continental.

It goes without saying that the Russian front was the greatest of the Führer's military 'ulcers'. Throughout the war not less than a million Germans were serving on the Eastern front at any one time, absorbing the bulk of his troops. In 1942 there were 72 per cent of the Wehrmacht and two-fifths of the Luftwaffe stationed in Russia.

After the failure to destroy the Red Army in 1941 many commanders advised withdrawal. Rundstedt told Hitler to be content with Poland but, like Napoleon before him, the Führer was convinced that he needed new and spectacular victories to retain his rule over Europe, while he was still determined to build a German colonial empire in the East. He had recruited fresh troops and German factories were turning out more arms; in 1942 the Wehrmacht would rise to three million, while war production would double. On 5 April Führer Directive 41, containing 'Operation Case Blue', was issued. Its overall plan was that while the armies in the centre would stand fast and those in the north take Leningrad, those in the south, heavily reinforced, would cross the Don to secure the Caucasian oil-fields and the passes through the Caucasus mountains – cutting Russia off from her main source of oil. This almost unbelievably ambitious project, Hitler's brain-child, came closer to success than is generally appreciated. During the early summer the Red Army's offensives ended in disaster along the entire front; it had lost seven million men in 1941, and now suffered further huge casualties. Case Blue began at the end of June. By the end of July the Germans were over the Don, one part of their forces swinging southward into the Caucasus, the other advancing on Stalingrad.

Like Napoleon's Spanish campaign, Hitler's operations had to be directed from hundreds of miles away. However, unlike the Emperor, he did not do so from a palace but was installed in a bleak frontier headquarters at Vinitsa on the Ukraine. He was more optimistic than the Emperor. Nevertheless, there were some resemblances – notably in the ferocious and costly activities of the partisans and in the terrible toll of veteran troops.

The Führer recognized that 'banditry' was almost as dangerous as the Red Army. In Führer Directive No. 46 of 18 August 1942 he ordered that the confidence of the local population should be won by handling them 'strictly but justly', and seeing that they had the bare necessities – otherwise more might join the partisans. However, he also warned against 'misplaced confidence in the native population'.

The Russians declined to abandon Stalingrad, whose loss would cut their country's supply lines in two. The Germans began their attack on 1 September, despite having advanced so far forward on such a narrow front that they risked encirclement. The Russians defended the city with amazing determination, continuing to fight under their factory fortresses after the buildings above them had been reduced to flaming rubble; combats of indescribable savagery took place in cellars, tunnels, lift-shafts and sewers.

Meanwhile the Red Army had amassed nearly a thousand tanks and a million men, outnumbering German forces within reach of Stalingrad by two to one. On 19-20 November 1942 they launched a classic pincer attack from both sides of the city, trapping 250,000 troops. The Führer believed the situation could be saved, just as it had been the previous winter, by ordering the Commander, General Paulus, to stay put and supplying him by air until he was relieved. The task was beyond the Luftwaffe's capability, while although Manstein's counter-attack got within forty miles of the city, it had failed by Christmas. Despite promotion to Field Marshal (in the hope that this would inspire him to commit suicide rather than give in), Paulus surrendered on 30 January 1943, together with twenty-four generals. In the meantime the Germans extricated themselves from the Caucasus, not without difficulty.

The more thoughtful and better-informed German officers now realized that it was impossible to win the war. Yet although it was defending a front of some 1,200 miles, the Wehrmacht remained formidable and superbly led. Even if Goering was correct in telling Goebbels in March 1943 'the Führer has aged fifteen years during three and a half years of war', he remained as determined as ever to continue the struggle. A major Russian salient penetrated the German front in the area around Kursk, and in July 1943 sixty-four divisions attacked in 'Operation Citadel'. However, the cannon-fire of the Red Army's superb tanks, dug hull deep into the ground, smashed into the Panthers, Tigers and Ferdinands as they advanced, and made the Germans break off the crucial offensive after a week in which they lost 2,500 tanks. The failure of Citadel meant that Hitler's Russian front was untenable. By the end of 1943 it had been driven back nearly 250 miles, the Russians recapturing such keypoints as Smolensk, Bryansk, Kiev and Kharkov, isolating German and Romanian troops in the Crimea. During the winter of 1943-4 the Red Army at last relieved Leningrad, besides regaining Odessa and the Crimea.

Like the Emperor, the Führer had other fronts, minor no doubt but none the less costly. The most important of these was the Battle of the Atlantic (for which there is no Napoleonic equivalent), a sustained and very nearly successful attempt by German submarines to starve Britain into submission by preventing supplies from reaching her. While the Führer had no control over the actual fighting, he was able to dictate strategy, emphasizing in Führer Directive No. 23 of February 1941 that sinking merchantmen was more important than attacking enemy warships, and the continuous use of minefields just as effective as torpedoing – 'By reducing the available enemy tonnage not only will the blockade, which is decisive to the war, be intensified, but enemy operations in Europe or Africa will be impeded.' The British were unable to master the U-boat menace until the spring of 1943 and then only with American help.

On land the Italians presented Hitler with two more fronts, first by involving him in North Africa and then Italy himself – changing sides when the Allies invaded their country. A Führer Directive of January 1941 decreed that Germany must go to the aid of the Italians 'for reasons strategic, political and psychological', Lieutenant-General Erwin Rommel arriving in Libya the following month with a detachment of what was later to be known as the 'Afrika Korps'. He went into action the day he landed. Although outnumbered and always with far fewer tanks (sometimes camouflaged *Volkswagens* took their place), his combined German and Italian force routed the British time and again, driving them out of Libya. In June 1943 he captured the stronghold of Tobruk, whose importance was as much psychological as strategic, and Hitler promoted him to Field Marshal. He prepared to invade Egypt, his ultimate objective being the Suez Canal. The Abwehr (or German counter-intelligence) was full of ingenious schemes, such as enlisting the Touareg tribes of the Sahara to fight against the British.

However, the Führer was not prepared – or could not afford – to let North Africa become a major front. He promised to send large reinforcements, but these never arrived. Had they come, in Rommel's opinion, 'We would have been strong enough to destroy the British in Egypt in the spring of 1942, and could have advanced into Iraq and cut the Russians off from Basra.' Nor would the Führer, despite Jodl's warnings, go to the expense of capturing Malta, so that British submarines stationed there were able to ensure the Afrika Korps was starved of supplies. Any hope of taking Egypt and the Suez Canal ended at El Alamein in the autumn of 1942 when Montgomery employed his enormous superiority in men, armour and aircraft to block, decimate and then pursue the Germans.

Unquestionably there was something of the Napoleonic marshal about Erwin Rommel, a resemblance which was not confined to his gifts as a soldier. The Führer's impact on him was very similar to that of the Emperor on many of his own commanders – especially those of humble origin like the Desert Fox. In all too many newsreels he can be seen fawning on Hitler, an impression confirmed by the diaries of Britain's 'favourite German soldier of World War II'. (Americans do not seem to have one.) Thanks to Dr Goebbels, who considered him 'an exemplary character', after taking Tobruk Rommel became a household name throughout Germany. The Führer approved highly of this hero-worship of a Nazi paladin. Napoleon would never have allowed such a thing, since he was invariably jealous of his commanders.

Rommel's success persuaded Hitler that North Africa could be held, an illusion strengthened by the rout of the Americans at the

Kasserine Pass in February 1943, after the Anglo-American invasion of Tunisia. Rommel left Africa in March on sick leave but could not have averted the defeat and surrender of the Afrika Korps in May. The Führer had lost 240,000 veterans who might have been of the utmost value to him elsewhere.

The invasion of Italy by the British and Americans during the second half of 1943 resulted in the removal of Mussolini by King Victor Emmanuel and the Fascist Grand Council. The coup shows the shrewdness of both Napoleon and Hitler in refusing to bring back monarchies which might dismiss them. Although the Italians had gone over to the other side, the skill of Field Marshal Kesselring – a far greater commander than Rommel, in some ways a twentieth-century German Wellington – in exploiting the Italian terrain, barred by mountain ridges and rivers, building the lines of Torres Vedras over and over again, long deprived the Allies of Italy.

The importance of the Balkans to the Führer is much too easily forgotten. He was always fearful that the Allies might launch an attack there, to take the pressure off the Russians, once they had overcome the Afrika Korps. Indeed, Winston Churchill had wanted the invasion of the 'soft underbelly of Europe' to take place in Yugoslavia rather than in Italy. Yugoslav partisans had been fighting the Germans since 1941, holding down numerous divisions. Admittedly, the occupation had the support of the Croats and the Ustaša fascists, together with that of many officers of the old Austro-Hungarian army who were only too ready to avenge themselves on the Serbs for the humiliations of 1918 – it could also rely on the Royal Bulgarian Air Force and the Albanian SS Skanderbeg Division. But the wild mountains and dense forests were ideal for guerrilla warfare, even crack Alpine troops finding it impossible to dislodge the partisans. Hitler dared not withdraw from territory so near Italy and the Romanian oilfields. As in Russia, he recognized that partisans could be as dangerous as regular troops.

Hungary was another potential Achilles heel. The Magyar nobles who ruled it had little natural sympathy for Herr Hitler, even if they were still more antipathetic to Bolshevism. The Führer disliked and distrusted them instinctively, resenting the courtly, old-fashioned German in which the Regent Admiral Horthy wrote to him. He cannot have forgotten how in 1941 Horthy's prime minister, Count Teleki, had shot himself in protest when his country was forced to join in the invasion of Yugoslavia. Hitler, moreover, was almost as uneasy about the Carpathian mountains, absolute control of which was essential for any successful defence of the Balkans. In the spring of 1944 he occupied the entire country.

In the later stages of their careers Napoleon and the Führer over-extended their troops on a truly massive scale, at a time when they were about to need every man they could muster. Perhaps inevitably, each man had entered upon an irrational and impossible grand strategy. Otherwise they might well have succeeded. Years of conflict had bled them white, sapping their armies' spirit, while each had grown too overweeningly arrogant, too far removed from reality, to function properly. They were now without flexibility, political or diplomatic.

Hitler became so stretched between Africa and Russia that these two original points of aim turned into the horns of a dilemma, and the strain precipitated his collapse in a way very similar to Napoleon's.

Sir Basil Liddell Hart, Strategy

Clausewitz would have approved the efforts of Hitler in the early years to use his armed forces as instruments of policy, but would have noted how the unlimited nature of his objectives made the war a total one far beyond his capacity to wage.

Sir Michael Howard, 'The Influence of Clausewitz'

10

The Wars of the Nations – 1813 and 1944

In the end Emperor and Führer found themselves confronted by coalitions whose strength was far greater than their own. Nevertheless, they prolonged the conflict until the very last, and there were moments when its outcome was far from certain. In 1813, faced by Russia, Prussia, Austria and Sweden on one front, by the British in Spain on the other, Napoleon had a fair chance of defeating the first and containing the second; even his opponents feared he might still be too strong, despite the débâcle in Russia. As it was, after his defeat in Germany he could have secured terms which would have left him much of his empire.

He was fighting for his empire, his dream of a European monarchy, although he had united most of Europe against him. Hitler too fought for his empire, his hegemony, posing as the continent's champion against 'Bolshevism'. If the Emperor had withdrawn behind France's 'natural frontiers' (the Rhine, the Alps and the Pyrenees) during the first months of 1813, before his enemies had had time to mobilize, they would surely have fallen out, Russia, Prussia and Austria squabbling for spoils in Eastern Europe and in Germany. Despite the Allies' demand for unconditional surrender in January 1943, if Hitler had withdrawn to the

1941 frontier in Poland, Stalin might well have come to an agreement with him, concentrating on gains in the Middle East. Yet neither Napoleon nor the Führer dared risk such blows to their prestige. Both knew that their subjects were longing for peace, and feared that if they got it they might demand political freedoms. Neither would contemplate any diminution of their overblown territory.

Where Hitler's situation differed was in its relation to America. Although the United States went to war with Britain in 1812, over interference with its merchant shipping, most North Americans detested the Emperor. However, they were too few, too poor and too far away. It was very different during the 1940s. As Bismarck had foretold, the decisive factor of the twentieth century was that Americans spoke English, even if many were anxious to avoid involvement in what they saw as purely European conflicts. In the event it was not they who declared war on the Führer but he on them. He did so from what may be described as quixotic loyalty to his Japanese ally. It was an infinitely worse miscalculation than his invasion of Russia, and ensured his defeat; otherwise he could undoubtedly have contained Britain and conquered the Soviet Union. Yet he was far from beaten, until a much later stage, even when the Anglo-American forces landed in Festung Europa on D Day 1944. With better luck he might easily have repulsed them all along the beaches, as indeed his troops did at Omaha Beach; only when the Allies broke out of their bridgeheads was disaster inevitable. Like Napoleon, he would never contemplate an ending to the war. Admittedly, from January 1943 the Allies agreed on demanding nothing less than unconditional surrender.

Napoleon always gambled on knocking his enemy out in a swift offensive. Clausewitz concluded: 'The political goal is the *end*, and warfare is a means leading to it.' However, by 1944, if not earlier, the Führer parted company over this with Napoleon, although he remained a gambler. Knowing that the ultimate conflict was lost, yet refusing to yield, Hitler had ceased to be a Clausewitzian, even if he continued to read him for tactical inspiration. He veered towards Clausewitz's most savage critic, General Erich von Ludendorff, who during 1916-18 had dominated the German Supreme Command. The General had abandoned Clausewitz's belief in a political aim, convinced that war was an end in itself – the 'expression of the nation's will to live'. This became Hitler's conviction too.

♔
N

In December 1812 an officer arrived at General Yorck von Wartenberg's headquarters in East Prussia. He brought a personal letter from the Russian chief of staff, showing that his troops were already moving to cut the Prussians off from the French. On recognizing the officer, the General shouted 'Keep away!' It was Major von Clausewitz. However, after he had read the letter – and after some persuasive words from his visitor – Yorck agreed to take his regiments over to the Russians. Prussia was technically still in alliance with the French but this Yorck decided to do 'even if it costs me my head!' Three months later the Prussian King and the Tsar met on the frontier, burst into tears and fell on one another's necks. On 28 March 1813 Frederick William III declared war on France, but instead of burning Berlin 'at the least insult' as ordered by his stepfather, Eugène de Beauharnais withdrew his troops behind the Elbe.

Napoleon's defeat in Russia and the destruction of the Grande Armée had dealt a blow as much moral as physical. He could be beaten! Nowhere did this realization dawn more intoxicatingly than

among the Germans, who for years had dreamt of ridding themselves of the bloodsucking French, with their billeting, confiscation,
conscription and firing-squads. From Russia, General Wittgenstein
sent a message addressed to every German, that there would be no
more class distinctions in a patriotic war against the invaders.
'Germans, we are opening up to you the ranks of the Prussian
army, where you will find labourers' sons fighting side by side with
princes' sons – any difference in class is obliterated by the words
"King, Liberty, Honour and Country".' It was almost the language of the French Revolution in reverse. All over Germany
nationalism burst into flame, patriotic songs thundering forth and
French soldiers being murdered, while every night guerrilla bands
went raiding. French officials began to slip away from Cassel with
what loot they could cram into their carriages.

Prussia and Russia started to mobilize in the spring. That underestimated soldier-politician Bernadotte saw that the time had come
for destroying his old rival. Sweden, the 'Baltic Prussia', still
produced excellent soldiers, and he landed 35,000 of them at Stralsund to march through Mecklenburg and join the Allies. Meanwhile
Wellington continued his remorseless advance across Spain towards
the Pyrenees.

However, the Emperor was far from defeated. Despite his losses in
Russia, he assembled a new army far more quickly than his opponents were able to mobilize – half the Russians were still on the other
side of the Vistula, while the Prussians had not yet been able to call
on their full strength. On paper it looked formidable enough; a field
army of 150,000 men and 372 cannon, with another 75,000 men
and 85 guns for garrisons. Yet he had cashed what has been described as his 'blank cheque on manpower'. His troops were no
longer veterans and not even adults, most of them being fifteen-
year-olds. His cavalry was pitifully inadequate, a mere 8,000
sabres mounted on third-rate hacks, in consequence of the loss of

horses in Russia.

Metternich was not so sure that Napoleon was finished, and was predisposed to favour his survival because of the dynastic alliance which made him the Austrian Emperor's son-in-law. In any case, the Austrian Chancellor was nervous about Prussia's ambition, the new German nationalism and 'rabble-rousing', fearful that Russian intervention in Europe might upset the balance of power. He was even prepared to guarantee the Confederation of the Rhine (including Bonaparte-ruled Westphalia), but France would have to give Warsaw, Lombardy and Illyria to Austria, and withdraw from the Rhein-Bund.

The Emperor was ready by the end of April 1813, having assembled his troops at Mainz. As always, his overall plan was to strike as soon as possible; he would aim for Danzig, crossing the Elbe and seizing control of the bridges over the Lower Vistula, in order to cut communications between Russia and Prussia. He hoped to knock them out before Austria could intervene. He took into account neither the poor quality of his troops nor his deficiency in cavalry, which would deprive him of essential information about enemy troop movements – he could no longer send a huge screen of light horse in front of him, spying out the land and concealing his own manoeuvres, as in former years.

Moving with his habitual speed, he crossed the Saale and marched east into Saxony, where the Allies had occupied King Frederick Augustus's capital of Dresden. On 1-2 May a third of his grape and canister 'shells' proved defective and yet he mauled Wittgenstein and Blücher so severely at Lützen that they retreated over the Elbe. (Major von Clausewitz was wounded behind the ear.) Yet the enemy had given as good as they got, inflicting no less casualties on the French, and escaping without losing a single prisoner or gun. On 6 May he entered Dresden, reinstating Frederick Augustus. Three weeks later at Bautzen he again defeated the

Allies, though he lost 15,000 men compared to the Allies' 10,000. Had Ney carried out his orders properly the enemy would have been annihilated. The Emperor muttered that his 'star' was setting. In particular he had been unpleasantly surprised by the stubborn ferocity with which the Prussians fought, remarking, 'The animals seem to have learnt something.' They withdrew from the battle as though from the parade ground. Nevertheless, he had no enemies left west of the Elbe.

The Free City of Hamburg had been so enthusiastic and unwise as to leave the Confederation of the Rhine, proclaiming its hostility to the Emperor. Davout occupied it, appropriating the entire funds of the Bank of Hamburg, demolishing suburban houses to build earth-works. The atrocities committed by the grim Marshal's troops were so vicious that the Hamburgers were still avenging them in 1870.

On 4 June Napoleon signed an armistice at Pläswitz for two months, the worst misjudgment of his entire career. He agreed to it because he was expecting more troops from Italy – above all more cavalry. 65,000 infantry arrived but only 2,000 sabres. Had he pursued Wittgenstein and Blücher into Bohemia he would almost certainly have routed them, destroying the coalition. As it was the Allies were able to mobilize more men of their own and wait for Austria.

In Clausewitz's view the Emperor was wrong in believing he could bluff Bernadotte and Blücher into staying on the defensive by placing shadow divisions opposite them and playing on their caution. In particular he failed to take into account Prussian hatred of the French.

Metternich stated his price at the Marcolini Palace in Dresden on 26 June, during a meeting which lasted several hours. Almost at once Napoleon, scowling, told him, 'So you want war. Good. You shall have it!' He continued that but for the possibility of Austrian intervention it would have been only too easy for him to make peace with Russia and Prussia. The Austrian chancellor reminded him again and again that everyone wanted peace, especially the French army. The Emperor insisted furiously, 'I will die before I give up a single inch of territory! Sovereigns born on their thrones can let themselves be defeated twenty times, and will always keep their crowns. I can't do that because I'm self-made.' A relentless Metternich pointed out to him that the French troops were mere children, that when they were dead there would be no one else left to conscript. The Emperor boasted, 'Someone like me doesn't care if he loses a million men', that if he was beaten, then 'I'm going to bury the world in my ruin!' (In reality he might have survived on the French throne had he given up the *Grand Empire* but he would certainly have lost his absolute power; when forced to grant a Constitution during the Hundred Days he grumbled that he would never have come back had he foreseen such a humiliation.) The Austrian Chancellor told him to open the windows so that everyone might hear him. He retorted that out of 300,000 men who had died in Russia only 30,000 had been French and the rest had been Poles or Germans. At this his guest – a Rhinelander – reminded Napoleon that he was a German too. The discussion was often extremely unpleasant, the Emperor asking Metternich how much Britain had paid him. The latter left, saying, 'You are doomed!' Nevertheless Napoleon sent an envoy to Prague to explore the possiblity of peace, even if he had no intention of signing one.

Despite his defiance, he was worried. After Bautzen he had told Marmont, 'The game is going wrong.' His uneasiness was shared by his staff. Metternich had noticed their anxiety during the meeting at the Marcolini Palace:

I find it difficult to convey adequately the painfully anxious look on the faces of the courtiers or on those of the gold braided generals assembled in the Emperor's apartments. The Prince of Neufchâtel

[Berthier, Chief of Staff] whispered to me, 'Don't forget that Europe needs peace, France especially – that's all she wants.

Murat was so concerned that he was negotiating secretly with the Austrians to save his Kingdom of Naples. Yet none of the Marshals contemplated a coup d'état. All owed their entire careers and positions to Napoleon.

At Reichenbach on the day after the meeting Austria reached a secret agreement with Russia, Prussia, Sweden and Britain to declare war on France if she refused to make peace. In July the Allies held a council of war at Schloss Trachenberg in Silesia to discuss the strategy and tactics they should adopt when hostilities reopened. Bernadotte and a Swedish general, Count Lowenhjelm, produced an inspired solution for dealing with the Emperor, based on the former's experience of Napoleon's methods in the days when he had served under him. It was to advance on the French army in a wide semicircle, attacking his flanks and any exposed corps, but to withdraw from any sector where the Emperor commanded in person. In the days before radio, when tactical response depended on what cavalry scouts could report, this would make it impossible for him to secure the decisive combat with which he had won all his victories.

The armistice ended on 10 August, Austria declaring war the following day. (News of the total defeat of the French in Spain and the knowledge that they could no longer switch troops from that front had decided Metternich to risk war.) The Allies' new strategy and tactics worked up to a point, though according to Clausewitz – who was there, on Blücher's staff – they were badly positioned and operating on too wide a front. The Emperor caught the Austrians under Schwarzenberg just outside Dresden on 26-28 August, driving back 220,000 men with 120,000 and inflicting nearly 40,000 casualties. A pursuit in the old style would have destroyed the Allies, but on the evening of the 28th Napoleon was stricken by food-poisoning and had to take to his bed in Dresden. Here he was informed that General Vandamme, pursuing too eagerly, had been defeated and taken prisoner at Kulm with 8,000 men, that General Macdonald had been routed by Blücher on the river Katzbach with the loss of 18,000 more. Bad news flooded into the sick man's room. Oudinot, advancing to stop Bernadotte from joining Blücher, was badly beaten by him at Grossbeeren, near Berlin. Ney then tried to block the Swedes, but was defeated at Dennewitz, losing a further 20,000 troops.

When the Emperor rose from his bed at the beginning of September the situation grew still worse. All the Allied armies succeeded in linking up, some 350,000 men. Bavaria changed sides, and its troops under General Wrede – who had been guarding Napoleon's rear – now threatened his retreat. The dwindling French army was starving and disease-ridden; its young soldiers could not take the pace, even if they could fight bravely enough. The Emperor abandoned Dresden in early October, realizing that he could no longer hold the river Elbe, and withdrawing to Leipzig, which was the key to North Germany. Here with 190,000 hungry men he awaited a vastly superior enemy; not only was he outnumbered but he had fewer cannon. A general engagement (the Germans would later name it 'The Battle of the Nations') commenced on 16 October outside Leipzig, on low, flat ground criss-crossed by streams and gardens, which offered no tactical advantage. During the first day the Allies launched six concentric attacks, the opposing armies bludgeoning each other mercilessly, mass colliding with mass. The French could make no impression on the enemy. Whether standing their ground or charging the Prussians fought with unrelenting ferocity; Clausewitz writes proudly, 'At Leipzig Blücher alone won the victory.' There was a lull on the second day, one of pouring rain during which Napoleon was uncharacteristically inactive. The French were down to 15,000 rounds (enough for only two hours), while ammunition and reinforcements were reaching the enemy all the time. The battle recommenced on the third day and the fighting was even more ferocious than on the first, beneath a relentless deluge. The Saxons, 3,000 strong, went over to the Allies, turning their 60 guns on the French. The Emperor's troops suffered such heavy casualties that when evening came he admitted that he had lost, ordering a general retreat. Although many of his men, including the badly wounded Prince Poniatowski, were drowned trying to swim the river Elster (where the single pontoon bridge had been prematurely demolished by panic-stricken sappers), he managed to fight his way back to France with a rabble of 70,000 broken men and boys. The Allies had inflicted 40,000 casualties on the battlefield, while taking another 20,000 Frenchmen prisoner. They had lost more men killed and wounded, but they could afford to replace them. Moreover, this was the first great battle in which Napoleon had received a total defeat.

He was in Paris again by 9 November. The *Grand Empire* no longer existed. The Confederation of the Rhine, including the Kingdom of Westphalia, had vanished like smoke; all that remained of the French domination were isolated garrisons whose troops were desperately needed in France. Switzerland, Holland and Northern Italy were rising in revolt, while Wellington was threatening France's southern frontier. The country faced invasion on all sides, although the roads of the period postponed serious campaigning during the winter weather. Nevertheless, as Sir Walter Scott wrote percipiently on 10 December, 'Bonaparte is that desperate gambler who will not rise while he has a stake left.'

As usual, Clausewitz's interpretation may be taken to imply that the Emperor had had a good chance of winning. He considers that at Dresden the Allied armies were only saved from the consequences of fighting on several fronts – in their frenzied efforts to envelop Napoleon – by General Vandamme's defeat on the Katzbach which made the Emperor decide to stay in Dresden. Clausewitz also believes that if the Emperor's onslaught on the first day at Dresden had succeeded the Allies would have been cut in two – their superiority in numbers was irrelevant. He knew what he was talking about, since he had been present, with Blücher's staff (as a liaison officer for the Russians). These pages in *Vom Kriege* would have made comforting reading for the Führer in 1944.

Both he and the Emperor displayed small understanding of their opponents, whether as races or individuals. Metternich was astounded by Napoleon's extraordinary ideas about the British, and ignorance of their institutions. The Emperor raged against the 'oligarchy' who ruled Britain, regarding them as doomed to extinction like the patricians of Venice. The British were 'a nation of shopkeepers', the common people 'crude and rough'. He was infuriated by the insulting articles in the London newspapers which were read out to him by his secretaries. Yet he none the less dreamt wistfully at times of peace with Britain, even though he knew it was impossible. As has been seen, he made half-hearted overtures in Spain in 1812. He sighed how matters might have been very different 'but for the death of Mr Fox'. He was also aware that a few Whigs had considerable sympathy for him, unable to appreciate that much of this sympathy came from a desire to irritate the Tory government. In 1815 he was to hope – vainly – that the Prince Regent would offer him a refuge. At no time did he show any insight whatever into the British character.

Like the Emperor, Hitler continued to insist to the end that he had no real quarrel with Britain. He also believed that he had friends there. Among these he numbered Sir Oswald Mosley and his Black

Shirts – 'some belonging to the best families' – and the aged Lloyd-George, 'a man of tremendous vision' who had told him that Britain had 'no alternative but to live on terms of friendship with Germany'. He entertained naïve hopes of the Duke of Windsor. 'If he had stayed everything would have been different. His abdication was a severe loss to us.' He was amazed that the British should have toppled 'so fine a pillar of strength'. (Goebbels lamented to Wilfred von Oven in 1944 that 'Were Edward Windsor on the throne today, supposing that under his rule it would ever have come to this war, he would long ago have undertaken the decisive move and our two peoples would be fighting side by side against the Bolshevik world enemy instead of tearing one another apart . . . Edward would not have allowed this ghastly spectacle to become reality.') The Führer could not grasp the limited political role of the monarchy in Britain and did not understand the Duke.

Just as Napoleon had hated Pitt, Hitler detested Churchill, an 'undisciplined swine who is drunk eight hours of every twenty-four', heaping insults on him. He was still more contemptuous of Roosevelt, 'a sick brain', sneering at the President's boast that he had 'noble Jewish blood' in his veins.' (He added, 'The completely negroid appearance of his wife is also a clear indication that she, too, is a half-caste.') Nevertheless, by 1943 Roosevelt had quadrupled the American army to nearly seven million men and American factories were producing 50,000 planes and 25,000 tanks a year, figures which were to increase with whirlwind rapidity.

The Emperor, perhaps not unnaturally, came to dislike the Tsar, whom he dismissed as false and untrustworthy. He never appreciated Alexander's difficulties, the precarious position of a hereditary autocrat. And he despised and feared the Russian people. After his victory at Lützen in May 1813 he was to tell his army (no doubt with his German and Polish troops very much in mind), 'We are going to throw those Tartars back into their own ghastly country, from which they must never emerge again. They must keep to their frozen steppes, the home of barbarianism and corruption, where man is reduced to the level of an animal.' On St Helena he expressed his dread that 'the cossacks will one day rule Europe.'

The Führer had an even lower opinion of Russians. 'The Slavs are a race of born slaves who feel the need of a master', he pronounced on many occasions. If other races had not imported the rudiments of organization, 'the Russians would still be living like rabbits'. On the other hand, he genuinely admired their leader, who was probably the sole world leader whom he did not underestimate. Stalin 'must command our unconditional respect. In his own way he is a hell of a fellow', Hitler told his private circle. He also called him 'a beast but a beast on the grand scale', and more than once described him as a genius. Speer sometimes suspected that the Führer felt sympathy and even solidarity for Stalin's régime, regarding him as 'a kind of colleague'. (A joke current in Berlin during the war went 'What's the difference between Nazi Germany and Socialist Russia? It's colder in Soviet Russia.')

German intelligence had long known that the Allies were planning to invade France but had not been able to discover when or where. With his uncanny intuition, the Führer guessed that the landing would be in Normandy. However, most of his generals were convinced it would be in the Pas de Calais. Despite his better judgment, he compromised, stationing his troops well back from the coast so that they could be moved swiftly to either sector. He had 77 divisions in France, a high proportion armoured, which he estimated should be twice as many men as the forces which the Allies could hope to ship across the Channel; he ignored the fact that these divisions were half-strength, and often composed of poor-quality troops. He chose two of his most trusted commanders to cope with whatever crisis might arise, Field Marshals von Rundstedt and Rommel. Even if the 'Atlantic Wall' was inadequate, there seemed to be an excellent chance of panzers speedily driving any Allied invasion back into the sea. Rundstedt wanted to evacuate France south of the Loire and bring all German troops there up to the north-west, so that if necessary he could launch a massive counter-attack. Hitler would not listen to such defeatist talk, since Vichy France was an essential part of his European empire. Nor would he let Rundstedt move a single armoured division without his express permission. As it was, Rundstedt never foresaw the enormous air superiority of the Allies. Like the Führer, Rommel was inclined to expect an attack on Normandy, though he thought it would be limited to an area around the port of Cherbourg to facilitate troop landing; he did not guess at the existence of the newly invented 'Mulberries', artificial harbours which could be moored at any point along the coast. He was confident that he could rout any invasion on the very first day.

In the event, when the invasion came on D-Day (6 June 1944) Rundstedt was not informed for many hours, while Rommel was absent visiting Hitler at Berchtesgaden. Most of the panzer divisions were the other side of the Seine. Nevertheless, troops on the spot fought magnificently, if without much co-ordination, and the Allies had great difficulty in pushing a bridgehead sufficiently far inland – a bridgehead strong enough to contain depots with food and ammunition which were out of range of German guns. They succeeded because the defenders had divided their forces to deal with both Normandy and Calais. Within a week they had built a bridgehead sixty miles wide and twelve deep. After another six weeks of savage fighting the German front collapsed, trapping 45,000 troops in the Falaise pocket. By the time Paris fell on 24 August German losses in France stood at 400,000. On 1 July, in response to Field Marshal Keitel's agonized question, 'What are we going to do?

What are we going to do?' Rundstedt had replied simply, 'Make peace, you fools. What else can you do?' He was removed from his post the following day. Horrified by the casualty reports, Rommel too had warned Hitler – 'the unequal struggle is drawing to its end!' Rommel himself was badly wounded in an attack by British aircraft on 17 July, retiring to a convalescence from which he never returned. (He was ordered to commit suicide for his suspected complicity in the July plot.)

Everywhere there was bad news, and it was now obvious to all but the most uninformed that Germany had lost the war. The Russians were advancing inexorably, in Italy Kesselring was steadily giving ground despite a brilliant campaign, and in the Pacific the Americans were moving ever closer to Japan. At last the muttering among certain circles in the Wehrmacht, among the nobility and among those with strong religious convictions was to receive concrete expression. Such opposition, which had existed in the army from 1938, had been ignored at first by the Führer because he was confident that he had established complete domination over the generals. Even though the Gestapo had known of potentially serious disaffection since as early as 1943, Hitler had not given it any attention.

The Führer failed to take into account the growing fear of the German people at the retribution in store for them. In his haunting poem of 1943, *Abendländische Elegie*, Hans Carossa voiced the terror they were beginning to feel. *'Wird Abend über uns, o Abendland?'* – 'what strange evening hangs over us, o western land? . . . people stand around sick at heart amid the turmoil.' (Spengler's prophecies of the fate of the *Abendland* now seemed only too convincing.) Admittedly the poet ended on a note of hope – 'but from the ruins a day of blessings will emerge in which we shall no longer have to hide from the light'. However, some Germans were not prepared to wait for a day of blessings to emerge from the ruins.

On 20 July Colonel Claus Schenk von Stauffenberg, a Catholic nobleman from Württemberg with only one eye, one arm and two fingers, placed a briefcase containing a small time-bomb beneath Hitler's conference table at Rastenberg in East Prussia. It exploded, but after the case had been moved. Under the impression that the Führer had been killed, Stauffenberg flew to Berlin to direct a coup which would, so it was hoped, install a conservative government under a regency for the Hohenzollerns, and that this would make peace with the Allies (on ridiculously over-optimistic terms). However, the coup was badly organized, and although Hitler suffered burns and a burst eardrum – he never regained his sense of balance – he survived. Despite some initial confusion in the capital, he quickly reasserted his authority.

The devilish nature of a tyrant was soon much in evidence. He had thousands of suspects arrested, especially among the nobility he so detested, and tried before 'People's Courts.' (This hatred and such names were the last vestiges of the Nazis' original socialism.) Many were condemned to death, to be hanged from meat-hooks with piano-wire. The Führer demanded, 'I want them strung up like slaughtered meat.' Their last moments were filmed so that he could watch them. Henceforward he would never again trust any non-Nazi officer, save for Rundstedt and one or two others, while his hatred of the German and Austrian nobility verged on mania. There was no longer any possibility of the Wehrmacht's generals staging a coup of the type which overthrew Napoleon at Fontainebleau in 1814. Hitler had become in truth 'the fate of Germany'.

Miraculously, the German front in the West was re-established. Immediately after the attempted coup of 20 July a message of loyalty had reached the Führer from one of his favourite soldiers. This was the 53-year-old Field Marshal Walter Model, the youngest to hold the rank in the Wehrmacht. A man of lower middle class origins and devoutly Nazi convictions, he had made his name on the Russian front as a ruthless master of defence who in a crisis could find troops from nowhere and then work miracles. He took over command in the West from Field Marshal von Kluge (who had committed suicide in despair) on 16 August 1944. Within a very few weeks he turned the German rout into as slow a retreat as was possible, taking advantage of the Allies' over-extended and often chaotic supply lines, and reducing the Allied offensive to one of attrition.

The Allies reached the German frontier on 12 September. The British tanks roared unexpectedly into Antwerp, whose port soon became a most valuable source of supplies for the Allies. But Model had strengthened German defences all along the front. A British attempt to get behind it, by dropping paratroops on Arnhem in southern Holland, ended in tragic failure at the end of the month. The Allies were further delayed by having to mop up pockets of German troops who fought with grim determination, while a general assault by all the Allied armies in November rapidly ground to a halt. The line of the Rhine remained unbroken, thanks to the efforts of Field Marshal Model.

Meanwhile in the East the situation was going from bad to worse. Contrary to expectations, the Russians had continued campaigning – and advancing – throughout the winter of 1943-4 and into the following spring. By May 1944 they had driven the Germans out of the Soviet Union. Their new summer offensive began a week after D-Day, and they were soon on the Vistula, threatening East Prussia. In August Finland sued for peace. There were coups d'état in Bulgaria and Romania, both going over to the side of the Soviet Union. Poland was invaded and Warsaw rose while Greece and Yugoslavia had to be evacuated. Many good troops were cut off in the Baltic states, no less than 26 desperately needed divisions, where they were to remain until the end of the war. The saviour of the Russian front, another convinced Nazi from the same lower middle class background as Model and a great favourite of Hitler, was Colonel-General Felix Schöner. He worked wonders in stabilizing a front which ran from the Gulf of Finland to East Prussia. He had much the same harsh ruthlessness and brutal drive as Model, sending many soldiers before the firing squad. Not only did he possess abundant energy and determination, but as one of the out-and-out Nazi generals he was a superb tool for the Führer, carrying out his orders to the letter.

Even so, by the end of 1944 Hitler still retained control of not only a large area of the Baltic States but of the entire heartland of *Mittel-Europa.* Western Poland, the Czech territories, Hungary and northern Yugoslavia all remained under his control.

But like Napoleon the Führer simply did not have enough troops left to defend his territories. The production of munitions was in chaos, although Speer worked miracles. If the Luftwaffe still received excellent new aircraft, there was rarely enough petrol to fly them. German cities were systematically flattened by the British and American air forces. Railways were disrupted, factories and oil plants obliterated – by September 1944 the latter's production had dropped to 10,000 tons of aviation spirit a month when the Luftwaffe needed 160,000. Meanwhile thousands of civilians died every night beneath an unceasing hail of bombs. Nevertheless, Hitler's will to win was unshaken, as was that of the German people as a whole – the bombing united them rather than cowed them, as it had the British during the Blitz of 1940. Above all, the Allies' policy of unconditional surrender made them go on fighting without any hope of victory.

Yet. according to Albert Speer, 'the more inexorably events moved towards catastrophe, the more inflexible he [Hitler] became, the more rigidly convinced that everything he decided on was right'. Speer also believed that the Führer was the only German leader who had no illusions about the Allies' insistence on

Germany's unconditional surrender. Jodl stated in May 1945 that it had been obvious to Hitler and to himself that 'victory could no longer be achieved' as early as the winter of 1941-2, when the German advance ground to a halt before the gates of Moscow. General Halder told Milton Schulman that in June 1942 he had acquired accurate information about the Russian armaments industry and the enormous pool of manpower on which the country could call. These were infinitely more formidable than the Germans had hitherto appreciated. Halder informed the Führer, no doubt with gloomy satisfaction, 'When I presented him with the figures of Russian tank production he went off the deep end. He was no longer a rational human being. I don't know whether he didn't want to understand or whether he didn't believe it. In any event, it was quite impossible to discuss such matters with him. He would foam at the mouth, threaten me with his fists and scream at the top of his lungs.' Admittedly, Hitler is known to have found the sour-faced Halder infuriating at the best of times, calling him 'a chronic know-all', and even during the triumphant campaign in France had subjected him to 'rages and screams'. Nevertheless, one suspects that he understood only too well, that Halder was merely confirming what he had already guessed. But he could not bring himself to deny his preordained role as the Wagnerian warlord who was going to lead his people to victory.

Despite their agreement with the West to accept nothing but unconditional surrender, during late 1943 the Russians had discreetly investigated the possibility of peace with Germany. In September a Russian diplomat approached German circles in Stockholm, and exploratory discussions took place. A possible agreement might have included German withdrawal from Russia to the frontier of June 1943, with such sweeteners as allowing the Russians to over-run Turkey and Persia. Stalin must have been seriously interested, since his agents would never have dared to act without approval and Ribbentrop was enthusiastic. The Führer would not consider it, to judge from a seemingly self-mocking remark to Ribbentrop: 'If I made an agreement with Russia to day, I would break it tomorrow. I just couldn't help it.' Perhaps this was a joke, in tune with Speer's anecdote about Ribbentrop's colleagues wished to present him with a jewelled casket containing copies of his treaties. They then realized that these treaties had nearly all been broken – Hitler's eyes 'filled with tears of laughter' when he heard the story. Yet we know that Goebbels was so anxious for peace with the Soviet Union that early in 1944 he presented him with a 40-page memorandum urging him to negotiate with Stalin. Hitler never read it, and refused to listen. He had already rejected Goebbels's advice in the autumn of 1943 to sound out Churchill, since 'we simply have to get out of a two-front war'.

The real reason why Napoleon would never even contemplate any form of peace is that he believed that surrendering territory would weaken his authority over his people, diminishing that absolute power which he loved above all else. He was a gambler on a gigantic scale. When he had lost his empire he still hoped to keep his country for himself, either by a single brilliant feat of arms or through some political miracle. The sufferings of his people, let alone those of conquered races, did not enter his mind.

Exactly the same considerations explain the Führer's behaviour in similar circumstances. He too was an absolutist, whose stakes were all or nothing, tortured by his obscene love of power. And he too lacked any compassion whatever for his fellow-men, to an even more terrible degree.

The bloody solution of the crisis, the effort for the destruction of the enemy's forces, is the first-born son of war.'

Clausewitz, Vom Kriege

When Etzel [Attila] sent his fiddlers to the Rhine, the news flew from land to land. By means of swift messengers he invited guests to his high tide. There many met their death.

Nibelungenlied

11

Red Ruin – 1814 and 1944-5

Gamblers almost invariably plunge when their luck is running out and both men were always prepared to risk everything on the throw of a dice rather than compromise. The fact that each was gambling with the fate of an entire nation was irrelevant. They had been brilliantly successful during the first half of their careers and neither could believe that fortune had deserted them; they would play the game out, until either they had broken the bank or were ruined beyond redemption. What was at stake was power, without which they did not consider life worth living.

At the beginning of 1814 Napoleon held only France and northern Italy. In public he admitted openly that he was ringed by foes – 'Wellington has invaded the south of France, the Russians threaten our northern frontier, and Prussians, Austrians and Bavarians are on our eastern.' The Allies offered him the 'natural frontiers' of France – the boundaries of the Alps, the Pyrenees and the Rhine if he would make peace. In practice this would mean evacuating northern Italy and an undertaking never to disturb Europe or go to war again. He refused these extraordinarily generous terms. He could not bring himself to part with the *Grand Empire*, to abandon his dream of hegemony over Europe. His former power had poisoned his reason beyond recovery.

Far from postponing their invasion until March or April, when the roads would be in better condition and their troops able to live off the countryside, the Allies began their invasion of northern France in December 1813. They mustered a joint army of nearly 400,000 men, with reserves at home of well over 400,000. And these figures did not take into account the army under Wellington which now numbered 160,000 British, German and Spanish troops. The Emperor had no choice but to leave southern France to cope with Wellington – his sole remaining hope lay in defeating the invaders in the north. His own forces amounted to slightly less than 120,000, of which the field army – with which he was going to have to fight for his very existence – was a bare 60,000. While there was a stiffening of veterans, most were boys even younger than the 'children' on whom Metternich had remarked, together with old soldiers in their fifties and sixties, some of them near-cripples from the Invalides. Napoleon had no illusions about their quality, telling the Senate that the boys were fit for nothing but hospitals.

The Legislative Body presented an address stating that France was suffering from destitution unparalleled in her entire history – 'commerce is destroyed, industry is dying'. Their master dismissed them, snarling, 'Is this the time to mull over past mistakes, when 200,000 Cossacks are crossing our frontier? It isn't a question of the individual's liberty or safety. What matters is the nation's independence!' Behind the scenes he admitted that France was finished. 'Rouse the nation? When the Revolution has destroyed the nobles and the priests, and when I myself have destroyed the Revolution?'

The 'home front' was in a disastrous state. For the first time his troops were living off the French countryside, requisitioning food and wine, transport and livestock and fodder. It did not add to the war's popularity. The Notables now regarded Napoleon as a dangerous liability, a view confirmed by the Allies' declaration in December 1813 that they were fighting the Emperor, not France. Probably the entire bourgeoisie had been unhappy with the régime since the vast increase in foreign commitments in 1808. Conscription was evaded more widely than ever, deserters being shot in batches every day. The *salons* seethed with disloyalty. Fouché and Talleyrand were already in touch with the Bourbons; Talleyrand commented, 'It's the beginning of the end!' Attempts to revive Revolutionary fervour – reintroducing the *Marseillaise*, long banned for its Jacobin associations – failed totally, even the Paris mob remaining unenthusiastic. There was strong resistance to swingeing new taxes. The Imperial treasury was nearly bankrupt, with an astronomical deficit. Only 10 million francs were left from the secret hoard of 75 million in gold which Napoleon kept in a vault beneath the Tuileries. (He had hoarded it out of pure greed; on St Helena he told General Bertrand, 'Money means everything.')

The capital grew terrified as refugees from the north flooded in, pushing what remained of their possessions in carts or clutching bundles. As usual the Emperor decided on an offensive campaign instead of going over to the defensive. He remarked to his chief of staff Berthier, 'I shall have to fight the campaign of Italy all over again.' His army was miserably inadequate, very different from that of 1797; unable to call on the 120,000 men cut off in German garrisons, he made do with adolescents who had never fired a gun before, hastily given an overcoat, a shako and a firearm; some of the latter were fowling pieces. Such boys were pitifully vulnerable, ignorant of what lay ahead – forced marches in the coldest winter in living memory across the flat plains of Champagne along roads ankle-deep in slush or mud, sleeping drenched by snow or rain beneath a freezing sky with no food, let alone shelter, to be found in the villages.

Despite such poor tools Napoleon savaged Blücher at St Dizier on 27 January 1814. Four days later, however, he was repulsed at La Rothière, being forced to fall back on Troyes. On 7 February the Allies delivered an ultimatum; this time he was no longer offered France's 'natural' boundaries but only the frontiers of 1789. When the Emperor's advisers suggested he should accept the terms he roared with rage, 'like a trapped lion', shouting that he would never give up the territory conquered by the Revolutionary armies, never leave France smaller than he had found her.

He possessed one valuable advantage over the invaders in knowing the ground over which the ensuing campaign would be fought, while he had much better maps. Blücher's 120,000 Prussians were dangerously extended in a long, thin column which reached from Châlons to La Ferté-sur-Jouarre. On 10 February he sliced through it at Champaubert, cutting Sacken off from Blücher, he then defeated Sacken on 11 February at Montmirail and on 13 February at Château-Thierry, driving him north in headlong retreat. The following day he hit Blücher so hard at Vauchamps that he almost severed his line of retreat, forcing the old warrior to take refuge inside Châlons. Marching his wretched young soldiers at an unheard-of pace, he intercepted Schwarzenberg's Austrians at Montereau, fifty miles south-east of Paris, striking with such ferocity on 16 February that he wiped out their rearguard. Another attack at Méry-sur-Seine sent the Austrians reeling back. Napoleon had won seven victories in eight days.

Understandably, he was elated, literally 'drunk with joy' after Champaubert, deluding himself that he would regain everything. 'The enemy are going to retreat over the Rhine much more quickly than they came and I shall be back on the Vistula,' he announced, to the horror of his generals. He had lost all sense of political reality.

The campaign was a bravura performance, even by Napoleonic standards of military genius. As he had promised, he had recovered all the mobility and flair for surprise which he had displayed in Italy in 1797. What makes it so astonishing is that for many years he had been showing signs of physical deterioration. Even during the Consulate the playwright Kotzebue had noticed that he was putting on weight, 'which does not suit a man like Bonaparte'. In 1808 the Duc de Broglie was shocked by the dramatic change in his appearance since those days: 'His torso was short and much thickened, his small legs fat, his face livid, his forehead balding and his profile like something on a Roman coin.' Nevertheless, his health seemed reasonably good, apart from occasional pains in the bladder (which the doctors attributed to the herpes he had contracted during the siege of Toulon). By 1811 he was stout to the point of being bloated, his complexion was yellow and his head was sunk on his shoulders. His obesity has been attributed to sharing Marie Louise's meals of many courses, while the other signs of weariness indicate that the burden of power was taking its toll. The Russian and German campaigns exhausted him still further; during the latter he seldom went to bed but slept in his carriage with his head tied in a handkerchief. The Imperial Post Master, the Comte de Lavalette, saw him on his return in November 1813 and thought him 'so downhearted and so worn out that it really frightened me'. Baron Fain confided in him that while Napoleon retired at eleven he always got up at three in the morning, working right through the day until he went to bed again at night. 'It can't go on', said Fain (who was his secretary). 'If it does, it will kill him.' How Napoleon summoned up the energy to fight the campaign of 1814 is a mystery.

Clearly he believed that he was going to win. Since he did not have enough troops for a knockout blow, his strategy was to disrupt the Allies' communications and prevent them from co-operating. Each time he had struck the enemy in the rear, and by skilfully concentrating his scanty forces had succeeded in routing opponents who outnumbered him by two or even three to one. Yet, as Clause-witz emphasizes, he underestimated 'old Blücher', who had been born in 1742 and whom he ridiculed still more than 'the Sepoy general' Wellington – 'he is just like a bull, glaring all around with rolling eyes and charging whenever he sees danger'. However, on St Helena Napoleon admitted grudgingly, 'The old ruffian always attacked me with the same fury and after the most terrible beatings would be on his feet again in a flash, ready for the fight.'

Throughout his career the Emperor had a tendency to underrate opponents, whether armies, statesmen or generals. The most obvious examples are his failure to appreciate the fighting qualities of Russian and British troops, the Machiavellianism of Metternich and the professionalism of Wellington. He was to lose in 1814 through not reckoning with the strategic sense of both Blücher and Schwarzenberg. In his opinion no enemy was worthy of him.

Blücher regrouped and advanced on Paris early in March. The Emperor attacked him so successfully that he took shelter behind the wall of Soissons. He emerged, to be beaten again at Craonne on 7 March, withdrawing to a strong position at Laon. Napoleon attacked him here on the following day, with 40,000 men against 100,000, this time launching a frontal assault, but failed to dislodge him, suffering casualties he could ill afford. Nevertheless, even if as he himself put it, the Young Guard – the one decent corps left to him – was 'melting away like snow', he drove Blücher back from Rheims on 13 March, and a week later fought an indecisive battle with Schwarzenberg at Arcis-sur-Aube. By now the boys whom he called his soldiers were collapsing from disease, hunger and sheer exhaustion to such an extent that he was down to 30,000 'men'; he had to find more troops or give up the struggle. As so often, he decided on a gamble. Learning that the Allies were marching on Paris, he decided not to meet them but to march east, reinforcing his army from local garrisons as he went, and cut their communications. He was confident the National Guard and the Parisian workers would fight for their city, that his brother Joseph was capable of directing its defence; at the worst Marshal Marmont had 8,000 infantry, 3,000 sabres and 60 cannon with which to delay them. Marmont reassured him, 'Sire, I can guarantee my army corps.' But Napoleon was unwise enough to send word of what he intended to Marie Louise in an uncoded note – 'I have decided to make for the Marne in order to drive the enemy back from Paris.' The note was intercepted by a Russian patrol, whereupon after an agitated debate the Allies decided to continue their drive on Paris. Marmont's attempt to stop them at La Ferté-Champenoise was easily brushed aside.

The Emperor had ordered that Paris must be defended to the last man, even if this meant that it would be reduced to rubble in the process.[29] It had no fortifications, not even street barricades, and Joseph Bonaparte was incapable of mobilizing the Parisians. There were 200 cannon standing idle in the Champs de Mars and a mere 60 on the heights of Montmartre. On 30 March Marmont signed an armistice to save the city from a general assault. Blücher and Schwarzenberg marched in the following day. It was the end.

On 9 March the Allies had signed a 'Grand Alliance', pledging themselves to fight on until they destroyed Napoleon Bonaparte and to reject any surrender other than unconditional. On 3 April the Senate, smoothly manipulated by Talleyrand, deposed the Emperor. Three days later it called upon Louis XVIII to ascend the throne of France.

As has been seen, as early as the spring of 1812 and even before the 'Campaign of Russia' Napoleon's senior officers had been very worried. There is no reason to disbelieve Metternich's testimony that by the summer of 1813 they were desperately anxious men. The last straw was their master's refusal to contemplate peace, with such remarks as 'Back on the Vistula.' When he hurried to Fontainebleau after the fall of Paris he might still conceivably have assembled a viable army from troops south of the Loire. But his marshals had had enough. We know very little of the officers' plot of 1814 apart from what Napoleon himself dictated on St Helena, yet one may at least guess that it had been brewing for some time. It is generally regarded as a spontaneous phenomenon, though it is more than likely that there was an original instigator – still unidentified.

The Emperor's version is that at Fontainebleau on 4 April, after taking a parade, Berthier told him the marshals wanted an audience. When they entered they were accompanied by the great officials of his Court, including Caulaincourt. One of the marshals then 'stammered' that everything was lost if he did not abdicate. 'The army is demoralized, exhausted and disorganized. Desertions are only too noticeable. We cannot consider returning to Paris. Any attempt to do so will shed blood uselessly.' What they did not say was that most junior officers were eager to go on fighting. The Emperor, who later claimed he did so to avoid civil war, wrote out his abdication. Even Marshals Berthier and Ney – 'Bravest of the Brave' – deserted him, although like everyone else they feared he might have them shot. He signed a further, unconditional, abdication on 11 April. The following day he tried to commit suicide with poison 'which I wore round my neck in a little silk bag' but agonizing pains brought on a nausea which made him vomit it up. On 20 April, after a theatrical farewell to the Imperial Guard he finally left Fontainebleau for the island of Elba (where the Allies had decided he must live). He told one of the guardsmen, 'I have abdicated but surrender nothing.'

One should not see any resemblance between the officers' plots of 1814 and 1944. Napoleon's relationship with his marshals was much more like that of Hitler with his party satraps than the Führer's relations with his generals. Wellington later suggested that the Emperor had been more 'in awe' of his marshals than was suspected, but this was simply not true. They owed everything to him, while in the last analysis he secretly despised them. This was Hitler's attitude to men like Goering and Himmler.

The story of 1814 was not a tale to amuse the Führer. 'I, perhaps better than anyone else, can well imagine the torments suffered by Napoleon,' he dictated to Bormann on 26 February 1945. He must have found *Vom Kriege* compulsive reading if he consulted the book during his own not unsimilar final crisis. In Clausewitz's view Napoleon was far from being beaten, at any rate in February 1814, despite the daunting odds against him and despite having to fight on French soil. (Wellington shared his opinion.) He thinks that his fatal mistake, after winning the battles at Champaubert, Montmirail and Vauchamps, was to switch his attentions from the Prussians to the Austrians:

> What would have been the result if, instead of turning from Blücher upon Schwarzenberg, he had tried another blow at Blücher, and pursued him to the Rhine? We are convinced that it would have completely changed the course of the campaign, and that the Allied army, instead of marching to Paris, would have retired behind the Rhine.

He attributes the Emperor's successes in 1814 against hugely superior numbers to a brilliant exploitation of the mistakes made by the Allies in dividing their forces. Clausewitz is quite certain that the fall of Paris was decisive, even if taking an enemy's capital does not win a war – as in the case of Moscow:

In 1814 by the capture of Bonaparte's capital the object of the war was attained. the political divisions which had their roots in Paris came into active operation, and an enormous split left the power of the Emperor to collapse of itself . . . through these causes the forces and defensive means of Bonaparte were suddenly very much diminished, the superiority of the Allies, therefore, just in the same measure increased, and any further resistance then became *impossible.*

As will be seen, the first passage may have inspired Hitler's last desperate Western offensive in the Ardennes, while the second may have influenced his decision to stay in Berlin.

Model, a 'dynamic genius' in Goebbels' eyes, had astounded the Allies by re-establishing Germany's western front. No doubt some of his success was due to carrying out the Führer's exhortations. On 16 September the latter ordered every able-bodied man to fight fanatically, warning his troops: 'There can no longer be any large-scale opposition on our part. All we can do is hold our positions and die.' Yet like Napoleon he was by nature incapable of remaining on the defensive. (Indeed, he had to go over to the offensive or the Reich would collapse sooner rather than later.) The Allies' new long-range fighter-bombers not only gave superiority in the air but by October had destroyed the last plants producing synthetic fuel; the scanty hoard which remained would soon be exhausted. Like the Emperor in March 1814, he decided to make one last throw, a final Western offensive, even if to mount it he had to borrow men and armour from the East – just as Napoleon had transferred the Young Guard from Spain. However, he let the troops facing the Russians keep their 88mm anti-aircraft guns (used as anti-tank weapons), weakening his new offensive's ability to deal with enemy aircraft. The tanks were given the lion's share of the fuel – there was very little to spare for the Luftwaffe. He chose the Ardennes, the scene of his triumph in 1940. The four defending

286

American divisions were under-strength and poorly supplied. He planned to attack along a 70-mile front, with a central *Schwerpunkt* of about 15 miles, his objective being Antwerp.

Although Field Marshal von Rundstedt, Commander in Chief West, thought it 'a nonsensical operation', the plan – drawn up by the OKW or Supreme Command on the Führer's instructions – was to be implemented by Field Marshal Model, by General of Panzer Troops Hasso von Manteuffel and by SS Colonel-General Sepp Dietrich. These were Hitler's chosen tools, all three prepared to implement his ideas. Yet privately they accepted Rundstedt's assessment – 'the available forces were too small'. Manteuffel told Liddell Hart, 'We were agreed in our objections to the plan', while Sepp Dietrich recalled ironically, 'All I had to do was to cross a river, capture Brussels, and then go on and take the port of Antwerp.' Even so, they were ready to try.

In contrast to their superiors, junior officers were full of confidence, elated by the prospect of attacking once again. The Führer strengthened their resolve by ordering any officer who doubted victory to hand over to a subordinate and fall in under his command. 'The war will decide whether the German people will continue to exist or perish', he warned them.

The second Ardennes offensive opened before dawn on 16 December, taking the Americans completely by surprise. They had settled into winter quarters, convinced that the Germans were by now incapable of mounting such an operation. Thick fog and mist prevented the Allies from exploiting their superiority in the air. At first the 300,000 Germans – some of them battle-hardened veterans of the Russian front – had dramatic success, disrupting the Americans' communications, cutting them off from their supplies. So alarmed were the latter that they called in Field Marshal Montgomery to take command of part of the front. However, after a week the Germans had failed to capture Bastogne, a vital communications centre, and Model saw that no further progress was going to be made; on Christmas Eve Rundstedt advised withdrawal. Hitler refused – this was his last throw. On Christmas Day the fog lifted, enabling Allied aircraft to decimate the panzers. German fuel ran out on 26 December, although some tanks came within a quarter of a mile of the American depot at Stavelot, which contained two and a half million gallons of petrol. Early in 1945 the Allies launched a counter-offensive, and by 16 January the gamble was over.

After the war Rundstedt called the defeat in the Ardennes 'Stalingrad No. 2'. The Germans had lost 120,000 men, together with 600 tanks and tracked guns – the entire reserve of armour for the Western front. German soldiers none the less went on fighting, without panzers or air cover, though more and more were surrendering; often they even lacked ammunition for their rifles. In the East the front was crumbling before the inexorable Russian onslaught, the Red Army crossing the Vistula on 18 January 1945. As vast numbers of German troops were captured their places were taken by members of the Hitler Jugend – boys sometimes as young as twelve, or the Volkssturm, a species of aged National Guard whose ranks included men in their sixties and seventies. At the end of January Albert Speer presented the Führer with a memorandum which stated that, with the loss of Upper Silesia, German factories could no longer provide the German army with sufficient ammunition, artillery or tanks. Hitler's response, 'in a cold cutting voice', was 'You must leave me to draw any conclusions about the state of the armaments' industry:'

His attitude is interpreted very differently by Goebbels and Speer, the two most informed witnesses during the final months of his life. The first, half crazed by his refusal to accept doom, shared his master's delusions. The second's autobiography may be always subtly self-exculpatory, but it gives an objective and indeed thoroughly convincing portrait of the Führer.

'Who knows when the moon may not crash into the earth and this whole planet go up in flames and ashes', Goebbels records Hitler as pontificating. 'Nevertheless it must be our mission to do our duty to the last.' Goebbels notes how at the beginning of March 1945 he 'is totally unshaken by the fearful blows to which we are now subjected. His steadfastness is admirable. If anyone can master this crisis he can.' The sorcerer's apprentice adds, however: 'The general mood in the Reich Chancellery is pretty dismal. I would rather not go again because the atmosphere is infectious. The generals hang their heads and the Führer alone holds his head high.'

Speer tells us how in the last half of March Hitler extorted from him an emotional and insincere agreement that the war could still be won. He describes his patron in the final months of his life as 'shrivelling up like on old man. His limbs trembled; he walked stooped, with dragging footsteps. Even his voice became quavering and lost its old masterfulness . . . His complexion was sallow, his face swollen; his uniform, which in the past he had kept scrupulously neat, was often neglected in this last period of his life and stained by the food he had eaten with a shaking hand.'

He threatened even his top advisers, not just ordinary Germans, that they would be shot as traitors if they said to anybody that the war was lost. He had the head of the Gestapo, Ernst Kaltenbrunner, present at every situation conference to cow those who might voice 'defeatist' opinions. During February and March he sometimes hinted he was taking steps to contact the Allies; Speer's view is that he was merely trying to reinforce the impression they were irreconcilable. He was hovering between an unbreakable will to win and enthusiasm for a suitably majestic funeral pyre.

So warped was his judgment by his terrible obsession with power that even in these last moments he refused to abandon the least fragment of what remained of his former empire. Such an attitude made

it impossible to defend the Reich's heartland. He resisted Guderian's frantic plea to ship the 26 divisions in Latvia back across the
Baltic, shouting furiously, 'We cannot give up those areas.'

All sources agree on the Führer's physical deterioration, which
accelerated after the assassination attempt of 1944. Manteuffel,
who had spent the previous Christmas as his guest, was horrified
when he visited him just before the Ardennes offensive – by the
'stooped figure with a pale and puffy face, hunched in his chair, his
hands trembling, his left arm subject to violent twitching which he
did his best to conceal'. Captain Gerhard Boldt, meeting him for the
first time in February 1945, records that he moved as though
senile, that his face wore a look of total exhaustion. Trevor-Roper
attributes it to turning night into day, and to drugs injected by his
doctors. If his sleep pattern had been irregular since his time as a
runner during the 1914 war, some of the drugs (belladonna and
strychnine) were undoubtedly harmful; Dr Brandt, who suspected he might have Parkinson's Disease, described the injections
as 'using the elixir of life years ahead of time'. John Keegan sug-
gests that the cause of this terrifying disintegration was primarily
psychological, the knowledge that he had not been worthy of the
German people. Yet he convinced Abert Speer and others that he
regarded the German people as having failed *him;* he told Speer in
March, 'The nation has proved to be the weaker and the future
belongs solely to the stronger eastern nation.'

In mid-March the Allies crossed the Rhine, and within a month
350,000 German troops surrendered to them. Model, the
'Führer's Fireman', shot himself. However, the Russians postponed their final assault, preferring to mop up East Prussia,
Hungary and Austria.

Amid the wreckage of his Thousand Year Reich Hitler still refused
to accept that he was finished. On 21 April Goebbels, equally
deluded, noted that 'a high ranking man from the Soviet Union in

Stockholm' had asked for talks but the Führer said no, arguing that such talks would be seen as a sign of weakness. Goebbels protested that talks would not tell the enemy anything which they did not know already. Hitler was adamant; talks would only encourage the British and Americans to co-operate more closely with the Soviets.

He had always shared the Emperor's fatal weakness for underestimating opponents, such as 'the drunkard Churchill and the criminal Roosevelt'. However, when news came on 13 April of the President's death, for a moment he thought it was proof that 'Providence' was watching over him, the political miracle for which he had been holding out; he awaited envoys from Harry S Truman. Even in the insane atmosphere of his bunker, it soon became clear that nothing had changed, but in his momentary euphoria he issued two final Führer Directives on 15 April. In the first, No. 73, explaining that Germany was likely to be cut in two, he announced that the area separated from him was to have its own commander in chief, though 'as far as communications will allow, the unified control of operations by myself personally, as hitherto, will not be altered'. In No. 74, which was to go down to company level to reach the troops, he exhorted them to fight on:

> In these hours, the whole German people looks to you, my fighters in the East, and only hopes that, thanks to your weapons, and under your leadership, the Bolshevik assault will be choked in a sea of blood.

There had been talk of an 'Alpine redoubt' in Bavaria into which the Nazi leadership and a picked force of dedicated troops were to withdraw to prolong the fight to the bitterest of all ends – in the conviction that 'Providence' would never abandon National Socialist Germany. While much of the south remained unoccupied by the Allies and contained mountainous country well suited for a last stand, the concept was almost certainly a device of Hitler to strengthen his followers' will to endure until he himself decided that that there was no further hope. Clausewitz had stressed how political opposition revived as soon as Napoleon was deprived of his capital, something the Führer must surely have feared. As it was Goering and Himmler were both plotting to take his place.

As his world crumbled around him in a hellish scenario of exploding bombs, crashing masonry and fire-storms Hitler stayed in his bunker 50 feet underground, clinging to the tatters of the power which had consumed him. (According to Otto Dietrich, he had a sign hung at the entrance to the bunker – 'No smoking'.) He played Wagner's *Götterdämmerung* on the gramophone, over and over again.

On 15 April, the same day as his two final Führer directives, three Russian armies started an offensive whose object was the capture of Berlin. In a vain attempt to beat them back, he juggled divisions existing only in his imagination on an operations map which bore no relation to reality. (Among his capital's few defenders were the Waffen SS, men of the Charlemagne Division.) By 25 April the city was completely surrounded, those within being cut off from all hope of rescue or escape.

Three days before the Führer had at last admitted that the war was lost. On 22 April, learning at the daily situation conference that Obergruppenführer Steiner's counter-attack would never happen, his control snapped. He shrieked and raved at his horrified 'courtiers' shouting that the army had betrayed him, that he was surrounded by traitors. The Third Reich was over, he cried, and he would stay and meet death in Berlin.

During the Emperor's flight from Russia in 1812 he speculated as to what the Allies would do if they caught him. 'Can you picture to yourself, Caulaincourt, the figure you would cut in an iron cage, in the main square of London?' He then had a fit of hysteria. Hitler had no illusions. He knew that he would be put on show and then executed. By 28 April 1945 the Russians were only half a mile away from the bunker. On 29 April, in the one chivalrous gesture of his entire life, he married Eva Braun. Next day both retired to their bedroom to die. Clutching a photograph of his mother, the Führer shot himself, while Eva took poison.

Amid his own ruin in 1814 Napoleon confided in a loyal supporter 'My dear fellow, if the Cossacks reach the gates of Paris it's the end of Emperor and Empire.' As it was, Tsar Alexander's Cossacks stabled their horses in Paris. In 1945 Stalin's Cossacks rode into Berlin. Neither capital need have entertained them had it not been for their rulers' madness. Determined to escape from a war on two fronts, both had been destroyed by such a war.

So long as his reign lasts there will be war.

Hippolyte Taine, Origines de la France contemporaine

I WILL TELL YOU NO MORE. LET THE DEAD LIE.
HOWEVER IT FARED AFTER WITH THE HUNS,
MY TALE IS ENDED. THIS IS THE
FALL OF THE NIBELUNGS.

Nibelungenlied

12

The Testaments

Napoleon Bonaparte and Adolf Hitler both left bequests, principally in the form of altered maps of Europe and political testaments. France and Germany suffered the miseries of enemy occupation but recovered from it, and from Emperor and Führer, with surprising speed – though Germany has remained split in two. Each dictator left a document in which he tried to justify himself and to shape the verdict of history. Napoleon succeeded, with disastrous consequences. Fortunately Hitler failed.

The great difference between the final stages of their careers is of course that the Emperor came back from exile, reascending his throne during the Hundred Days to lead his army – strengthened by repatriated veterans from all over Europe – to final defeat at Waterloo. If he spent his last years in a miserable captivity, there was never any question of trying him and condemning him to death. Had Hitler returned in 1946 from some obscure refuge he would have found only ruins, with no army or party to welcome him home.

Napoleon's personal will is predominantly domestic in its concern with his family and its countless small legacies – including that of his heart preserved in spirits to Marie Louise. He refers *en passant* to 'the French nation I have loved so dearly' and tells his son 'never to forget that he was born a French prince'. Yet there are malevolent notes, such as the statement 'I die before my time, murdered by the English oligarchy and its hired assassin', the bequest of 100,000 francs to a French sergeant who tried to murder the Duke of Wellington or the declaration that he would have the Duc d'Enghien shot all over again 'in like circumstances'. Hitler too left a personal will, appointing Martin Bormann his executor, instructing him to ensure that his relatives, his mother-in-law and his secretaries were assured of 'a petit-bourgeois standard of living'. [*ein kleines bürgerliches Leben*]. In addition, they bequeathed political testaments.

The Emperor's was in the form of a Napoleonic legend, subtly designed to create a Bonapartist political faith which would attract supporters and place his son on the throne of France. He did so by means of a long series of apologias which he dictated to his companions in exile, the first and most influential series being the *Mémorial de Sainte Hélène*, which became a best-seller as soon as it appeared in 1823, and went on selling throughout the century. Dissatisfaction with restored Bourbons, memories of the days when French troops marched triumphantly into every European capital, and the Romantic movement ensured the myth's appeal. Chained like Prometheus to his 'abominable rock', Napoleon became an increasingly heroic figure in French eyes. The ballads of Béranger, *'Parlez-nous de lui, grand'mère'* and Victor Hugo, *'Toujours lui! lui partout'*, helped to gild the story as well as spread it. In 1840 his body was brought back to France on King Louis-Philippe's instructions and enshrined in its vast tomb at the Invalides – to which the Führer would one day go on pilgrimage. The Bonapartist message was simple enough; prosperity at home, military glory abroad.

'I have saved the revolution as it lay dying, I have cleansed it of its crimes and have held it up to the people, shining with glory', he boasted on St Helena. 'I have given France and Europe new ideas which will never be forgotten.' His wars of conquest had really been campaigns of liberation, intended to unify the peoples of Europe in a single great brotherhood. A note of self-exculpation mingled with the self-glorification. 'However much I may be misrepresented, silenced or mutilated, my enemies will find it difficult to make me disappear. Deeds speak like the sun.' He had ennobled nations, strengthened the throne, opened up a career for everybody with talent. 'What can I be accused of, that some writer won't be able to acquit me? . . . That I've been too fond of war? He'll be able to show that I always acted to defend myself. That I tried to make myself ruler of the world? It happened by pure accident, because of circumstances and because my enemies pushed me, step by step.' No doubt historians would find him guilty of ambition but it was the ambition to ensure that reason triumphed, to 'consecrate' the full flowering of all human abilities.

'Far from achieving the aims of the revolution whose heir he happened to become, he never even caught sight of them,' Jean-Charles Bailleul wrote of Napoleon. The extent to which he doctored the truth is illustrated by the contrast between his public and private attitudes to religion. In his will he declares, 'I die in the Apostolic and Roman faith, in whose bosom I was born more than fifty years ago.' He also instructed the Abbé Vignali to give him communion and extreme unction on his deathbed. Yet in August 1817 he had confided in Baron Gourgaud 'I don't believe Jesus ever existed', and on 27 March 1821 (five weeks before his death) told Count Bertrand, 'I find it a great consolation that I have no imaginary terrors, no fear of the future.'

However, the legend was widely accepted in France where the working class and petit-bourgeoisie looked back with nostalgia to the Empire's comparative material plenty; conscription had ensured a good market for labour, while the price of bread had been kept down. In retrospect it appeared as a time of well-paid employment and cheap food when contrasted with the hardship of Restoration or Orleanist France, whose degrading poverty is preserved in Hugo's *Les Misérables*. Nevertheless, the second Napoleonic empire, proclaimed in 1851, was born on St Helena.

The myth had acquired extraordinary potency. Even today it continues to fascinate. As its creator himself said, 'What a romance my life has been!' Nevertheless, Bonapartism proved a disaster when his nephew Napoleon III tried to put the creed into practice. Although he had genuine concern for the poor, his régime grew steadily more unpopular at home, while the aggressively nationalist foreign policy which was his uncle's legacy proved increasingly unsuccessful, until it finally destroyed the Second Empire with the Franco-Prussian war of 1870-1.

Confined to his bunker in a devastated country, the Führer was in very different circumstances at the end of his life. He disinherited his original heir, Goering, together with Himmler, for intrigue, expelling them from the Party. He appointed Grand Admiral Doenitz to succeed him as Führer, while Goebbels was to be Chancellor.

His monologues on why Germany had lost the war, taken down between February and early April 1945, are generally regarded as his 'testament'. Like the Emperor, Hitler cynically shrugs off all guilt. Neither he nor anyone else in Germany had wanted war in 1939. He blamed Britain and the 'Jew-ridden half-American drunkard Churchill' for not having worked to unit Europe by allying with Germany; in fighting him Britain had ensured America's entrance into the war; otherwise she would have stayed neutral. As for invading Russia, his 'own personal nightmare' had been that Stalin might take the initiative. He accused his officers of failing Germany by surrendering too easily – in ironical contrast to his often voiced opinion that in 1918 Germany had failed the army. Nevertheless, the conflict 'in spite of all the setbacks will one day go down in history as the most glorious and heroic manifestation of a people's will to live'. After the war there would be only two great powers capable of confronting each other, the United States and the Soviet Union. 'The laws of both history and geography will compel these two powers to a trial of strength, either military or in the fields of economics and ideology' – inevitably both would seek German support.

Unlike Napoleon – and this is surely the strongest and most merciful contrast – no legend came out of the Führer bunker. Yet there is an odd quality of mystery which is missing in Napoleon's case. His father's bastardy prompted wild tales of his grandfather having been a Jew from Graz called Frankenberger, even a Baron Rothschild. (At one point he himself took these tales very seriously.) The full details of his subterranean life in Vienna and Munich before 1914 will never be established; the files of the Viennese police list him as a homosexual, while it is claimed he visited Liverpool. In 1918 he is said to have contemplated joining the Spartacists. He is supposed to have promised to restore Crown Prince Rupprecht to the throne of Bavaria – Rupprecht certainly offered him a dukedom. None other than the Nuncio, the future Pope Pius XII, is rumoured to have told him monarchy was finished, that he should create his own type of state. No one has ever discovered the precise nature of the relationship with Geli Raubal, or that with Eva Braun. It was months before the story of his last days was established. Even now no one is sure the charred remains found by the Russians were his body.

Ultimately the two men are united by their reaction to the French Revolution, for it was Rousseau's explosive concept of the General Will coupled with the breakdown of the social order which in the long run created both Emperor and Führer. The former ensured the demolition of Christian Europe, while the latter completed it. However much Goebbels might boast, 'We have abolished 1789', no less than Napoleonic France Nazi Germany stemmed from the

Revolution. Lieutenant Bonaparte's horror, Jacobin though he then was, at the storming of the Tuileries by the *sans-culottes* in 1792 was echoed by Corporal Hitler's revulsion at the disorder which convulsed his adopted country in November 1918. Yet each claimed that he embodied the people's will.

Napoleon saw himself as offering a via media between the *ancien régime* and the Terror. He claimed to have 'cleansed' the revolution, combining with it what was best from the past, morally regenerated by Revolutionary ideals. Yet for all his protestations, he accepted the Revolution only because it had made his career possible, and because those who had profited from it were ready to support his régime.

Similarly, Hitler argued that he was steering a middle path between capitalism and Marxism. National Socialists claimed that their political and social programme had thwarted the machinations of international finance, while at the same time defeating the evil consequences of the French Revolution as embodied in its children – liberalism and, above all, Bolshevism. The Führer regarded himself as both a conservative and a socialist. He has been described as ultra-modern in his day – a label he would not have rejected – yet he was modern only in discarding everything which had preceded him. For all its pretensions, the Brown Revolution merely served to confirm that of 1789. It was the same crowns and the same support which Emperor and Führer 'picked up from the gutter'.

In his search for the 'Napoleonic secret' Clausewitz sometimes seems to suggest that the Emperor would have liked to achieve his ambitions by another means than war. (This is surely the meaning of a sibylline sentence in *Vom Kriege*, 'The political goal is the *end*, and warfare is a means leading to it, and a means can never be thought of without a certain end.') It has been said that a twentieth-century Bonaparte might have succeeded in doing so. The Führer's career contradicts this view – he began with politics, hoping to get what he wanted without going to war, and finished by regarding war as an end in itself.

Hitler's dictatorship was the first dictatorship of an industrial state in this age of modern technology, a dictatorship which employed to perfection the instruments of technology to dominate its own people.' Albert Speer emphasized at Nuremberg, 'Telephone, teletype and radio made it possible to transmit the commands of the highest levels directly to the lowest organs where because of their high authority they were executed uncritically. Thus many officers and squads received their evil commands in this direct manner.' In the past dictators had needed the assistance of high quality at even the lower levels, men who could think and act independently, but now 'The authoritarian system in the age of technology can do without such men . . . Thus the type of uncritical receiver of orders is created.' Who can say what Napoleon might not have done with such instruments? The question underlines the difficulty of comparison.

Both men were enigmas on a vast scale. We can at least guess that each was fascinated by himself, dramatizing his own career in his imagination. Hippolyte Taine – of all Frenchmen the most critical of the Napoleonic myth – discerns a total, all-consuming egotism. The Emperor insisted on monopolizing all executive and legislative power, on 'the annihilation of all moral authority save his own', on the silencing of all public opinion and of every individual voice, the destruction of any initiative other than his own. He 'loved the French people' only in as far as they served his ambition. This book has stressed the role played by Wagnerian music and drama throughout Hitler's life. In his early days they offered an escape from a futile existence, while later they provided an extraordinary secret background, enabling him to live out his very strange – and to him very real – dream-world of Teutonic myth, which in his mind shaded imperceptibly into German history. No doubt he saw himself not merely as Rienzi but as Lohengrin, and even on occasion as Wotan. Few people have been more intoxicated by Wagner, not even Ludwig II of Bavaria. The operas embodied the very essence of Germany for him, endowing his nationalism with a heady quality of feverish mysticism, which lasted until the last days of his life. Albert Speer said of the Third Reich, 'It was only an opera.'

Neither man recognized any moral boundaries. Napoleon pretended to have principles, but what he dictated to Las Cases for public consumption was very different from his real opinions. Even if the Führer did infinitely greater evil, the difference in guilt is one of scale. No accurate estimate exists of the casualties which resulted from the Emperor's career, but they must have run into millions, in a Europe far less populated than during the mid-twentieth century. Between 1804 and 1815 at least 1,700,000 French soldiers died on active service; the true figure is probably nearer two million. Certainly well over two million of Napoleon's allies and opponents were killed. Such figures are enormous when one remembers that there was no mechanized transport – soldiers rode or marched to the front. When all is said and done, the Emperor did not leave monuments like mounds of corpses as tall as a house at Belsen or the gas ovens at Treblinka and Auschwitz.

We have a better idea of the mortality which resulted from Hitler's ambition. According to Stalin at least seven million Russian civilians perished, many as a result of deliberately induced famine, together with three and half million Russian soldiers who died in prisoner-of-war camps. Over five million Jews were murdered, more than half the Jewry of 'New Europe', besides three million non-Jewish Poles.

In 1823 during his pro-Bourbon period Victor Hugo, not yet a convert to the Napoleonic legend, composed a florid ode to 'Buonaparte'. He had seemed 'a living plague' [*un fléau vivant*],

had reigned by 'flame and iron' as 'a warrior without faith' wrote
the poet. 'Crowned in blood . . . he made a sceptre of his sword,
used his tent as a throne.' Hugo declaims how the Emperor 'took
the path of glory, took the path of crime, and fell to disaster . . . like
some meteor which did not follow the course of the sun.' All this
could be applied to the Führer.

In 1945, when Hitler's Germany was deservedly ending in
horror, Professor Schramm asked his wife to type out for him a
chilling passage in Goethe's *Dichtung und Wahrheit*. 'The most
fearful manifestation of the demonic, however, is seen when it
dominates an individual human being. In the course of my life, I
have been able to observe several . . . they emanate a monstrous
force and exercise incredible power over all creatures . . . All moral
powers combined are impotent against them. In vain do the more
enlightened among men attempt to discredit them as deluded or
deceptive – the masses will be drawn to them . . . they can be overcome only by the universe itself, against which they have taken up
arms.' The passage ends with the proverb *Nemo contra deum nisi
deus ipse* – 'No one can do something against God who is not God
himself.' Naturally, Schramm applied Goethe's reflections to Adolf
Hitler. Yet they had been written with Napoleon Bonaparte in mind.

Speer stresses how modern communications made possible the
Führer-state. If this really is the reason why Hitler was able to do
so much more evil than Napoleon – or even only one of the reasons –
then technological progress should ensure that the next 'national
saviour' on a world scale will be infinitely more terrible. Antichrist
is yet to come. Perhaps the Emperor and the Führer were merely
forerunners.

Notes

The following are deliberately selective, only intended to give the more obscure sources or as afterthoughts.

1. (p. 8) Martin Gilbert, in *Winston S. Churchill 1939-1941* (p. 844) quotes from Churchill's introduction to a volume of Pitt's speeches:

    > A Nazi victory would be an immeasurably worse disaster for us and for all mankind than Napoleon's victory could ever have been. As modern France, and not France only knows Napoleon could construct as well as destroy. There can be no comparison, indeed, in the scale of civilisation between the Nazi system and that of the Napoleonic Empire; nor could the humane, free-spirited French people ever have become the docile instruments of such barbarism as now issues from Berlin.

2. (p. 13) See R. Aron, *Penser la guerre*, Paris, 1976.

3. (p. 13) And other strategists too, according to Keitel:

    > *Er studierte auch während des Krieges in Nächten in all den grossen General-stabswerken von Moltke, Schlieffen und Clausewitz.* Maser, p. 196.

4. (p. 15) See Taine, *Les origines de la France contemporaine. La régime moderne,* tome 1, pp. 111-12.

5. (p. 16) Jacques Charles Bailleul (1762-1843), a former member of the Convention and of the Council of Five Hundred.

6. (p. 62) Letter of Major W.E.L. Seward MC, of Unter den Linden 56, Berlin, dated 17 August 1926. [Later he was suspected by the Gestapo of

having been a British agent and in 1936 was warned by a friend in the SS not to return to Germany.)

7. (p. 83) 'It's not my job to do justice,' Goering told the Prussian police in February 1933, 'it's my business to annihilate and exterminate'. In the same speech he informed them: 'From now on every bullet fired from a political gun is my bullet. If that's called murder, then I commit murder, since it's me who orders it.'

8. (p. 89) Desperate attempts have been made to discredit Mme de Rémusat's memoirs ever since their publication in 1880. But if some letters written under the Empire express admiration for Napoleon and if the book was rewritten in 1818 – the original having been burnt during the Hundred Days – she wrote her memoirs without any thought of being published.

9. (p. 100) It fits the mordant humour of both Talleyrand and Fouché, though some authorities credit the jibe to the jurist Count Boulay de la Meurthe. However, in his memoirs Fouché says specifically:

> ' "It's more than a crime," I observed, "it's a mistake!" '
> Words which I record because they have been repeated and attributed to others.

10. (p. 110) Information from W.E.L. Seward.

11. (p. 111) Personal information from the Prince's widow.

12. (p. 111) Otto Dietrich, the Nazi party's former press chief and Goebbels's right-hand man writes in very similar vein:

> In Hitler's soul, sincere warmth and icy heartlessness, love of his fellow creatures and ruthless harshness, dwelt side by side.

13. (p. 112) Otto Dietrich comments on the Führer's outbursts 'Death penalties or the concentration camp were as often the result of his uncontrollable rages as of his "ice-cold" reflections – to use his own phrase.'

14. (p. 118) Information from W.E.L. Seward.

15. (p. 120) 'I swear by God this holy oath, that I will render unconditional obedience to the Führer of the German Reich, Adolf Hitler, supreme

commander of the armed forces and that, as a brave soldier, I will be ready at any time to stake my life for this oath.'

16.   (p. 123) See Maser p. 199 for a discussion of his library.

17.   (p. 124) 'For decades he promoted humane treatment for animals,' wrote Otto Dietrich. Nazi Germany was to be the first state to forbid hunting an animal with hounds.

18.   (p. 126) If some historians are to be believed, Napoleon's attitude to Jews was more complex, even if the general consensus is that he was fundamentally benevolent towards them. For a survey of the literature on this aspect see Tulard pp. 377-8.

19.   (p. 140) For all his 'philosophical' attitude and urbanity of style, Clausewitz's approach was brutal enough. 'Philanthropists may easily imagine that there is a skilful method of disarming and overcoming the enemy without bloodshed, and that this is the proper tendency of the Art of War . . . This is an error which must be extirpated.' Or 'Let us not hear of generals who conquer without bloodshed.'

20.   (p. 154) 'There can be no doubt on this subject,' Field Marshal von Manstein stated after the War. 'Hitler always wanted to avoid a struggle with England and the British Empire.'

21.   (p. 155) See T.H. Geer, *What Roosevelt Thought* (Michigan, 1958), pp. 181-2.

22.   (p. 158) This is A.J.P. Taylor's final opinion – see 'Second Thoughts' in the revised edition of his *Origins of the Second World War*.

23.   (p. 165) See J.I. Shulim, *The Old Dominion and Napoleon Bonaparte*.

24.   (p. 171) William Wordsworth, Sonnet XVI.

25.   (p. 217) One must distinguish between Continental Blockade and Continental System; the exclusion of Britain from Europe and the French political and economic domination of Europe, even if the first led to the second.

26. (p. 222) See Taine, *Les origines de la France contemporaine. La régime moderne,* tome 2, pp. 188-9.

27. (p. 235) Personal information.

28. (p. 239) Information from Colonel Beauclerk, now the Duke of St Albans. Oberführer D'Alquen later hanged himself in his cell.

29. (p. 283) On 15 January 1814 he dictated instructions for fortifying Paris which, if necessary, must 'be buried in its own ruins'. See M. Guerrini, *Napoléon et Paris,* Paris, 1967.

Select Bibliography

NAPOLEON

Bainville, J., *Le Dix-huit Brumaire*, Paris, 1925.

Bainville, J., *Napoléon*, Paris, 1931.

Balzac, H. de, *Une ténébreuse affaire*, Paris, 1841.

Barras, P. de, *Mémoires de Barras*, Paris, 1895.

Bausset, L.F.J., *Mémoires anecdotiques*, Paris, 1827-9.

Bertrand, H.G., *Cahiers de Sainte-Hélène*, Paris, 1949.

Bourgeois, E., *Manuel de politique étrangère*, Paris, 1898.

Bourrienne, L. de, *Mémoires de M. de Bourrienne*, Paris, 1831.

Broglie, Duc de, *Souvenirs du feu duc de Broglie*, Paris, 1886.

Caulaincourt, L. de, *Mémoires*, Paris, 1933.

Chaptal, J.A., *Mes souvenirs sur Napoléon*, Paris, 1893.

Chuquet, A., *La Jeunesse de Napoléon*, Paris, 1897.

Fain, A., *Mémoires du Baron Fain*, Paris, 1908.

Fouché, J., *Mémoires*, Paris, 1945.

Fox, C.J., *Memorials and Correspondence*, London, 1854.

Geyl, P., *Napoleon For and Against*, London, 1949.

Gourgaud, G., *Journal de Sainte-Hélène*, Paris, 1944.

Haussonville, J.O.B. de, *L'église romaine et le premier Empire*, Paris, 1868-70.

Houssaye, H., *1814*, Paris, 1888.

Jomini, H., *Vie politique et militaire de Napoléon*, Paris, 1827.

Précis politique et militaire des campagnes de 1812 à 1814, Paris, 1886.

Las Cases, M.J.E.A.D. de, *Le Mémorial de Sainte-Hélène*, Paris, 1951.

Lefebvre, G., *Napoléon*, Paris, 1936.

Lockhart, J.G., *Life of Napoleon Buonaparte*, London, 1829.

Marmont, A.F.L.V. de, *Mémoires*, Paris, 1857.

Masson, F., *Napoléon et sa famille*, Paris, 1897-1919. *Napoléon Inconnu*, Paris, 1895.

Méneval, C.F., *Mémoires*, Paris, 1894.

Metternich-Winneburg, Prince Klemens von, *Mémoires, documents et écrits divers*, Paris, 1880-4.

Mounier, P.E., *Souvenirs intimes du baron Mounier*, Paris, 1896.

Napoleon I, *Correspondence*, Paris, 1858-69.

Napoleon I, *Correspondence militaire*, Paris, 1876-7.

Pitt, W., *Orations on the French War*, London, 1906.

Pradt, Abbé D.D. de, *Histoire de l'ambassade dans le grand-duché de Varsovie en 1812*, Paris, 1815.

Rémusat, C.E.J. de, *Mémoires, 1802-8*, Paris, 1880.

Roederer, P.L., *Journal*, Paris, 1909. *Mémoires*, Paris, 1942.

Shulim, J.I., *The Old Dominion and Napoleon Bonaparte*, New York, 1952.

Staël, G. de, *Mémoires*, Paris, 1818.

Stendhal, *Mémoires sur Napoléon*, Paris, 1930.

Stendhal, *Vie de Napoléon*, Paris, 1930.

Taine, H., *Les Origines de la France contemporaine*, Paris, 1891-4.

Talleyrand-Périgord, Prince C.M. de, *Mémoires*, Paris, 1891-2.

Tulard, J., *Napoléon*, Paris, 1977.

Vandal, A., *L'Avènement de Bonaparte*, Paris, 1903.

Vandal, A., *Napoléon et Alexandre Ier*, Paris, 1909-10.

HITLER

Aster, S., *The Making of the Second World War*, London, 1973.

Bezymenski, L., *The Death of Adolph Hitler*, New York, 1968.

Boldt, G., *Hitler's Last Days*, London, 1973.

Bullock, A., *A Study in Tyranny*, London and New York, 1964.

Carr, W., *Hitler: A Study in Personality and Politics*, London, 1978.

Churchill, Sir W., *Arms and the Covenant. Speeches . . .*, London, 1938.

Churchill, Sir W., *Into Battle: Speeches . . .*, London, 1941.

Churchill, Sir W., *The Unrelenting Struggle: Speeches . . .*, London, 1942.

Churchill, Sir W., *The End of the Beginning: War Speeches . . .*, London, 1943.

Ciano, G., *Ciano's Diaries 1939-43*, London, 1947.

Cooper, G., *The German Army 1933-45*, London, 1978.

Craig, G., *Germany 1866-1945*, Oxford, 1978.

Deakin, F.W., *The Brutal Friendship*, London, 1962.

Dietrich, O., *The Hitler I Knew*, London, 1955.

Erickson, J., *The Road to Stalingrad*, London, 1975.

Fest, J., *Hitler*, New York, 1974.

Fest, J., *The Face of the Third Reich*, London, 1970.

François-Poncet, A., *The Fateful Years*, London, 1949.

Gilbert, M., *Winston S. Churchill 1922-39*, London, 1976.

Gilbert, M., *Winston S. Churchill 1939-1941*, London, 1983.

Gilbert, M., *Winston S. Churchill 1941-1945*, London, 1986.

Goebbels, J., *The Diary of Joseph Goebbels 1925-6*, London, 1962.

Goebbels, J., *The Goebbels Diaries 1942-3*, London, 1949.

Guderian, H., *Panzer Leader*, London, 1952.

Halder, F., *Hitler as War Lord*, London, 1950.

Hanfstaengl, E., *Hitler, the Missing Years*, London, 1957.

Henderson, N., *Failure of a Mission*, London, 1940.

Hitler, A., *Mein Kampf*, London, 1972.

Hitler, A., *Hitler's Table Talk 1941-44*, ed. H.R. Trevor-Rover, London, 1953.

Hitler, A., *The Speeches of Adolf Hitler, 1922-39*, ed. N.H. Baynes, Oxford, 1942.

Hitler, A., *Hitler's War Directives*, ed. H.R. Trevor-Roper, London, 1964.

Hitler, A., *The Testament of Adolf Hitler*, London, 1961.

Hitler, A., *Hitler's Secret Book*, New York, 1961.

Irving, D., *Hitler's War*, London, 1977.

Jetzinger, F., *Hitler's Youth*, London, 1958.

Kubizek, A., *Young Hitler*, New York, 1955.

Langer, W., *The Mind of Adolf Hitler*, London, 1972.

Leach, B., *German Strategy against Russia, 1931-41*, Oxford, 1973.

Liddell Hart, B.H., *The Other Side of the Hill*, London, 1951.

Liddell Hart, B.H., *History of the Second World War*, London, 1972.

Liddell Hart, B.H., *Strategy: the indirect approach*, London, 1954.

Lüdecke, K.G.W., *I Knew Hitler*, London, 1938.

Maser, W., *Adolf Hitler: Legende, Mythos, Wirklichkeit*, Munich, 1971.

Milward, A., *The German Economy at War* , New York, 1964.

Paget, R.H., *Manstein, his Campaigns and his Trial*, London, 1951.

Papen, F. von, *Memoirs*, London, 1952.

Rauschning, H., *Hitler Speaks*, London, 1939.

Rauschning, H., *Germany's Revolution of Destruction*, London, 1939.

Clausewitz

Clausewitz's great work, *Vom Kriege*, was first published in Berlin between 1832 and 1834. An English translation by Colonel J.J. Graham appeared in 1873, the best-known edition being that (with an introduction by Colonel F.N. Maude) of 1908. An excellent new translation by Sir Michael Howard and P. Paret was published in 1977; although this is sometimes more accurate, I have nevertheless used the Graham version since it has been the standard English text for over a century.

His historical writings are little known. A definitive edition of *Der Feldzug von 1812 in Russland und die Befreiungskriege von 1813-15* appeared in Berlin in 1906 (with an introduction by General von Schlieffen). A not altogether reliable English translation, *The Campaign of 1812 in Russia*, was published in London in 1843 while *La Campagne de 1814*, which came out in Paris in 1914, is also confined to a single year.

Index